"*Just Cutting It Straight* offers lucid, thoughtful, and directional understandings of familiar Old Testament scriptures. Dr. T.D. Stubblefield has unselfishly given readers a window into his personal theology by sharing this wonderful collection of sermon outlines that will expand and elevate the preaching and teaching of the Gospel for generations yet born."

Gerald L. Smith, Ph.D.
Professor of History
University of Kentucky
Co-editor, *The Kentucky African American Encyclopedia* and
The Papers of Martin Luther King, Jr., Volume VI: Advocate of the Social Gospel

"I had the distinct privilege and honor to 'sit at the feet' of Pastor T. D. Stubblefield for more than a decade. Two things are crystal clear: first, he has a stratospherically high regard for the Word of God. And second, Dr. Stubblefield is a gifted, imaginative and animated orator and preacher-teacher of our glorious gospel. As he would often say, "All good preaching is good teaching." Don't he fooled by the brevity of this work as much is packed in this small but significant literary piece. In this piece, expositor Stubblefield provides those who wish to hone their craft of preaching the Old Testament Scriptures the fruit of his theological and biblical insight and his proven exegetical and homiletical skills. As such, those who reflect and imbibe this teaching will preach the Old Testament Scriptures with newfound clarity and power."

Luke B. Bobo, Ph.D.
Director of Resource and Curriculum Development,
Made to Flourish
Author of *A Layperson's Guide to Biblical Interpretation* and
Living Salty and Light-filled Lives in the Workplace

"Once again, in *Just Cutting It Straight* by T.D. Stubblefield, we are able to witness firsthand the gift of preaching, and what a gift it is! We are able to witness firsthand, a dynamic preacher who is influencing preaching and teaching today. We are able to witness firsthand, preaching and teaching from a pastor's heart. We are able to witness firsthand the priority, passion, and power of preaching. We are able to witness firsthand Pastor Stubblefield's passion for exposition of scripture. A bond servant of the text, Dr. Stubblefield writes according to the thought of the original author.

In *Just Cutting It Straight* you will be able to discover how to prepare and plan a sermon. You will be able to prepare and plan what role culture plays in shaping your sermon. You will not only see how scripture develops but what I really like about it, it will also help your own interpretative skills grow. As "iron sharpens iron," you cannot help but become a better preacher yourself. You will discover as you read *Just Cutting It Straight* the components of a sermon, explanation, illustration and application at its best. The diversity of sermons in *Just Cutting It Straight* challenges you and encourages not only you, but your people as well. You will discover how to move consecutively through a text which ultimately forces you to deal with subjects that you might not otherwise deal with, which is the beauty of expository preaching. As Pastor Stubblefield so ably does, he brings the meaning of the text to bear upon the biblical needs that the text is addressing and then connects those biblical needs to the contemporary needs of people today. In other words, Pastor Stubblefield in *Just Cutting It Straight* is not preaching and teaching for information only, but for transformation purposes.

Augustine says we ought to say what God says, and in *Just Cutting It Straight* Pastor Stubblefield is saying, "This is not me as a preacher talking. This is what God says to you based upon what this text means." For anybody who wants to be a good preacher, this is a must read and a book that must be in your personal library. It is powerful, personal and dynamic.

Rev. Dr. Carlton R. Caldwell, Senior Pastor
Galilee Missionary Baptist Church

Author of *We Are All Ministers – Moving Members from Pews to Purpose* and
Little by Little

Just
Cutting It
Straight

OUTLINES FOR PREACHING
AND TEACHING FROM THE
OLD TESTAMENT

T. D. Stubblefield

Just Cutting It Straight
Copyright © 2016 T. D. Stubblefield Ministries, L.L.C.

ISBN-13: 978-0-692-64548-2

Library of Congress Control Number: 2016902528

All Scripture quotations, unless otherwise indicated, are taken from the Holy Bible, King James Version.

Scripture quotations marked NIV are taken from the Holy Bible, New International Version.
© 1973, 1978, 1984, 2011.

Scripture quotations marked MSG are taken from The Message by Eugene Peterson.
© 1993, 1994, 1995, 1996, 2000, 2001, 2002.

Scripture quotations marked TLB are taken from The Living Bible.
© 1971.

Scripture quotations are taken from the Moffatt Translation.
© 1922, 1924, 1926, 1935.

Cover Design by Brandy Jackson

Printed in the United States by
Mira Digital Publishing
Chesterfield, Missouri 63005

CONTENTS

Old Testament Outlines

ACKNOWLEDGEMENTS

I am truly humbled to share these expositional excavations from the Old Testament with a wider audience. I thank God for the First Baptist Church of Chesterfield (Missouri) Faith Family. For more than sixteen years now, they have provided the pastoral, inspirational and experiential anvil on which many of these outlines were formed and forged. The dedicated labor of love from Kimberly Hodge-Bell (Project Manager), Brandy Jackson (Graphic Designer) and Monique Smith (Editor) is inestimable. Finally, I thank God for my wife Judy, my life partner, soul mate, compelling constant and mother of our four children. Her inspiration and insight are indelibly etched on this volume and in my heart.

INTRODUCTION

Growing up on a farm in rural West Tennessee, my grandfather taught me when I was a young boy the proper technique when chopping or cutting wood with an axe. He emphasized how important it was to cut with and not against the grain. This is in essence what the Apostle Paul admonishes his son in the ministry, Timothy, to do when he challenges him with these words,

2 Timothy 2:15 (KJV)
[15] Study to shew thyself approved unto God, a workman that needeth not to be ashamed, rightly dividing the word of truth.

The Greek word translated "rightly dividing" in this verse means literally "to cut a straight road or path." It is a challenge or summons to every preacher and teacher of the Bible to exercise diligence and discipline when interpreting the Scriptures in its parts or as a whole.

As one who has been called to serve the local church as a pastor-teacher for the past thirty-four years I have, when preaching and teaching, always aimed to find the grain of the text and its larger context and "cut it straight." This begins in my preparation and extends to and through my presentation of the transcendent truths and powerful principles of the Word of God. This practice has assured that the development of the Bible text that the Lord deposits in my spirit is always driven by the text. Scholars describe this as expositional or textual preaching and teaching.

In the following pages, I humbly share some of these textual and expositional offerings with a wider audience. These expanded outlines are drawn from Old Testament passages that I have shared with the people of God that I have been given pastoral and spiritual oversight of, and with the larger body of Christ in revivals, conferences and conventions.

The narratives, history, poetry and prophecies that comprise the first thirty-nine books of the Bible speak with timeless relevance to our contemporary situation. They are magnificent mirrors which reflect our images as flawed, finite, fragile and fickle creatures yet fearfully and wonderfully made in the image of God. But they are also wide windows that we can look through and survey the panoramic horizon of promise and possibility which is inherent in the salvific plan that has its inception in the Old Testament but finds its fulfillment in the New.

Relative to the experiences of our spiritual predecessors under the old covenant, the Bible says, "These things happened to them as examples and were written down as warnings for us, on whom the fulfillment of the ages has come." (1 Corinthians 10:11 NIV). We can learn from them because, "What was will be again, what happened will happen again. There's nothing new on this earth. Year after year it's the same old thing" (Ecclesiastes 1:9 MSG). These outlines for preaching and teaching aim to leverage the lessons of the past in order to fan and fortify our faith in the present.

To conserve space, in some cases when a particular passage is cited, its larger context is indicated in brackets. In most of the outlines, an introductory porch is included that provides an entry point into the movements or grain of the text. In some instances, sub points are provided for clarity and continuity. The alliteration I use is secondary to the textual development and has become a signature characteristic of my approach to preaching and teaching. The text always drives the points in the sermon or lesson. The alliteration and titles only serve to provide a conceptual closet for the audience to remember and store what has been shared.

These outlines are offered as sermon or lesson starters and are inherently elastic allowing space for the exercise of any reader's own unique gifts and perspectives. Phillip Brook's classic definition of preaching as "the communication of truth through personality" is a reminder that every communicator of the Word of God has been blessed by God with a unique imprint that cannot be mimicked or matched. I challenge you to embrace this truth but to be always mindful that as we exercise our gifts, our personalities should never become so translucent that they set in eclipse or hide the truth of the Word of God, which must always be exposed by "cutting it straight."

OLD TESTAMENT OUTLINES

– 1 –
Am I My Brother's (Sister's) Keeper?

Genesis 4:9 [1-9] (KJV)
⁹ And the LORD said unto Cain, Where *is* Abel thy brother?
And he said, I know not: *Am* I my brother's keeper?

In our text, Cain asks this question to God. His tone and demeanor was mocking, arrogant, sarcastic and unrepentant. He had just murdered his brother Abel. On what path did he traverse to plummet to these unprecedented and despicable depths? There are four things to consider in this text.

I.   A fractured fellowship

    a. Two brothers at odds because of envy and arrogance. Sound familiar?

II. A frightening foe

    a. "sin crouches at the door"

III. A family failure

    a. Friction can be fatal.

IV. A fervent faith

    a. Abel was a righteous man according to Hebrews 11:5

– 2 –
When God Elevates Our Faith

Genesis 15:5-6 [1-6] (NIV)
⁵ He took him outside and said, "Look up at the heavens and count the stars — if indeed you can count them." Then he said to him, "So shall your offspring be." ⁶ Abram believed the LORD, and he credited it to him as righteousness.

This passage records a strategic moment in the life of Abram later named Abraham. Since the day God spoke to him in the land of Ur, his life had been driven by faith and not by facts. Three things God did to elevate Abram's faith.

I.   He changed his environment (verse 5a)

II.   He challenged his expectations (verse 5b)

III.   He credited his example (verse 6)

- 3 -

Don't Look Back!

Genesis 19:16-17 (KJV)

[16] And while he lingered, the men laid hold upon his hand, and upon the hand of his wife, and upon the hand of his two daughters; the LORD being merciful unto him: and they brought him forth, and set him without the city. [17] And it came to pass, when they had brought them forth abroad, that he said, Escape for thy life; look not behind thee, neither stay thou in all the plain; escape to the mountain, lest thou be consumed.

The actions of Lot and his wife serve as a warning to us not only of the dangers of looking back but what is required of us if we are to move forward according to the will of God. Four things we must do to avoid the mistake that Lot's wife made and to escape our past.

I.   Get Up

II.   Get Out

III.   Get To

IV.   Get Through

- 4 -
Footnotes to a Father's Failure

Genesis 27:33 [30-36] (NIV)

[36] Esau said, "Isn't he rightly named Jacob? He has deceived me these two times: He took my birthright, and now he's taken my blessing!" Then he asked, "Haven't you reserved any blessing for me?"

Isaac can be described as "the mediocre son of a great father and the mediocre father of a great son." When we meet him in the Bible, he is a beacon of light and a well of possibility. There is no reason to believe that he would not experience great success in life and favor from God. But good starts don't necessarily guarantee strong finishes. What happened to him? There are four mistakes that Isaac made that created crisis and chaos in his family.

I.   He failed to focus

II.   He failed to fortify

    a. He chose favoritism over faith

    b. He chose information over intimacy

III. He failed to fathom (vs. 36b)

    a. While his ability to bless was exhausted, God has unlimited capacity to meet us at our point of need. This is what he should have told Esau when he asked, "hast thou not reserved a blessing for me?" (verse 36).

- 5 -
Supersizing Our Faith and Downsizing Our Fears

Genesis 32:26-27 [24-28] (KJV)

[26] And he said, Let me go, for the day breaketh. And he said, I will not let thee go, except thou bless me. [27] And he said unto him, What *is* thy name? And he said, Jacob.

The Word of God does not discount, diminish or disregard the reality of our fears but provides the supernatural resources we need to face any challenge. Faced with a challenge he could not overcome by his wit, cunning or manipulation, Jacob experienced four things that supersized his faith and downsized his fears.

I.   He was exposed to a stabilizing insight

    a. He received "insider information" and realized that he was not alone.

II. He experienced a supernatural intervention

    a. The angel of the Lord appeared to him. This is what biblical scholars call a "Christophany" – a pre-incarnate appearance of the second member of the Godhead.

III. He exercised a surrendered inadequacy

    a. He surrendered to God; his name was changed.

– 6 –

God is Working Behind the Scenes

Genesis 42:36 (NIV)

[36] Their father Jacob said to them, "You have deprived me of my children. Joseph is no more and Simeon is no more, and now you want to take Benjamin. Everything is against me!"

Faced with tragic and inexplicable loss, Jacob like us was unable to grasp the reality of God's presence, plan and provision. When we believe God is working behind the scenes, we will experience three things.

I.   God's presence is greater than our problems

II. Gods' plan is greater than our perspectives

III. God's provision is greater than our poverty

Our Father is Still Alive!
(A Father's Day Sermon)

Genesis 43:26-28 (NIV)

²⁶ When Joseph came home, they presented to him the gifts they had brought into the house, and they bowed down before him to the ground. ²⁷ He asked them how they were, and then he said, "How is your aged father you told me about? Is he still living?" ²⁸ They replied, "Your servant our father is still alive and well." And they bowed low to pay him honor.

Joseph's question to his brothers concerning his aging father rings and resonates with relevance for us today. "Is he still living?" prompts consideration and reflection along three lines.

I.   The father he endeared

II.   The favor he enjoyed

III.   The future he embraced

Don't Get Ahead of God

Exodus 13:20-22 [17-22] (KJV)

²⁰ And they took their journey from Succoth, and encamped in Etham, in the edge of the wilderness. ²¹ And the LORD went before them by day in a pillar of a cloud, to lead them the way; and by night in a pillar of fire, to give them light; to go by day and night: ²² He took not away the pillar of the cloud by day, nor the pillar of fire by night, *from* before the people.

In this text, Moses and the children of Israel were led by God into a new beginning. It is obvious in the text at a number of points that God was in charge as He moved them from captivity to Canaan. Moses displays exemplary leadership skills here because he did not get ahead of God. There are three reasons why we should not get ahead of God.

I.   There are dangers we cannot discern (verses 17, 18)

II.   There is data we cannot dismiss (verse 19a)

III.   There are demonstrations we cannot doubt (verses 19b, 21-22)

– 9 –

The Stand Still in Still Standing

Exodus 14:13 [10-14] (KJV)

13 And Moses said unto the people, Fear ye not, stand still, and see the salvation of the LORD, which he will shew to you to day: for the Egyptians whom ye have seen to day, ye shall see them again no more for ever. 14 The LORD shall fight for you, and ye shall hold your peace.

The Hebrew word translated "stand still" in verse 13 means "to stand or withstand." When we encounter the Israelites in this text, Moses's orders them to "stand still." After a furious but futile assault by Pharaoh and his legions, at the end of this passage we find Moses and the people of God he leads "still standing." This thought and theme ushers us down five corridors in this passage.

I.   The "stand still" of hobbling attachment

    a.   While the Israelites were out of Egypt, Egypt was not out of them!

II.   The "stand still" of heroic assurance

    a.   His faith motivated him to demonstrate courage and confidence in this situation.

III.   The "stand still" of heavenly assistance and alliance

    a.   God summoned an atmospheric alliance that pushed the waters back and up.

IV.   The "stand still" of humbling awe and adoration

    a.   The women danced on the sea shore!

V. The "stand still" of hopeful anticipation

    a. There are seven occurrences of the phrase "stand still" in the Word of God. See Exodus 14:13; Numbers 9:8; 1 Samuel 12:7; 14:9; Job 37:14; Acts 8:38. In five of these occurrences, man is speaking to God. But in two of them, God is speaking to man. God orders Job to "Hearken unto this, O Job: stand still, and consider the wondrous works of God. This is not just a command to Job but a timeless summons to every child of God.

– 10 –

The Day the Church Stopped Giving (A Stewardship Sermon)

Exodus 36:6-7 (NIV)

[6] Then Moses gave an order and they sent this word throughout the camp: "No man or woman is to make anything else as an offering for the sanctuary." And so the people were restrained from bringing more, [7] because what they already had was more than enough to do all the work.

In a remarkable account in the Old Testament, Moses commanded the people to stop giving! This is the day that Israel "upsized" their giving and gave an "over-the-top" offering. What would happen if every church did the same? The generous financial and material response of the Israelites involved four characteristics.

    I.   The means of their giving

        a. They were blessed when they left Egypt by their former oppressors

    II.   The motivation for their giving

        a. Their hearts were stirred up and they were willing

    III.   The measure of their giving

a. They gave more than enough

I. The mode of their giving

a. They gave a heave offering which was elevated up toward the sky

– 11 –

Where to Go to Give Up?
(Sabbaticals for Sinners)

Numbers 35:9-11 (NIV)

[9] Then the LORD said to Moses:
[10] "Speak to the Israelites and say to them:
'When you cross the Jordan into Canaan,
[11] select some towns to be your cities of refuge, to which a person who has killed someone accidentally may flee.'"

This passage has application for humanity's incessant search and longing for respite, refuge, and rest. The institutionalizing of this need in the nation of Israel through "cities of refuge" encompass three characteristics.

I. The principles that perpetuate rest

II. The premises that protect and preserve rest

III. The pattern that promises rest

a. Six cities of refuge are outlined in this and corresponding passages. Where is the seventh city? Ultimately it is not a place but a Person who says, "Come unto me and I will give you rest."

– 12 –
An Oversized Church with an Undersized Faith

Deuteronomy 32:15 [15-20] (KJV)

¹⁵ But Jeshurun waxed fat, and kicked: thou art waxen fat, thou art grown thick, thou art covered *with fatness*; then he forsook God *which* made him, and lightly esteemed the Rock of his salvation.

For the nation of Israel, God's called out (church) people in the Old Testament, prosperity became a greater test than adversity. Referred here as "Jeshurun" which means "the upright one," Israel abandoned God when they became prosperous or grew fat or oversized. Their lapse was characterized by three things.

I.   The fat of forgetfulness

II. The fat of idolatry

III. The fat of disobedience

– 13 –
The Making of a Minister (Pastor's Anniversary)

Joshua 1:1-2 [1-11] (KJV)

¹ Now after the death of Moses the servant of the LORD it came to pass, that the LORD spake unto Joshua the son of Nun, Moses' minister, saying, ² Moses my servant is dead; now therefore arise, go over this Jordan, thou, and all this people, unto the land which I do give to them, *even* to the children of Israel.

The Hebrew of this text is strongly suggestive that authentic ministry is more functional than formal; more progressive than passive. The word ascribed to Joshua and translated "minister" is the Hebrew word SHARATH and is in fact a verb in the text and not a noun; literally, "the one who ministered to or assisted Moses." Joshua's ascendancy is the culmination of a forty-year process and program of modeling, molding and mentoring. This text reveals five things about the making of a minister.

I.   The motivation of the minister (verse 1a)

II.   The mortality of the minister (verses 1a, 2a)

III.   The mandate of the minister (verse 3)

IV.   The meditation of the minister (verse 8a)

V.   The multiplication of the minister (verses 10-11)

– 14 –

Moving Forward Against All Odds
(Pastor's Anniversary)

Joshua 3:1 [3:1-17} (NIV)

**¹ Early in the morning Joshua and all the Israelites
set out from Shittim and went to the Jordan,
where they camped before crossing over.**

Joshua and two million Israelites fresh out of slavery stood on the brink of the Promised Land. Their dilemma was exacerbated because as they marched toward Canaan, they arrived at the Jordan River during the rainy season when the waters were at flood stage. The odds against a successful crossing were very high. But they were able to move forward against daunting odds because of four reasons in this text.

I.   Commitment for moving forward (3:1-4)

II.   Consecration for moving forward (3:5-6)

III.   Confidence for moving forward (3:7-13)

IV.   Consequence for moving forward (3:14-17)

– 15 –

When Walls Come Tumbling Down

Joshua 6:1-5 (NIV)

[1] Now Jericho was tightly shut up because of the Israelites. No one went out and no one came in. [2] Then the LORD said to Joshua, "See, I have delivered Jericho into your hands, along with its king and its fighting men. [3] March around the city once with all the armed men. Do this for six days. [4] Have seven priests carry trumpets of rams' horns in front of the ark. On the seventh day, march around the city seven times, with the priests blowing the trumpets. [5] When you hear them sound a long blast on the trumpets, have all the people give a loud shout; then the wall of the city will collapse and the people will go up, every man straight in."

Walled cities separated the people of Israel from the promise of blessing abundance. The most formidable of the wall cities they faced was Jericho. But this text reminds us that walls come down when:

I.   When the man (woman) of God worships the person of God

II.   When the plan of God secures the promises of God

III. When the people of God shout to the glory of God

– 16 –

A Faithful Man

Joshua 14:12 [6-15] (NIV)

[12] "Now give me this hill country that the LORD promised me that day. You yourself heard then that the Anakites were there and their cities were large and fortified, but, the LORD helping me, I will drive them out just as he said."

Caleb, at the age of eighty-five years old, was for his generation and ours a compelling example of faithfulness. What are the divinely nurtured attributes in this text that support the assertion that Caleb was a "faithful man?"

I.   He was a devoted man (verse 8)

II.   He was a delivered man (verse 10)

III. He was a daring man (verse 11)

IV.   He was a delighted man (verse 13)

– 17 –

A Father with Favor (A Father's Day Sermon)

Joshua 24:15 (KJV)

[15] And if it seem evil unto you to serve the LORD, choose you this day whom ye will serve; whether the gods which your fathers served that *were* on the other side of the flood, or the gods of the Amorites, in whose land ye dwell: but as for me and my house, we will serve the LORD.

This text and its larger context in the book of Joshua are strongly suggestive of the sources or streams of Joshua's favor.

I.   His sense of history

    a. See context in 23:1 – 24:14

II.   His sense of himself

    a. "but as for me"

III. His standing of headship

    a. "and my house"

IV.   His singleness of heart

    a. "we will serve the LORD"

– 18 –
When Failure Meets Favor

Judges 16:21-22 (NIV)

²¹ Then the Philistines seized him, gouged out his eyes and took him down to Gaza. Binding him with bronze shackles, they set him to grinding in the prison. ²² But the hair on his head began to grow again after it had been shaved.

There are four movements in this text and its larger context that provides strong clues from Samson's life about how failure can meet favor.

I.   The face of failure (13:1-25)

II.   The fact of failure (14:1 – 15:20)

III.   The folly of failure (16:1-21)

IV.   The forgiveness of failure (16:22-31)

– 19 –
Facing North When Life is Going South

Ruth 1:16-18 (NIV)

¹⁶ But Ruth replied, "Don't urge me to leave you or to turn back from you. Where you go I will go, and where you stay I will stay. Your people will be my people and your God my God. ¹⁷ Where you die I will die, and there I will be buried. May the LORD deal with me, be it ever so severely, if anything but death separates you and me." ¹⁸ When Naomi realized that Ruth was determined to go with her, she stopped urging her.

It is not a difficult thing to be faithful to our commitments and to others when everything is going well but Ruth was faithful while facing some very difficult, disillusioning and disappointing circumstances. When she and Naomi's life started going south she faced north.

I.   She dealt with difficult circumstances

II.   She demonstrated a decisive commitment

III. She discovered a determined champion

– 20 –

Recipe for a Blessing (A Mother's Day Sermon)

1 Samuel 1:17-18 (KJV)

[17] Then Eli answered and said, Go in peace: and the God of Israel grant *thee* thy petition that thou hast asked of him. [18] And she said, Let thine handmaid find grace in thy sight. So the woman went her way, and did eat, and her countenance was no more *sad*.

Hannah's name means "grace or kindness." She lived in Ramoth Gilead which means "heights." She was married to a man whose name means "The Lord created" and she was taunted and teased by a rival whose name means "pearl or coral." A tasty spiritual cuisine is served up in this passage. It is undeniably a recipe for a blessing. Hannah used the recipe and was blessed beyond measure.

I.   Develop a healthy discontent

II.   Disregard harmful and hurtful distractions and detractors

III. Desire holy delicacies

IV.   Deploy heavenly dynamics

V.   Display humbling detachment

     a. Hannah received the priestly blessing from Eli and went back home glad. There was a new bounce in her step and a swagger in her stagger. Her mood had changed from apathy and anxiety to anticipation.

Looking Up When Life is Looking Down

2 Samuel 5:22-24 [20-25] (KJV)

[22] And the Philistines came up yet again, and spread themselves in the valley of Rephaim. [23] And when David enquired of the LORD, he said, Thou shalt not go up; *but* fetch a compass behind them, and come upon them over against the mulberry trees.
[24] And let it be, when thou hearest the sound of a going in the tops of the mulberry trees, that then thou shalt bestir thyself: for then shall the LORD go out before thee, to smite the host of the Philistines.

At the core of his being, David knew something that often eludes so many of us in our materialistic modern culture. Immersed in our circumstances, our strife and our struggles, we are prone to forget that God moves in mysterious ways above and beyond all we can rationally comprehend. David knew how to look up when life was looking down. When the child of God does this, three things happen according to this text.

I.   It frustrates our foes

II.   It fixes our focus

III. It fortifies our faith

Costly Worship

2 Samuel 24:24 [18-25; 1 Chronicles 21:18-30] (KJV)

[24] And the king said unto Araunah, Nay; but I will surely buy *it* of thee at a price: neither will I offer burnt offerings unto the LORD my God of that which doth cost me nothing. So David bought the threshingfloor and the oxen for fifty shekels of silver.

Cost cutting, bargain basement, coupon cutting worshippers frequent churches far too often on Sundays. David's worship was costly and not convenient. What can we learn from his experience?

I. The revelation that compelled his worship

II. The recognition that commended his worship

III. The refusal that complemented his worship

IV. The rewards that confirmed his worship

    a. "and the plague was stayed from Israel" (verse 25)

– 23 –

When Brooks Dry Up

1 Kings 17:6-7 (KJV)

⁶ And the ravens brought him bread and flesh in the morning, and bread and flesh in the evening; and he drank of the brook. ⁷ And it came to pass after a while, that the brook dried up, because there had been no rain in the land.

Elijah was a committed, consecrated and courageous servant of God. He was called to be a prophet to the apostate Northern Kingdom of Israel. Yet, he had to learn to trust God when the brook dried up. Life so many of us, Elijah's faith was strengthened during this crisis by:

I. The experience of God's purposes

II. The evidence of God's promises

III. The expression of God's power

– 24 –

Guess Who's Coming to Dinner?

1 Kings 17:8-11 (NIV)

⁸ Then the word of the LORD came to him: ⁹ "Go at once to Zarephath of Sidon and stay there. I have commanded a widow in that place to supply you with food." ¹⁰ So he went to Zarephath. When he came to the town gate, a widow was there gathering sticks. He called to her and asked,

"Would you bring me a little water in a jar so I may have a drink?" [11] As she was going to get it, he called, "And bring me, please, a piece of bread."

A widow from the town of Zarephath experienced a miracle when she trusted God and fulfilled the request of the prophet Elijah who was providentially placed in her presence during a difficult and dire situation. Elijah was not the main guest at the dinner that evening but God Himself, who performed the miracle. There are five movements in this narrative; four are explicit and the fifth one is anticipated.

I.   The devoted prophet

II.   The disheartening predicament

III.   The daring pronouncement

IV.   The dynamic provision

V.   The delightful prospect

       a. Jesus came to this world, sat at the spiritual table He built, served the spiritual meal He bought and fed the world He saved!

– 25 –

The Showdown at Mount Carmel

1 Kings 18:21 [21-40] (KJV)

[21] And Elijah came unto all the people, and said, How long halt ye between two opinions? if the LORD *be* God, follow him: but if Baal, *then* follow him. And the people answered him not a word.

Elijah stood tall for God and won the showdown with the false prophets that he summoned to Mount Carmel. Three things happened that day.

I.   The prophet was magnetized

       a. By a compelling consciousness of a consecrated call

    b. By a compassionate concern for a crippled community

II.   God was magnified

    a. By Elijah's bold assault in enemy territory

    b. By Elijah's refusal to sacrifice on the worlds' altar

    c. By Elijah's affirmation of community

    d. By Elijah's faith perception

    e. By Elijah's reliance of believing prayer

III.   The people were mesmerized

IV.   Celebration

    a. The greatest showdown in human history took place on a hill called Calvary!

– 26 –

How to Handle the Breaks in Life

2 Kings 4:1[1-7] (KJV)

[1] Now there cried a certain woman of the wives of the sons of the prophets unto Elisha, saying, Thy servant my husband is dead; and thou knowest that thy servant did fear the LORD: and the creditor is come to take unto him my two sons to be bondmen.

This woman's experience teaches us how to handle the breaks in life.

I.   She experienced a breakdown

    a. Breakdowns occur when life writes us a bill we cannot pay.

II.   She experienced a breakthrough

    a. "What do you have in the house?"

III.   She experienced a break-in

    a. The more she poured out, the more God poured in!

IV.   She experience a breakout

  a. She paid her bills and "lived on the rest!"

– 27 –

What to Do When Life Loses Its Edge

2 Kings 6:5 [1-7] (KJV)

⁵But as one was felling a beam, the axe head fell into the water: and he cried, and said, Alas, master! for it was borrowed.

The late Dr. Stephen Olford noted that this text is a reminder that God "matches the misery of human tragedy with the miracle of divine victory." The axe in this narrative was lost. It did not belong to the one who was using it. The sacrificial or stewardship principle in life that is implicit in this passage requires three things of us.

I.   Remember what is loaned

II.   Recognize what is lost

III.   Receive what is located (recovered; redeemed)

  a. God is in the lost and found business!

– 28 –

What to Do with an Oversized Load

2 Kings 19:1-3 [14-16] (NIV)

¹When King Hezekiah heard this, he tore his clothes and put on sackcloth and went into the temple of the LORD. ²He sent Eliakim the palace administrator, Shebna the secretary and the leading priests, all wearing sackcloth, to the prophet Isaiah son of Amoz. ³They told him, "This is what Hezekiah says: 'This day is a day of distress and rebuke and disgrace, as when children come to the point of birth and there is no strength to deliver them.'"

In this passage with the Assyrian army massed at the gates of the city, King Hezekiah was faced with an oversized load. Israel was outmanned and outgunned. What was a king supposed to do?

I.   He faced his futility

II.   He fortified his facts

III.   He forwarded his fears

IV.   He fulfilled his future

        a.   In 2 Kings 19:29-31, God reminded Hezekiah that everything would be alright. An oversized load is no match for an oversized God!

– 29 –

How to Handle Life's Interruptions

2 Kings 20:1 [1-11] (NIV)

[1] In those days Hezekiah became ill and was at the point of death. The prophet Isaiah son of Amoz went to him and said, "This is what the LORD says: Put your house in order, because you are going to die; you will not recover."

King Hezekiah's sickness demonstrates our vulnerability to the contingencies of life. No amount of status or security can buffer us or insulate us from the call at three o'clock in the morning that turns our lives upside down. Four things we can learn from Hezekiah's experience.

I.   The reality we must accept

II.   The role and responsibility we must acknowledge

        a.   He respected the message from the prophet

III.   The remedy we must apply

        a.   He demonstrates the purposeful perpetuation of a pleasing pattern of powerful prayer as he "turned to the wall."

IV.   The results we must authenticate

a. God provides proof and pardon for our interruptions

- 30 -
Moving from Baggage to Blessing
1 Chronicles 4:9-10 (NIV)

⁹ Jabez was more honorable than his brothers. His mother had named him Jabez, saying, "I gave birth to him in pain." ¹⁰ Jabez cried out to the God of Israel, "Oh, that you would bless me and enlarge my territory! Let your hand be with me, and keep me from harm so that I will be free from pain." And God granted his request.

In this passage, Jabez whose name means "he makes sorrowful" had baggage but it did not keep him from experiencing blessing. He was able to move from baggage to blessing. How did this happen for him? How can it happen for us?

I. Tag it ("His mother had named him Jabez ... ")

 a. By giving him this rather distinctive and dubious name, Jabez's mother forced him to face daily the unpalatable circumstances surrounding his birth.

II. Tell it ("Jabez cried out to God ... ")

 a. Jabez's prayer was the outward cry of an inward sigh

III. Try it ("Oh that you would bless me ... ")

 a. He asked God to come up close and personal in his life – "to bless me"; this is not religion by proxy

IV. Treasure it ("And God granted his request")

 a. What do you do when God expands your territory?

Celebrating Our Connections

1 Chronicles 12:32 (KJV)

³² And of the children of Issachar, *which were men* that had understanding of the times, to know what Israel ought to do; the heads of them *were* two hundred; and all their brethren *were* at their commandment.

One of the most compelling connections and potent partnerships in the Bible is that between David and his "mighty men." None were mightier or more magnificent than the men of Issachar. This band of brothers came to David's side while the anointed and future king of Israel forayed for safety and survival in the wilderness during his ascent to power. What were the connections these men shared?

I.   They were connected by a common frailty

II.   They were connected by a common foe

III. They were connected by a common fervor

    a. The men of Issachar not only understood the times in which they lived but also commanded the families under their charge; like E. F. Hutton, when they spoke, their kinsmen were moved to action!

IV.   They were connected by a common future

The Fix for a Flawed Faith

2 Chronicles 7:14 [11-16] (NIV)

¹⁴ if my people, who are called by my name, will humble themselves and pray and seek my face and turn from their wicked ways, then will I hear from heaven and will forgive their sin and will heal their land.

When Solomon became king, succeeding his father, he wanted to experience God's continued favor and blessing in the event of any contingency, emergency or national crisis. He understood that our faith can sometimes become flawed and frayed by unwise choices and unsavory circumstances. How can a flawed faith be fixed according to this passage?

I.   The assurance of the presence of God

II.   The affirmation of the people of God

III.   The appropriation of the pardon of God

IV.   The anticipation of the promise of God

     a.   "I will heal their land."

- 33 -

Taking the Fight to the High Ground

2 Chronicles 20:15 [5-15] (NIV)

15 He said: "Listen, King Jehoshaphat and all who live in Judah and Jerusalem! This is what the LORD says to you: 'Do not be afraid or discouraged because of this vast army. For the battle is not yours, but God's.'"

This text is one of the most remarkable narratives in the entire Bible! It is the record of an astounding and unusual [by "unusual" I mean unorthodox] military victory by the armies of ancient Israel. King Jehoshaphat was victorious because he was directed by God to take the fight he faced to spiritual "high ground." He did this by deploying three powerful dynamics.

I.   He engaged in powerful petitioning or praying (verses 5 – 13)

II.   He sought relevant reconnaissance or revelation (verses 13 – 19)

III.   He prioritized wonderful worship (verses 20 – 22a)

     a.   The worshippers marched to the battlefield in front of the warriors

IV.   He experienced satisfying surrender (verse 22b)

    a.   It is reported of the enemy that day, "and they were defeated." Every child of God can surrender and experience satisfaction by embracing the promise that God will fight our battles!

– 34 –

Answering God's Curtain Call

Job 1:20-22 [13-22] (NIV)

[20] At this, Job got up and tore his robe and shaved his head. Then he fell to the ground in worship [21] and said: "Naked I came from my mother's womb, and naked I will depart. The LORD gave and the LORD has taken away; may the name of the LORD be praised." [22] In all this, Job did not sin by charging God with wrongdoing.

At God's unction, Job moves to center stage in this compelling drama. He is the defendant in a high profile case that has riveted the attention of both heaven and hell. Job is a righteous man chosen to answer God's curtain call. Job demonstrates how we should respond when trouble and trial rushes in like a tidal wave or tsunami into our lives.

I.   Job worshipped – evoked the Transcendent (verse 20a)

II.   Job witnessed – exposed the truth (verse 21b)

III.   Job waited – exercised the trust (verse 22)

– 35 –

Putting Our Problems in His Hands

Job 2:7-10 (KJV)

[7] So went Satan forth from the presence of the LORD, and smote Job with sore boils from the sole of his foot unto his crown. [8] And he took him a potsherd to scrape himself withal; and he sat down among the ashes. [9] Then said his wife unto him, Dost thou still

retain thine integrity? curse God, and die. [10] But he said unto her, Thou speakest as one of the foolish women speaketh. What? shall we receive good at the hand of God, and shall we not receive evil? In all this did not Job sin with his lips.

The Book of Job opens with Satan alleging before God that Job, the pride of heaven, is on the take. Satan insists that if the divine protections, privileges and perks God has afforded Job are taken away, Job's faith will wither and not be able to withstand the assault of evil. Unknown to Job, God gives His permission for Job to be tested. In successive waves, he experiences the loss of property, profit and person. His livestock is taken, servants killed and all his sons and daughters perished when a great wind toppled the house they had gathered in. This was Job's 9/11 and certainly not expected on the day when he had just gotten up early and offered prayers and burnt offering to God for each of his children. Job's experience and response to evil in his life reveals three things.

I.   The reality of evil

II.   The reach of evil

III.   The redemption of evil

        a. Job put his problems in God's hands with the profound recognition that they were in His hands first. In God's hand's evil is recycled, restrained and redeemed.

– 36 –

The Worth in Waiting
(First Sermon of the New Year)

Job 14:14-15 (KJV)

[14] If a man die, shall he live *again*? all the days of my appointed time will I wait, till my change come. [15] Thou shalt call, and I will answer thee: thou wilt have a desire to the work of thine hands.

We live in the age of instant gratification. The whole notion of waiting for anything has become for many unpleasant and undesirable. We like things fast – fast foods, fast track, convenience store, quick cash, payday loans, drive through, instant coffee, and express mail. But Job reminds us in a compelling text that there is worth in waiting.

I.   The worth of unique perspective ("all the days of my appointed time")

II.   The worth of urgent priority ("will I wait")

III.   The worth of undeniable promise and prospect ("till my change come")

       a.   Job viewed death as a release and reprieve from the burdens of life. It would be like an honorary discharge or changing of the guard.

IV.   The worth of unrelenting passion ("thou wilt have a desire to the work of thy hand")

       a.   Eugene Peterson's wonderful paraphrase of verse 15 is "Homesick with longing for the creature you made, you'll call and I'll answer."

       b.   Our hope and joy is not ultimately dependent on what we do but what God does. God is relentless in His care for us!

– 37 –

The Face of Favor

Psalm 1:1-3 (KJV)

[1] Blessed *is* the man that walketh not in the counsel of the ungodly, nor standeth in the way of sinners, nor sitteth in the seat of the scornful. [2] But his delight *is* in the law of the LORD; and in his law doth he meditate day and night. [3] And he shall be like a tree planted by the rivers of water, that bringeth forth his fruit in his season; his leaf also shall not wither; and whatsoever he doeth shall prosper.

The dictionary defines "favor" as "an act of kindness; approval; acceptance; fair treatment; the condition of being liked." Who doesn't want favor? In the spiritual life, we often confuse worldly success with divine favor. The two concepts are not synonymous or interchangeable. One of the most striking portraits in the Bible of favor or blessedness is the first Psalm. In these three short verses, we are looking indeed into the face of favor. There are three dimensions of this compelling biblical portrait of favor.

I.   His vigilance (verse 1)

II. His volume (verse 2)

III. His victory (verse 3)

    a. Through preparation

      i. He was planted; indeed "transplanted" there

    b. Through presentation

      i. He brought forth fruit in his season

    c. Through preservation

      i. "his leaf also shall not wither; and whatsoever he doeth shall prosper."

– 38 –

Witness Protection

Psalm 27:5 [1-14] (KJV)

⁵ For in the time of trouble he shall hide me in his pavilion: in the secret of his tabernacle shall he hide me; he shall set me up upon a rock.

This is a psalm written by David when he was on the run; when his back was against the wall. Facing extreme adversity and a wanted man, he found solace and security in his faith in God. When the psalm is surveyed in its wide spiritual expanse, it features three movements – (1) what life does, (2) what God does and (3) what we can do. David experience's "witness protection" on four levels.

I.   The reality that haunts us

II.   The refuge that hides us

III.   The "Rock" that holds us

IV.   The remedy that helps us

– 39 –

The Flavor of Favor

Psalm 34:8 [1-10] (KJV)

**8 O taste and see that the LORD *is* good:
blessed *is* the man *that* trusteth in him.**

Based on the prescript to this psalm, to preserve his life and the loves of his men, David while on the run from King Saul pretended to be a madman in the presences of a pagan king and potential adversary. Perhaps he wrote these words as an apologetic to assure anyone who witnessed his magnificent mirage that, as it related to the things that really mattered, he was not a madman but clothed and in his right mind. In doing so, he exposes the flavor of favor.

I.   The flavor of tried (proven) experience

II.   The flavor of transcendent (preeminent) essence

III.   The flavor of transforming (promising) expectation

A Life Directed by God

Psalm 37:23-26 (NIV)

[23] If the LORD delights in a man's way, he makes his steps firm; [24] though he stumble, he will not fall, for the LORD upholds him with his hand. [25] I was young and now I am old, yet I have never seen the righteous forsaken or their children begging bread. [26] They are always generous and lend freely; their children will be blessed.

If your life, family, marriage, career or ministry was a featured film or a major cinematic production, would you not want the best director available to manage the project? Someone who has extensive credits to His name and a proven track record? A life directed by God:

I.   Encourages God's delight (stanza 23)

II. Experiences God's deliverance (stanza 24)

III. Enjoys God's dependability (verse 25)

IV. Expresses God's disposition (verse 26)

When Deep Calls

Psalm 42:7 [1-8] (NIV)

[7] Deep calls to deep in the roar of your waterfalls; all your waves and breakers have swept over me.

Beneath the chaos of the psalmist's circumstances emerges a remarkable portrait of spiritual maturity. It is not his passion as he leads worshippers into the sanctuary that is viewed here but rather the private and very personal pain he experiences as the songwriter would say, *"When waves of affliction sink over the soul and sunlight is hidden from view."* He is having his own Job experience. He is in a torrential storm at sea and it seems the LORD is sleep and cares not that he perishes. Deep called on the writer of this psalm. That is deep trial, deep suffering, deep tribulation and deep anguish. And when deep called, his faith was tested and tempered.

I.   The character of human experience (stanzas 1-4, 5a)

II.   The confession of hopeful expectation (stanzas 5b, 6)

III.   The confidence of heavenly engagement (stanzas 7, 8)

   a. His problems were unceasing and overwhelming; one wave followed another; each echoing the ferocity and terror of the other; bodily pain caused mental anguish; demonic insinuations inspired dark fears; outward tribulation harmonized with internal anguish; like the Apostle Paul who described how he experienced the deep, there were "fightings without and fears within." This man's soul was drowning in an unyielding flood and torrent of trouble. But that is not how the story ends … !

– 42 –

Getting to Then

Psalm 51:13 (KJV)

[13] *Then* will I teach transgressors thy ways;
and sinners shall be converted unto thee.

Psalm 51:19 (KJV)

[19] Then shalt thou be pleased with the sacrifices of righteousness, with burnt offering and whole burnt offering: then shall they offer bullocks upon thine altar.

This psalm is a pungent and profound reminder that sin is more than just "missing the mark." While this is the classic definition, it is obvious that when we miss one thing we hit another. Sin has consequences. Sin is misdirection; dislocation; a misguiding that detours and deters us from where God wants us to be. David had missed his exit in a flood of lustful gratification and the subsequent cover-up. The old Black preacher said it well, "Sin will make you do things you don't want to do; pay more than you want to pay, go places you don't want to go and stay longer than you want to stay." **In the spiritual life, THEN is**

- A vacancy sign for weary travelers
- A mile marker along our march to maturity
- A rest stop on the expressway of Christian experience
- A pleasing punctuation in the sentence of salvation
- A place where prodigals return home to the love of their Father

THEN is a spiritual location that is the supreme goal of the believer's life; that point where God is pleased with our offering. David had detoured from this point and place but the record is that he desired to reach this destination. Twice in this psalm, he begins a stanza with the word "then." In one instance, "then" is supplied by the translators but the inference is still there. How then do we get to <u>then</u>?

I.   The reality of convicting confrontation

II.   The recognition of crippling condition

III. The result of cleansing confession

IV.   The reward of consecrated commitment

    a. This is the place of treasured transformation and the point where God transforms our willing availability by renewing of our minds. It is the place where "mercy and truth meet together" (Psalm 85:10).

Closed to Through Traffic

Psalm 55:6-8 (KJV)

⁶ And I said, Oh that I had wings like a dove!
for then would I fly away, and be at rest.
⁷ Lo, *then* would I wander far off,
and remain in the wilderness. Selah.
⁸ I would hasten my escape from the windy storm *and* tempest.

Scholars characterize this psalm as an individual lament or "song of sorrow." It is almost universally agreed that David penned these words during the Absalom rebellion. It was perhaps the darkest period of his reign when his favored son and potential heir to the throne turned against him, led the nation in a revolt, attempted to usurp his power and take his crown. David is at his wits end and expresses a desire to run away; to take flight and to leave it all behind. It is not unlikely that these words formed on his lips during the heat of the crisis as he spotted a dove flying freely and flawlessly in midflight in the Palestinian sky. David moves from "How can I get out of this?" to "What can I get out of this?"

I.   What life will do (stanzas 1-5, 9-15, 19b-21)

II.   What prayer will do (stanzas 16-19a)

III. What God will do (stanzas 22-23)

   a. Jesus was on a mission that was divinely determined and destined. He travelled down through forty-two generations and came to an exit that was closed because of sin, suffering and death. He did not detour but ignored the sign, "closed to through traffic" and exited at the end of a ramp named Calvary and there He died!

Insight for the Uptight

Psalm 73:16-17 (KJV)

¹⁶ When I thought to know this, it *was* too painful for me; ¹⁷ Until I went into the sanctuary of God; *then* understood I their end.

Psalm 73 launches the third of five divisions of the Psalms or Psalter. It is ascribed to Asaph, a Levite, who many expositors believe was a worship leader in the Temple during the reign of King David. See 1 Chronicles 15:16-19. His passion and prominence as a leader in this arena was imperiled by an uptightness that had spawned a crisis of faith.

I.   The crisis he faced (stanzas 1-15)

II.   The clarity he found (stanzas 16-22)

III.   The confession he framed (stanzas 23-28)

How to Make It Through a Bad Day

Psalm 77:11-13 [11-20] (KJV)

¹¹ I will remember the works of the LORD:
surely I will remember thy wonders of old.
¹² I will meditate also of all thy work, and talk of thy doings. ¹³
Thy way, O God, *is* in the sanctuary:
who *is so* great a God as *our* God?

The author of this Psalm is having a "bad day." In the first section or paragraph of the psalm, stanzas 1 – 10, he graphically expresses his sense of being overwhelmed; overmatched; overrun and overcome by his circumstances. In stanza 2, he characterizes this moment in his personal history as "the day of my trouble." So distressed was he that his "soul refused to be comforted" (stanza 2b). He has difficulty speaking and trouble speaking. And, worst of all, his faith in God has been shaken and shredded for he expresses his worst doubts and fears about being forsaken and forgotten by God. How could he lead the people in worship if he had questions about God's dealings?

The author identified in the subtitle of the Psalm is Asaph. He was a Levite who served with others as a musician and worship leader in the sanctuary during David's reign. Twelve of the one hundred fifty psalms are attributed to him (50, 73 – 83). Eleven of those psalms launch the third book of the Psalter.

This brother was having a bad day. He couldn't get away from trouble. While praying, you might say that Asaph experienced an epiphany of insight that helped him to exit the darkness of his despair and make it through his bad day. There was a change in the tenants that leased space in his mental, emotional and spiritual penthouse.

- Mercy moved in and misery moved out
- Delight moved in and discouragement moved out
- Clarity moved in and confusion moved out
- Assurance moved in and anxiety moved out
- Faith moved in and fear moved out

This takes place as a result of two seismic and significant shifts in the latter part of the Psalm. These clues in stanzas 13 and 19 provide timeless truths and permanent principles for anyone who wants to know how to make it through a bad day. You want to know what they are.

I.   Bless God in the sanctuary of His holiness

II.   Believe God in the sea of His hiddenness

- 46 -

Business at Baca

Psalm 84:5-8 (NIV)

[5] Blessed are those whose strength is in you, who have set their hearts on pilgrimage. [6] As they pass through the Valley of Baca, they make it a place of springs; the autumn rains also cover it with pools. [7] They go from strength to strength, till each appears before God in Zion. [8] Hear my prayer, O LORD God Almighty; listen to me, O God of Jacob. Selah

Psalm 84 is a moving portrayal of the life of the pilgrim-believer who longs to visit the temple of God in Jerusalem.

I.   The desire that arrested him

II.   The difficulty that assails him

III.   The destiny that awaited him This is the only psalm in the Psalter that is attributed to Moses; the vigilant, valiant, virtuous vanguard of Israel's faith. I call it the **"pulsar"** psalm for there are at least fifteen (15) references to date, time, or chronology. When reading this psalm, listen to its thrust and theme intently with your heart, and you can almost hear it go "tick tock, tick tock".

    a.   The Lord gives us grace and glory

    b.   "I'd rather be a doorkeeper ... "

- 47 -

Making the Most of the Moment

Psalms 90:12 (NIV)

[12] Teach us to number our days aright, that we may gain a heart of wisdom.

This is the only psalm in the Psalter that is attributed to Moses; the vigilant, valiant, virtuous vanguard of Israel's faith. I call it the **"pulsar"** psalm for there are at least fifteen (15) references to date, time, or chronology. When reading this psalm, listen to the thrust and theme with heart, and you can almost hear it go "tick tock, tick tock …

I.   The transcendent orientation ("teach us")

II.   The transactional operation ("to number our days")

III.   The transformational obligation ("that we may gain a heart of wisdom")

– 48 –

Living Life by the Numbers (An Alternative Approach)

Psalm 90:12 (KJV)

[12] **So teach *us* to number our days,
that we may apply *our* hearts unto wisdom.**

Moses, the assumed author of this psalm was challenging his readers to live their lives by the numbers. He did not have the lottery in view or some other gambling venture or venue but rather the spiritual well-being of the flock God had called him to shepherd. The oldest of the Psalms, it was written most likely in connection with Israel's failure to trust God and enter into the Promise Land. God judged them. He made the nation wander for forty years in the wilderness until all the people who had been over twenty years of age at Kadesh-barnea died.

Noted Bible scholar, Warren Wiersbe believes that this psalm is Moses' personal reaction to the crisis; he turned to God in prayer and sought an eternal abiding place in the Lord. When a life is lived by the numbers it is:

I.   A maturing life

II.   A measured life

III.   A meaningful life

How Good is God?

Psalm 100:5 [1-5] (KJV)

**⁵ For the LORD *is* good; his mercy *is* everlasting;
and his truth *endureth* to all generations.**

The identity of the author of this psalm is shrouded in anonymity. We don't know who he was, yet it is obvious that he furrowed through any doubt, disillusionment, desperation or disappointment and arrived at a place where the essential question for him was not "What good is God?" but rather he is answering the question implied in his magnificent and moving praise and thanksgiving, "How good is God?"

I.   God is good because of God's exalted essence

II.   God is good because of God's matchless mercy

III.   God is good because of God's amazing availability

      a.   God will never leave you or forsake you. Wherever you go, whatever you do, God is already there; waiting, willing, wanting and working for us. He is good because as the songwriter says, "He was there all the time!"

How to Avoid a Spiritual Foreclosure

Psalm 116:12 [1-19] (KJV)

**¹² What shall I render unto the LORD
for all his benefits toward me?**

Most interpreters believe this is an individual psalm of thanksgiving, which at that point in time was celebrated in the communal experience of the people of God. The psalmist is responding to deliverance from a "near death" experience. Twice in the psalm does he declare, "I will pay my vows unto the Lord now in the presence of all his people" (stanzas 14; 18). This statement represents on the part of the psalmist the recognition of a payment due notice. The psalmist makes four payments in this passage.

I. The payment called satisfaction (stanzas 1-8)

II. The payment called service (stanzas 9-11, 16)

III. The payment called sacrifice (stanza 13)

IV. The payment called security (stanza 15)

  a. What begins with satisfaction, ends with security. Security is the last payment in the text. The psalmist expresses his secure confidence in God. He has taken care of him in life; God will take care of him in death. He says, "Precious in the sight of the Lord is the death of His saints" (stanza 15).

- 51 -

The Outlook for the Uplook
(First Sermon of the New Year)

Psalm 121:1-8 (KJV)

[1] I will lift up mine eyes unto the hills, from whence cometh my help. [2] My help *cometh* from the LORD, which made heaven and earth. [3] He will not suffer thy foot to be moved: he that keepeth thee will not slumber. [4] Behold, he that keepeth Israel shall neither slumber nor sleep. [5] The LORD *is* thy keeper: the LORD *is* thy shade upon thy right hand. [6] The sun shall not smite thee by day, nor the moon by night. [7] The LORD shall preserve thee from all evil: he shall preserve thy soul. [8] The LORD shall preserve thy going out and thy coming in from this time forth, and even for evermore.

The movement (uplook) in this psalm constitutes assurances that will encourage our "outlook" as we face the changes and challenges of the days ahead.

I. The expression of a personal awareness (stanzas 1-2)

II.   The experience of a powerful availability (stanzas 5-8)

    a. God puts swagger in our stagger. One reason is because our "Keeper does not sleep."

III.   The expectation of promising assurance (stanza 9)

    b. Three times in the last three stanzas of the psalm do we find the word "preserve." It translates the Hebrew word <u>shamar</u> which means "to keep." Our salvation is sure and secure today because God has keeping power.

- 52 -
The Anatomy of a Blessing

Psalm 133:1-3 (KJV)

[1] Behold, how good and how pleasant *it is* for brethren to dwell together in unity! [2] *It is* like the precious ointment upon the head, that ran down upon the beard, *even* Aaron's beard: that went down to the skirts of his garments; [3] As the dew of Hermon, *and as the dew* that descended upon the mountains of Zion: for there the LORD commanded the blessing, *even* life for evermore.

Psalm 133 is foundational to understanding the true character of divine blessing. It shares with Ephesians 1:3 a conceptual coalescence that constitutes a spiritual biopsy of what authentic blessing from God looks like.

I.   The character that elevates it

II.   The community that encourages it

III.   The coordinates that empower it

IV.   The currents that expand it

V.   The command that engages it

    a. "<u>There</u>, the LORD commanded the blessing"

The Day the Choir Stopped Singing

Psalm 137:4 [1-6] (KJV)
4 How shall we sing the LORD'S song in a strange land?

Many believe that this psalm was written in the 6th century B.C. by a former exile who had returned to Jerusalem. As the psalmist looks back on this painful experience, there is not only deep love for Yahweh but deep hatred for his captors. Israel was a worshipping community; indeed one grand "mass choir" called like us "to make a joyful noise unto the Lord … to enter his gates with thanksgiving and his courts with praise" (Psalm 100). But in captivity with only the prospect of singing "songs in the night" (Job 35:10), the choir stopped singing. Why?

I. They were moved out but not moved on

II. They sat down but did not stand up

III. They remembered the past but forgot the promise

IV. They stopped worshipping and started worrying

V. They asked a question but forgot the answer

  a. How can I …

    i. Worship in the wasteland

    ii. Find melody in the misery

    iii. Hit high notes in the lowlands

    iv. Keep my pitch when I am in the ditch

    v. Find my range in the land called Strange

    vi. Resign to worship when I am really weary

    vii. Handle my harp rather than hang my head

    viii. Remember and yet not forget?

  b. You and I can only truly sing when "It's in my heart, this melody of love divine."

- 54 -

A High Definition Faith in a Low Definition World

Psalm 139:23-24 [1-24] (KJV)

[23] Search me, O God, and know my heart: try me, and know my thoughts: [24] And see if *there be any* wicked way in me, and lead me in the way everlasting.

By all accounts, David was a man of "high definition" faith. This is not only the testimony of the Lord who distinctly dubbed him as "a man after God's own heart" but of the Bible as well. You can't read the Psalms and not reach this conclusion. This psalm provides a clue today to what made David's faith "high definition."

I.   The revelation of a supreme authority (stanzas 1a,4, 21)

II.   The reality of a sobering appraisal (stanzas 1b-6, 14-18)

III.   The rewards of a satisfying availability (stanzas 7-13)

IV.   The request for searching apprehension (stanzas 23-25)

    a. David moves from celebrating God's comprehension to requesting God's apprehension; compare Philippians 3:13. He asks the Lord to touch him; to frisk him; pat him down and make sure he is not packing!

- 55 -

Dangerous Intersection

Proverbs 14:12 (KJV)

[12] There is a way which seemeth right unto a man, but the end thereof *are* the ways of death.

A few years ago, I was driving along on a two lane highway; it was overcast, raining and damp. I remember being preoccupied and distracted that day with my head flooded with thoughts and my heart flooded with emotions. On this particular day, I observed a road sign that summoned me out of the misty, meandering moisture of that rainy day. Road signs don't talk, don't walk, beg or beckon but on this day the words etched on the sign seared and seethed like a scorching coal into the inner sanctum of my consciousness. The sign read "Dangerous Intersection". I asked myself, "Why would the state post such a sign?" Low visibilities, sharp curve, slick surface, heavy traffic, a history of accidents or mounting fatalities are all reasons for such a warning. Quickly deferring my analysis of the "why", I focused on the immediate and more urgent response which was to slow down; adjust my speed; and stay alert.

Experience wedded exposition as that distant memory of some years ago drew alongside the words of this text. These words represent a warning. Solomon, the wisdom writer who had made his share of mistakes, knew a dangerous intersection when he saw one. So alert was he to its dangers that this verse is repeated verbatim in Proverbs 16:25.

I.   The problem of perception

II.   The presence of peril

III.   The promise of protection

    a.   The most dangerous intersection in human history was located at a hill called Calvary. There, the worst in man collided with the best in God. It was at this intersection that light penetrated darkness; that truth trounced evil and where sin abounded but grace abounded much more. It was at the cross where our Savior died!

- 56 -

Avoiding Life's Dead Ends

Proverbs 16:25 (KJV)

[25] There is a way that seemeth right unto a man, but the end thereof *are* the ways of death.

This verse occurs twice in the Book of Proverbs. See 14:12 for the other occurrence. I am sure the repetition and reiteration has significance if for no other reason than special emphasis and reinforcement of a fundamental message. In Chapter 14, it follows a verse that contrasts the fortunes of the house of the wicked and the tabernacle of the righteous; in Chapter 16, it is an addendum to a verse that underscores the value of positive and "pleasant words."

But the fundamental truth our passage bears witness to is that our decisions and choices in life have consequences. Life is a path or road that we take and wrong turns can be costly and even deadly. We must choose our way carefully and prayerfully otherwise we will end up literally at a "dead end." There are three things the text tells us that we must do if we are to avoid "dead ends" in life.

I.   Choose THE way and not "a" way

II.   Choose GOD'S way and not "my" way

III.   Choose the FREE WAY and not the "toll" way

    a.   The "ways of death" is a spiritual toll in time and eternity. Why pay a toll when you can travel free? When you are God's child, and have the pass that only He can give us, you might have to slow down but you will never be pulled over, ticketed or arrested.

- 57 -

What Faith is Not Afraid to Do

Ecclesiastes 11:1-2 (NLT)

[1] **Send your grain across the seas, and in time, profits will flow back to you. [2] But divide your investments among many places, for you do not know what risks might lie ahead.**

For ten chapters in the Book of Ecclesiastes, Solomon paints a rather dismal and disillusioning portrait of what life is all about. In his excellent commentary on this passage, Dr. Warren Wiersbe lists four arguments that King Solomon uses to support this portrayal of life. They are (1) the monotony of life; (2) the vanity of wisdom; (3) the futility of wealth and (4) the certainty of death.

The problem is that his premises and arguments are all horizontal and totally excludes God from the picture. Being the wise man that he was, beginning at the eleventh chapter and the passage we read tonight, Solomon invites God to center stage. When he extends this invitation, the horizons of his understanding open up and his perspective changes radically.

The man or woman of faith does not cower in the corners of life and is not ultimately defined or intimidated by the shadows of uncertainty that hover and haunt our path in this world of sin and suffering. Solomon uses two metaphors to illustrate his adventuresome perspective and positive outlook. The two are the life of the merchant and the life of the farmer. In both instances, success in either endeavor requires a faith that is not afraid. It is the first one that solicits our attention this evening. It is the activity of the merchant who sends his ships out to sea. Solomon, who had a navy of his own and traded goods with neighboring countries, understood this type of endeavor, the risks that were involved and the profits that could be made. For me, and I pray for you too, it is a moving metaphor for what faith is not afraid to do.

I.   Faith is not afraid to live boldly (verse 1a)

II.   Faith is not afraid to live broadly (verse 2)

III. Faith is not afraid to live blindly (verses 1b, 2b)

IV.   Faith is not afraid to live bountifully (verse 1b)

- 58 -

God's Cleaning Service

Isaiah 1:16-20 (KJV)

[16] Wash you, make you clean; put away the evil of your doings from before mine eyes; cease to do evil; [17] Learn to do well; seek judgment, relieve the oppressed, judge the fatherless, plead for the widow. [18] Come now, and let us reason together, saith the LORD: though your sins be as scarlet, they shall be as white as snow; though they be red like crimson, they shall be as wool. [19] If ye be willing and obedient, ye shall eat the good

of the land: ²⁰ **But if ye refuse and rebel, ye shall be devoured with the sword: for the mouth of the LORD hath spoken** *it.*

In the passage before us, God calls heaven and earth as silent witnesses in a judicial convocation against Israel. The indictment is that because of sin, Israel is sick from the soles of her feet to the crown of her head. Yet she wearies God with a incessant religious ritual that denies the reality of her relationship to the Holy One of Israel. What should have been a parade of praise was a shallow charade of pretense and a superficial cycle of religious frenzy. In v. 16, God essentially calls for Israel to "clean up your act." God lifts up before Israel the promise of pardon. Through the prophet Isaiah, God tells the people "clean up your act and I will help you." In this passage, God offers God's own cleaning service to address the spiritual ills and ails of His chosen people. He did it then and He is still doing it right here and right now. Why do we need God's Cleaning Service?

I.   The problem of crippling contamination (verse 15)

II.   The possibility of comprehensive cleaning (verses 16-18)

III.   The provision of commendable consideration (verse 19)

- 59 -
Overcoming an Identity Crisis
Isaiah 6:1 [1-8] (KJV)
¹ **In the year that king Uzziah died I saw also the Lord sitting upon a throne, high and lifted up, and his train filled the temple.**

Our text today is set in the eighth century B.C. The great King Uzziah is dead; whether it is the civil death he experienced after contracting leprosy as a result of his arrogant usurping of the priestly office or his actual physical death, expositors are not sure but this passage records that the nation and the prophet Isaiah are mourning his demise and death. Exegetical and expositional engagement of this text crescendos around verse 8, "Also I heard the voice of the Lord, saying, Whom shall I send, and who will go for us? Then said I, Here am I; send me".

But on the way to "here am I" or, to use a more contemporary rendering, "here I am", Isaiah experiences two more affirmations of his prophetic ministry that helped him to resolve a critical identity crisis precipitated by the death of the notable king.

I.   Who I am (a creature before my Creator – verses 1-4)

II.   How I am (a sinner before my Savior – verses 5-7)

III.   Here I am (a servant before my Sovereign – verse 8)

– 60 –
Surviving a Spiritual Eclipse
Isaiah 21:11-12 (KJV)

[11] **The burden of Dumah. He calleth to me out of Seir, Watchman, what of the night? Watchman, what of the night?** [12] **The watchman said, The morning cometh, and also the night: if ye will enquire, enquire ye: return, come.**

The Edomites were experiencing a dark spiritual night and Isaiah the prophet speaks a word to them in due season. This prophetic pronouncement occurs in a chapter that also includes prophecies concerning Babylon and Arabia. This spiritual nugget provides clear direction about how to make it through the night and survive a spiritual eclipse.

I.   The problem that transmits the night

II.   The preacher that translates the night

III.   The promise that transcends the night

    a.   The prophet said "Morning is coming, but also the night." There is no justification here for nightless mornings and morningless nights but rather the affirmation that in life, night and morning coexist. No wonder the Psalmist said, "Weeping may endure for a night but joy comes in the morning" (Psalm 30:5b).

– 61 –
The God Who Waits

Isaiah 30:18 (KJV)

¹⁸ And therefore will the LORD wait, that he may be gracious unto you, and therefore will he be exalted, that he may have mercy upon you: for the LORD *is* a God of judgment: blessed *are* all they that wait for him.

Israel is in the throes of national upheaval facing imminent destruction and devastation as a judgment from God. While turning to Egypt for assistance, the nation faces a looming, lumbering threat from her nemesis Assyria. Isaiah reminds them that God is waiting on them.

I.   To experience His pardon

II.   To enjoy His provision

III.   To explore His precepts

IV.   To expect His presence

– 62 –
No Matches Found!

Isaiah 40:25 [18-31] (KJV)

²⁵ To whom then will ye liken me, or shall I be equal? saith the Holy One.

The prophet Isaiah is reinforcing to a once proud and pompous people the very hard lesson that their disobedience and defection had taught them and brought them-that there is none like God. Search if you will among the vast array of nations of the world or among the pantheon of illusive idols and distant deities and there are "no matches found." God has no equals!

I.   In the magnitude of His counsel (verses 3-5, 6-8; 13-14)

II.   In the majesty of His creation (verses 2, 21-22)

III. In the mastery of His competition (verses 15-20, 23-24)

IV. In the measure of His comfort (verses 1-2, 9-11; 27-31)

– 63 –

The Price of Our Pardon

Isaiah 53:5 (KJV)

⁵ But he *was* wounded for our transgressions, *he was* bruised for our iniquities: the chastisement of our peace *was* upon him; and with his stripes we are healed.

What is the price of our pardon? The answer to this question is given in a central passage in one of the most compelling chapters in the Bible.

I. The price of our pardon was high (His suffering)

II. The price of our pardon was heavy (His substitution)

III. The price of our pardon was honored (His sufficiency)

    a. The text ends with these words, "With his stripes we are healed." This is not a reference to physical healing; Jesus can do that too but here we are reminded that only Jesus can heal a sin sick soul. He paid the price that no one else could pay. That price was paid in full, accepted and a receipt printed on Calvary with the words emblazoned on it, "It is finished!"

– 64 –

An Extreme Makeover

Jeremiah 18:1-4 [1-6] (KJV)

¹ The word which came to Jeremiah from the LORD, saying, ² Arise, and go down to the potter's house, and there I will cause thee to hear my words.

³Then I went down to the potter's house, and, behold, he wrought a work on the wheels. ⁴And the vessel that he made of clay was marred in the hand of the potter: so he made it again another vessel, as seemed good to the potter to make *it*.

In this text, through his appointed and anointed prophet Jeremiah, God offers apostate Israel an extreme makeover. This prophecy does not only teach spiritual truth but also presents a religious personality. God sends Jeremiah to school. His first on the job training assignment takes place at the potter's house.

I.   A divine dispensation

    a. "The word which came to Jeremiah from the Lord"

II. A distinctive deployment

    b. "Arise and go down"

III. A dynamic development

    c. Describe the work of the near Eastern potter

IV. A disturbing disruption

    d. "Marred in the hand of the potter"

V.   A delightful destiny

    e. "As the clay is in the potter's hand, so are ye in mine hand"

– 65 –

A Man on Fire

Jeremiah 20:7-9 (NIV)

⁷O LORD, you deceived me, and I was deceived; you overpowered me and prevailed. I am ridiculed all day long; everyone mocks me. ⁸Whenever I speak, I cry out proclaiming violence and destruction. So the word of the LORD has brought me insult and reproach all day long. ⁹But if I say, "I will not mention him or speak any more in his name," his word is in my heart like a fire, a fire shut up in my bones. I am weary of holding it in; indeed, I cannot.

Jeremiah whose name means "Yahweh establishes" was ordained to be a prophet even before he was formed in his mother's womb. His calling had pre-natal and post-natal implications. Often described as "the weeping prophet" because he was given to tumultuous sweeps and swings of emotion, Jeremiah was a man on fire.

I.   He was in a fire (his intimidation – verses 7-8)

II.   He was out of fire (his resignation – verse 9a)

III. He had a fire (his determination – verse 9b)

    a. Deep in his heart he experienced an irrepressible resolve; an unshakeable sense of certainty that metastasized and settled in his bones that bolstered his prophetic calling, character and career.

– 66 –
The Hope That Holds Us Hostage
Lamentations 3:22-24 (KJV)

[22] *It is of* the LORD'S mercies that we are not consumed, because his compassions fail not. [23] *They are* new every morning: great *is* thy faithfulness. [24] The LORD *is* my portion, saith my soul; therefore will I hope in him.

This text is the epicenter of the memorable parade that occurred six hundred years before Jesus rode into Jerusalem on Palm Sunday. This parade took place on the occasion of the destruction of the city of Jerusalem in 587 B.C. as the soon-to-be exiles were marched captive from their homes to a foreign land. Jeremiah was one of those and he records his experience in the Book of Lamentations. In the miser of this historic moment and the haunting uncertainty that resonates from the calamity and catastrophe all around him, the prophet finds home and encouragement in the constancy and faithfulness of God.

I.   The Lord's mercies (verse 22)

II.   The Lord's mornings (verse 23)

III.   The Lord's measure (verse 24)

   a.   The LORD is my portion! He was not saying
        that someone else did not have a portion; that
        he had some monopoly or franchise on the
        blessings of God, but the prophet acknowledges
        his awareness of Gods' measure or portion in
        the context of his own personal experience. We
        should all do likewise.

– 67 –

Experiencing Rest in the Ruins

Lamentations 3:21-24 (KJV)

[21] This I recall to my mind, therefore have I hope. [22] *It is of*
the LORD'S mercies that we are not consumed, because his
compassions fail not. [23] *They are* new every morning: great *is*
thy faithfulness. [24] The LORD *is* my portion, saith my soul;
therefore will I hope in him.

We would love it if life was one perpetual party or festival
full of fun, food and fellowship but this text is a reminder that we
are a fallen people and we live in a fallen world. We don't have to
look far to find ruin. No life is safe from it; no marriage is immune
from it; no family is exempt from it; no church is insulated from it!

•   Ruin is one phone call away
•   Ruin is one doctor's visit away
•   Ruin is one MRI away
•   Ruin is one drunk driver away
•   Ruin is one layoff away
•   Ruin is one gunman or bullet away
•   Ruin is one bad decision away

On the other hand, the word "rest" is alluring, inviting,
consoling, comforting and peaceful; both ruin and rest permeate
this text; they collide and converge around a colossal catastrophe.
It is 587 B.C. and the clock has struck midnight in the life of

the Southern Kingdom. The prophet Jeremiah is overrun and overwhelmed by ruin; now exiled from his homeland and having to sing the Lord's song in a strange land, he recalls the calamitous and catastrophic failure of a nation that had been destined for greatness; perhaps he was taking this failure personally for it had happened on his watch.

I.   The focus of the rest

II.   The fact of the rest

III. The face of the rest

    a. Jeremiah's lament is intimately personal. It is not a concept or a covenant that is in his purview, but a real person.

– 68 –

Standing Tall in a Difficult Situation

Daniel 6:23 (NIV)

[23] The king was overjoyed and gave orders to lift Daniel out of the den. And when Daniel was lifted from the den, no wound was found on him, because he had trusted in his God.

So many Christians, stand for nothing and fall for everything. Cf. Ephesians 4:14. You and I will be tested. Are you prepared to stand tall when you face your difficult situation? Daniel was! Now a senior statesman; in the sunset of a brilliant career, when facing his difficult situation, he did three things that every Christian should aspire to.

I.   He stood out

II.   He stood up

III. He stood on

    a. He stood on the solid foundation of his faith in God. His actions here inculcated years of experience with God. He remembered how his Hebrew companions had defied a similar edict and were thrown into a burning, fiery furnace. He remembered how God showed up in the midst of the fire and delivered them. Daniel remembered his visions of a new world order where God would make all His enemies His footstool.

– 69 –

MapQuest to Misery

Jonah 1:1-3 (NIV)

¹ The word of the LORD came to Jonah son of Amittai: ² "Go to the great city of Nineveh and preach against it, because its wickedness has come up before me." ³ But Jonah ran away from the LORD and headed for Tarshish. He went down to Joppa, where he found a ship bound for that port. After paying the fare, he went aboard and sailed for Tarshish to flee from the LORD.

The prophet Jonah was directionally disoriented. His disorientation and disassociation from God was precipitated by four (4) choices.

I.   Hearing rather than heeding

II.   Career rather than calling

III.   Fleeing rather than following

IV.   Paying rather than praying

      a.   It is one thing to experience misery; it is something altogether different to pay for the privilege! Jonah paid for passage to Tarshish. He did not use frequent flier miles but paid. He did not win a ticket in a sweepstakes or lottery but paid. He did not stowaway aboard ship but paid. He eventually prayed and found mercy for his misery.

The Stretch That Overcomes Our Stress

Habakkuk 3:16-19 [3-19] (NIV)

[16] I heard and my heart pounded, my lips quivered at the sound; decay crept into my bones, and my legs trembled. Yet I will wait patiently for the day of calamity to come on the nation invading us. [17] Though the fig tree does not bud and there are no grapes on the vines, though the olive crop fails and the fields produce no food, though there are no sheep in the pen and no cattle in the stalls, [18] yet I will rejoice in the LORD, I will be joyful in God my Savior. [19] The Sovereign LORD is my strength; he makes my feet like the feet of a deer, he enables me to go on the heights. For the director of music. On my stringed instruments.

The prophet Habakkuk did not confront the people but confronted God as he wrestled with the problem of evil and suffering around him. He is the only prophet in the Old Testament whose message is directed to God. In Chapter 1, he is disturbed; Chapter 2 – discerning and in Chapter 3, he is determined. As he posted, positioned and postured himself for God's response (Chapter 1 -2), God's final word was *"the just shall live by faith."* This verse is quoted three times in the New Testament (Hebrews 10:38; Romans 1:17; Galatians 3:17)

We live in a "stressed out" world. Many in the church are experiencing stress. Adversity is what life does to us but stress is what we do to ourselves. We must be able to counter the stresses of life with the stretch of faith.

I. The stretch of purposeful witnessing (verses 3-15)

II. The stretch of patient waiting (verse 16b)

III. The stretch of passionate worshipping (verse 18)

    a. The variegated fractions of Habakkuk's experience when divided by the integer of God's incomparable work and wisdom reduced the prophet to his least spiritual common denominator which was "worship."

Marketing in the Cyber Age

Marketing in the Cyber Age

The Why, the What and the How

Kurt Rohner

JOHN WILEY & SONS

Chichester · New York · Weinheim · Brisbane · Toronto · Singapore

Other Wiley Editorial Offices

John Wiley & Sons, Inc., 605 Third Avenue,
New York, NY 10158-0012, USA

WILEY-VCH Verlag GmbH, Pappelallee 3,
D-69469 Weinheim, Germany

Jacaranda Wiley Ltd, 33 Park Road, Milton,
Queensland 4064, Australia

John Wiley & Sons (Canada) Ltd, 22 Worcester Road,
Rexdale, Ontario M9W 1L1, Canada

John Wiley & Sons (Asia) Pte Ltd, 2 Clementi Loop #02-01,
Jin Xing Distripark, Singapore 129809

Library of Congress Cataloging-in-Publication Data
Rohner, Kurt, 1954-
  [Cyber-Marketing. English]
  Marketing in the cyber age : the why, the what, and the how / K.
Rohner.
    p. cm.
  Includes bibliographical references and index.
  ISBN 0-471-97023-9 (paper)
  1. Telemarketing. 2. Database marketing. 3. Internet marketing.
  I. Title.
HF5415.1265.R6413 1998
658.8'4--dc21   98–3083
                                                      CIP

British Library Cataloguing in Publication Data

A catalogue record for this book is available from the British Library

ISBN 0-471-97023-9

Typeset by Klaus Lutsch, Munich, Germany.
Printed and bound in Great Britain by Bookcraft (Bath) Ltd, Midsomer Norton, Somerset.
This book is printed on acid-free paper responsibly manufactured from sustainable forestry, in which at least two trees are planted for each one used in paper production.

To Mailey, Papa and Mama

CONTENTS

FOREWORD AND ACKNOWLEDGEMENTS

Impulses for innovations in the field of information technology originate for the most part in the USA, therefore any books on this subject will also hail mainly from that part of the world. And this is certainly the case. However, in today's networked world the availability of knowledge and information across the globe, via the Internet among other media, does not pose any problems. Justifiably or not – a point which is open to debate – Switzerland has an image of self-seclusion, an image that is not supported by its economic situation in general nor by the commercial awareness of its managers who use the means provided by telecommunications and information technology (IT), or telematics, quickly and efficiently. This means that experiences gained in practice create a solid platform from which to share these experiences. I am sure that, viewed from this angle, this book will be well received by the public.

My special thanks go to Barbara M.V. Esam and to Carol and Frank Gilges who have tackled the difficult task of translation with understanding and perception.

My immediate thanks go to Robert P. Kübler, whose critical though encouraging comments were a great help for me in the earliest stages of writing my first book. My thanks go, too, to a number of other helpers and especially to my wife, Mailey.

I should be pleased to receive any suggestions and additions under *http://www.teletrust.ch* where you will also find further detailed information on the book.

Bern and Neuheim, Switzerland, 1998

INTRODUCTION

The advent of the information age has been trumpeted for years. The revolution which has occurred in the way information is handled has brought about the transformation of the industrial era into the information era. The industrial community has undergone a mutation and become the information or communication society, in which information processing and the mastery of knowledge is possible by means of the computer, enabling communication to take place on world-wide networks at any level, any time, anywhere and without any difficulty whatsoever.

This powerful change is not a tangible entity that we can grasp directly with our hands. It is certainly happening before our eyes, but the process seems to be invisible. Many people who are affected by it, fail to interpret the daily signs of the transition from the industrial society to the information society in their new entirety. Other contemporaries of ours – such as businesspeople and politicians – are finding themselves pressured to such an extent to simply link up to the high level industrialisation of the so-called 'developed countries' or, at the very least, not to disassociate themselves from it, that they hardly have breath left for questions about how to actually get into the information age.

It is in the nature of a front-line report to highlight the salient points of this revolutionary entry into the information age as they affect the marketing sector, as well as the foreseeable developments. In this time of transition old paradigms are being replaced by new ones. The current change of paradigms is altering the rules of economic activity radically and lastingly. Changes of paradigms have been rare until now. Some 200 years ago the industrial revolution replaced the paradigms of the agricultural economy which had existed for centuries. At that time, just as today, the change that occurred in the time of transition took place almost imperceptibly. A seesaw moving in slow motion is a fitting analogy for this. Tipping the balance initiates a new position. But, unlike a seesaw with two people on it, a change in paradigms is irreversible, once a new position has been reached. New patterns of perception, thought and action are imperative if we are to achieve commercial success in cyber space.

The term 'cyber space' was coined by the science fiction author William Gibson in his novel *Neuromancer,* which appeared in 1984[1]. In his story the brains of computer hackers make direct contact with company databases. The information bases present their data in a realistic environment and the protagonists in the novel travel through the apparently real data environment as if it were a real world which they can perceive by their senses. The word 'cyber' has its roots in the English word 'cybernetics'. Cybernetics as a branch of science was established by the mathematician Norbert Wiener in 1946. This interdisciplinary, scientific approach explores the functions and inter-relationships of control and communication in animals, man, machines, organisations and, more generally speaking, systems.

Cybernetics in its original form had concentrated particularly on coupling and control systems in servo-mechanisms and automation. With the development of the computer the principles were adopted to form a basis for computer science. The possible applications of the theory of cybernetics in brain research were recognised very early on and the concepts were subsequently adapted within this scientific area. It was on the basis of these findings that 'artificial intelligence' was developed some two decades ago as a special area of computer science.[2] Within this special branch of computer science, highly complex decision-making processes are copied and transferred to computers in an attempt to imbue them with a certain ability to make decisions when faced with complex queries. Artificial intelligence was a media event at the end of the 1980s.[3]

The term 'cyber space' was taken over some years ago by the computer industry. Cyber space is a digital, artifically created reality. This is experienced by man through his senses and is very difficult to distinguish from true reality. For this reason we very often speak of virtual reality. It is the kind of reality that exists only in the mind – not materially – and which can be distinguished from fantasy in that it is not an individual experience, but instead one which is shared by a number of people. For purposes of linking up to virtual reality, the appropriate terminal equipment for transmitting pictures, sound, taste and, to some extent, heat is directly connected to the human sensory organs. Audio equipment and screens mounted on head visors, as well as bodysuits, shoes and gloves fitted with sensors, all play their part.

The concept of the cyber world made its commercial debut in the games sector. This was for a number of different reasons. One was the fact that it was possible to achieve the required quantities relatively easily within this sector. Also, children and young people are more receptive to the cyber world; at the end of the day, fantasy and virtual reality are still much closer to one another in the minds of children than in the heads of adults who have been groomed to worship at the shrine of rationality. Furthermore, there is a large and widening gap between 'state of the art' professional information technology as used within a company context and the technological options generally available. The commercial possibilities of cyber technology have become the object of much interest for the film industry. As will be seen from the following chapters, the cyber world is currently making its way into conventional economic activities via multimedia, hypermedia and global information networks. 'Multimedia' means storing and distributing data, language, pictures, texts and films or videos in digital form and reproducing them for the viewer or communicating the information contained in these different media digitally in package form via cable, satellite or radio. The term 'hypermedia' means that direct links exist between the different media.

In the information era with all its new digitial opportunities, marketing in the electronic markets of virtual reality will be totally removed from marketing today. The arena of success is transferred into the virtual world. This is where the public and the market exist digitally. Customers and potential buyers communicate on a multimedia basis and move around within the cyber world. The marketing of the future, marketing within this new reality, the only successful marketing, will be cyber marketing.

Dealing with values, ideas and expectancies represents an important aspect of today's traditional marketing. But the orientation of values as well as expectations are basically nothing more than the creation and communication of information which will ultimately be checked for its effectiveness. Companies can no longer imagine life without data and information on markets, the environment, competitors and customers. The communications and advertising sectors represent an important service industry which use a wide variety of classic communication media to position companies or products or conduct promotions with a view to increasing sales.

The first three chapters of the book deal with the WHY – the causes, contents and basic definitions of the factors, thoughts and concepts which form the paradigms of the information era. The three chapters which go to make up the second part, Perspectives, examine existing marketing tools, the WHAT, which are of central importance to cyber marketing or which already satisfy the new paradigms in respect of their current availability and are thus suitable for the specific creation of a cyber marketing scheme which is able to offer effective competition. The last three chapters in Part III deal with the practical implementation of cyber marketing – the HOW.

The transformation from the industrial to the information era is multi-dimensional: from an economic viewpoint, the TIME industry re-shapes itself; from a political point of view, it is governments that create competitive positions nationally. In this transformation, however, the people concerned have their vision somewhat obscured. What they are able to perceive immediately is the significance of the Internet as presented by the media in addition to the universally recognised future position of the computer industry, as well as the changes within the television sector which are beginning to emerge. The first chapter gives an insight into the origins of the communication society and outlines the origins of the new economic paradigms of the information era.

Marketing awareness is closely allied to the social conditions of the relevant era. The various changes in the perception of marketing are highlighted in the introduction to Chapter 2, in particular the transition from the industrial era to the information society. The extent of this transformation is revolutionising marketing and leading from a marketing approach directed at the masses to one directed at the individual. The development of the new paradigms is taking place in synchrony with the new electronic markets, created on the technological front within the information and communications sectors. The principles of information awareness, the factors within the network society which are critical for success and the rules of thumb in cyber marketing, are crucial for companies as far as their success is concerned. They form the framework of cyber marketing in which the new marketing instruments are applied.

The information highways[4] which are developing (as well as data highways) maximise communication possibilities and add a new dimension to the concept of communication. This is detailed in Chapter 3, which shows how companies can progress from data to information and conveys the guiding principles for a better understanding of the information age, which is based on data. Since it is only on

the basis of data that information can thrive and communication survive, the definition of these and other concepts, such as the information value chain and information content, is important in terms of the various different aspects.

Database marketing in its modern practical application is based on a solid foundation of information technology and is mainly geared to mass marketing. Chapter 4 discloses the reasons why current database marketing is no longer meeting the
requirements of the information age and how database marketing in the cyber age
can become an à-la-carte meeting with the customer. This will succeed if contact
between the supplier and the prospective purchaser takes place at a highly
informed level and is aimed at long-term customer retention. For purposes of practical database marketing, the pre-requisites, some examples, the most frequent
mistakes and the basics of data protection legislation are discussed.

Chapter 5, Electronic Marketing, examines important current communication
options and forms of technology, such as telemarketing, videotext, multimedia,
hypertext, CD-ROMs, all of which are set to become more important in the future.
The existing instruments are briefly assessed in the light of the new paradigms. The
basic ability to deal with multimedia will play a dominant role in the future. The
media necessary to transfer the spoken word, sounds, pictures and films have so far
been technologies of a diverse nature which could not be integrated as well as different media. This is set to change. The future capacities on the communication
networks will greatly increase the importance of multimedia, i.e. the combination
of pictures, sound, written text and video films in digital form. It is for this reason
that multimedia is considered to be the basic technology of the information era.
Companies will, sooner or later, have to get to grips with multimedia if they want
to master cyber marketing.

Internet, the avenue into the cyber world, is exciting, brand-new, revolutionary
and is dealt with in Chapter 6. 'Internet' is an abbreviation for 'inter-networked'
and the term has become established world-wide in many languages in its short-
ened form of 'Internet', 'Inet' or simply 'the Net'. It is the term which signifies a
large number of computer networks of different types connecting together to
encompass the entire world. The Internet causes the death of distance. The users
connected speak to one another, visit one another and yet – regardless of this –
each one remains in his own little corner somewhere in the world. The Internet is
not a fleeting fashion – no more so than the personal computer – but is the impetus for powerful changes in economies and within society in the lives of every one
of us. Familiarity with the various services offered on the Internet is something
which belongs in every cybernaut's rucksack. The Internet has both a tactical and
a strategic significance as far as marketing is concerned. From the tactical point of
view, the Net, represented by the World Wide Web (WWW), stands for a new and
alternative form of marketing communication within the classic marketing mix.
The strategic importance of the Net lies in its function of preparing the ground for
cyber marketing. Hence the basic question 'Internet – yes or no?' does not arise.
All we have to decide is when to get on. Depending on the company's objectives,
there will be different options for getting on as well as further development scenarios.

One basic economic principle also applies to the cyber world and that is that only companies with profits in the bottom line survive. It is not, therefore, technology alone that decides the issue but business acumen and the ability to conduct successful business under the new conditions. Marketing, construed as a science or as a doctrine, can provide the necessary insights and guidelines for this, the knowledge of which is part of the craft of marketing. Knowing how to use marketing science as a tool and how to implement it is vital to a company's success. However, many marketing people are not able to bring a vision into line with the profit-orientated targets on the company's balance sheet. A marketing programme is the shortest route from marketing idea to bank account. Chapter 8 deals with the concept of the marketing programme which, used as a framework for action, can increase profits. The principles of setting targets, the allocation of resources, revenue statements, marketing planning and preparations for implementation, performance and monitoring are the most important points on the action grid in cyber marketing.

Many entrepreneurs and managers have given themselves stomach ulcers through dealing with software projects within the information technology sector. Chapter 8 shows how (unpleasant) surprises can be avoided when dealing with IT projects in cyber marketing and how the risks can be controlled. So far the practical guidelines for clients have been very successful. The diversity of tasks in cyber marketing means that success will only accompany projects which are dealt with by teams of specialists. Human ability to communicate is therefore important – either within real groups of people or in virtual teams whose members are scattered all over the world but who nevertheless, together, are able to achieve top performance.

Chapter 9 contains a summary of cyber marketing for a particular caste of people in an everyday working situation. The core points of cyber marketing are presented for those who, whilst they may be responsible for making decisions, often do not know what the consequences of those decisions will be – i.e. the bosses. As bosses they learn what they may expect and what they have to enforce to ensure that their decisions are reflected in good results.

I – Paradigms, the Why

1 THE NETWORK SOCIETY TAKES OVER FROM THE CONSUMER SOCIETY

What are the characteristics of the new age? They include the transition from the society of the masses to the society of the individual through the new technical opportunities which have presented themselves. The limited importance of communication and information within the economic process is being transformed into dominance. This is bringing about massive changes both for society and for the individual, not only in his role as a supplier but also as a customer for commercial services.

From Consumption to Communication

Communication is the expression, transfer and exchange of information of any kind between living beings. In the information age this takes place between people personally or with the help of as well as between technical systems. Communication has a central significance for the human existence. Without communication, social intercourse, the formulation of political demands and objectives, science, culture, social behaviour and, indeed, morality itself, are not possible. Communication conveys feelings, knowledge, wishes, opinion, but at the same time power. The fact that politicians have, in every age, striven to control the means of mass communication is no pure chance. Our thoughts here turn to television and radio stations in particular. In non-democratic states this happens by means of intimidation, disabling or taking over transmitters and the associated media personnel. In democratic states legislation has evolved to prevent misuse, granting almost inviolable freedom to the media. Media representatives enjoy a relatively high level of power based on the freedom of the press and it is this which, in addition to the three institutionalised powers of political structure and economy, equates to a fifth force within the state and the society.

A human being cannot not communicate. Body signals, facial expression, the spoken word or, in certain situations, silence, represent communication in its original, natural form. The lack of precision, unreliability and risk of loss, all of which may apply to oral delivery, have been countered by the use of handwritten records. This may be defined as the beginning of 'technical' communication. Communication, in the sense of a source of information available to people in general on a practically unlimited basis, began in the fifteenth century with Gutenberg's invention of letterpress printing. The print media, in particular the press, were dominant for centuries as the sole means of mass communication. They had no competition. The period from 1837 saw the introduction of long-distance telegraph transmissions augmented, as from 1877, by the telephone. However, it was only with the advent of radio and television, which happened in Europe during the 1920s and 1950s respectively, that long-distance communication really took a decisive step forwards. The perception of democracy in certain states and the limited availability of frequencies led to radio and television which, unlike the print media, were initially organised under public law and this was the way they remained. It was not until the 1980s that private suppliers won themselves the right to operate broadcasting media to the same extent – a wholly logical and, for a free society, probably absolutely necessary development.

In addition to the development of computer technology, the meteoric rise of telecommunications marks the next significant step on the road to the information society, in particular the use of communications technology to transmit data via the (initially) analogue and (now increasingly) digital communications network. In only a few years, the fax, for example, has become just as much a part of our everyday life as the telephone.

The economic dimension formation of the TIME industry

The global information infrastructure (GII) is viewed differently, depending on individual opinion.[5] One branch of industry sees the high performance networks, linking computers together world-wide, as a structure of paramount importance, and it is to this that the network of computer networks – the Internet – belongs. An alternative perception sees in the GII the multimedia networks which, based on the use of increased band widths to extend transmission capacity, are emerging from modern telephone networks. The multimedia networks transmit video films together with data, speech, pictures and text. A third standpoint has its attention firmly fixed on the cable TV networks. These television networks are shortly to be extended to provide tele-interaction networks. It will no longer simply be unintelligent television sets that are attached to them, but interactive television equipment, personal computers and video telephones, all of which offer very attractive possibilities in terms of communication. Responsible for formulating the three standpoints are three very different industries – the computer or information technology industry, the telecommunications industry and the entertainment or media industry are girding themselves for a gigantic battle for dominance in the information era. A common and significant feature is that the networks of all three industries are digital networks. The competitition for the power of the networks and – bringing up the rear – for wireless communication is in full swing. Wireless communication is effected either terrestrially or via satellite. This is set to play a significant role. Nevertheless, communication will be principally by means of fixed networks. It is for this reason that a battle has already begun to oust competitors, even before demand has fully set in. One thing is certain, however – capacity will be available for the customers. The trend of communication costs will show a decided fall. Who will walk away from the field of battle as the victor? Research carried out in 1994 showed that, out of a basic 1985 million communication units installed, 58.4% were TV equipment, 32.5% telephone connections and 9.1% personal computers.[6] We do not know who out of the three rival industries is going to be the victor – what is certain is that the customer will benefit whatever happens.

Another important development in modern communication technology is the computer readable digital data carrier, first and foremost the CD-ROM, externally indistinguishable from the familiar audio compact disc. The CD-ROM will, in the long or short term, oust the medium of print in the professional/scientific sector, if the content of a space-consuming and work-intensive 30-volume loose-leaf collection of the Swiss Court Rulings – at present updated quarterly – is offered on a small silver disc. The Collection of Laws and Decrees which currently fills several cupboards can be stored on three CDs! Using keywords, passages of text can be accessed in a matter of seconds: hard times for the print media. Spares catalogues, price lists, mail order catalogues, technical handbooks, directories of each and every kind, encyclopaedias – in short, any collection of data where people need to look up items, conduct researches for a specific reason, rather than reading them from A to Z – is better accommodated in the CD-ROM format than using the medium of paper, which, when all is said and done, takes up space as well as consuming precious raw materials.

When people talk about the information society, what they mean primarily is the world-wide linking of a theoretically infinite number of computers via a modernised telephone network (e.g. ISDN) by modem (equipment which transforms digital into analogue signals or vice versa for purposes of remote data transmission).

The de-regulation of telecommunication in the USA and Europe means that the TIME industry (Telecommunication, Information technology, Media, Entertainment) will be able to re-shape itself completely in the immediate future (see figure 1). Deregulation brought about the political preconditions which were predetermined by the possibility of digitalisation in communication technology. Mergers, such as the one that took place in 1995 between Walt Disney and Capital Cities/ABC, are the first signs of this trend. Time Warner, the largest media group in the world (Time, Fortune, Warner Bros.), is banking on its 'Full Service Network'.

THE TIME INDUSTRY

The information era will be dominated to a significant extent by the TIME industry. In a similar way to the automobile sector in the industrial era, the TIME enterprises are becoming a pivot for the entire economic scene. All economic areas and sectors are being affected by the market performance of the TIME-sector enterprises, and it is this which is set to become the basic industrial driving force of the next few decades. Banks, manufacturing companies and the agricultural economy will be affected by this fundamental development, not only in terms of their isolated activities but also in terms of their finished net output – the same applies at state level. The global com-

Figure 1 The TIME industry

Industry	Strengths	Shortcomings	Immediate goals	Strategic vision
Tele-communications	Networks (ISDN) Standards Customerbase	Agility Marketing Software Contents	Customer retention Proving of Contents Deregulation Globalisation	Dominance in networks Switching and billing
Information Technology	Agility Marketing Software Innovation of base technology	Standardisation Contents	Customerbase Providing of Contents	Dominance in software, computing and devices (PC, networks, etc.)
Media	Marketing Customerbase Market attention	Fragmentation Digital technology in their networks	Modernisation of networks Software	Dominance in consumer networks (ITV)
Entertainment	Contents	Agility Networks for the distribution of contents	Alliances with telecommunication industry	Dominance in contents

petitiveness of the individual states will be shaped by the prevailing political circumstances for converting the potential offered by research, development, the education system, the economic development and the communications infrastructure, nationally into successful factors within the TIME industry sector and, at the same time, ensure the link to the global information highways.

With the options offered by the information highway social implications may be expected which, overall, represent not only possibilities but also risks. Marketing in this new social environment will differ quite radically from marketing in the industrial society.

The political dimension

The Conference of Ministers of the G7 Nations held a meeting in Brussels on the subject of the Information Society. In their concluding message dated 27th February 1995 'the Ministers selected eleven pilot projects and endorsed eight principles to realise their common vision of a global information society':

1. Promoting dynamic competition.
2. Encouraging private investment.
3. Defining an adaptable regulatory framework.
4. Providing open access to networks whilst ...
5. Ensuring universal provision of and access to services.
6. Promoting equality of opportunity.
7. Promoting diversity of content.
8. Recognising the necessity of world-wide cooperation, with particular attention to less developed countries.[7]

These statements clearly indicate one thing: measures related to the transition to the information society figure on the agendas of various governments and in the plans of many enterprises.

The elements of the 'information highway' which American Vice-President Al Gore made a central domestic project of the Clinton administration in 1994, are providing additional impulses for the USA over and above that country's already existing technological predominance within the TIME industry.

One of the stated aims of American education policy is to connect every classroom to the information highway by some time in 1998. As of the year 2010 all adult citizens will, as a matter of course, be handling computers, digital telecommunication and digital television sets. These media will be as much a part of their leisure as well as working time as the telephone is now in terms of its almost irreplaceable position in all our lives.

The American nation is making conscious preparations for the new developments and is endeavouring to actively shape the future. The discussion of framework conditions and the effects of the information society on marketing thus deals with a fact and not with fiction.

The dimension of personal involvement

The fact that today we are faced with a fast-track, internationalised, scientifically advanced industrial society-cum-meritocracy in transition to an information society, necessarily means that every human being is swamped with huge quantities of information. It has become a most difficult task, but at the same time one that is necessary to life, to ensure that each individual makes the correct selection from the mass of information, a selection which is right for him and which complies with his own needs and his own business – a flood of choices, consisting to a major extent of junk information.

Within the information society the individual is not allowed to give up in the face of this tide of information. The answer cannot be increasing and exclusive specialisation. Never was there a greater need for a tendency towards becoming generalists who do not lose sight of the whole, however many highly specialised individual aspects there are. The idealised picture of the introverted specialist of the industrial society will give way to the demands of the information society. It requires, in addition to a high degree of specialisation, a high level of universality. This is possible today, as easy access to specialist knowledge from any sector is available at any time – by accessing databases through the computer network. The painstaking and time-consuming rummaging in scientific libraries, in universities for instance, will give way to specific research in databases via the data network, information which, regardless of opening times, is available right round the clock on one's very own desk.

Information is becoming increasingly important but it is becoming less manageable, whether it is required for commercial, scientific or other purposes. If we proceed at a steady pace, what is known as the half life of topicality, i.e. the time up to which only half of the information or knowledge content has still not been superseded and is still relevant, becomes shorter and shorter. The mass of information can no longer be managed by the individual using traditional means, and good personal organisation and a suitably adapted infrastructure are called for. One method is to concentrate on a few (hopefully carefully) selected publications, periodicals or authors with the risk of potential gaps in knowledge. The other way is to turn one's back on one's own long-term specialist knowledge and handle any acute requirement for information on an individual basis by calling up the relevant information via the Internet or similar communication paths. A combination of two paths is possibly the best approach and is also a sensible way of ensuring that one is connected to the explosion of science and information. The well-informed specialist with permanent access to specific specialised information is set to emerge as a type of the information society. No one can read all the specialist magazines, but anyone can call up information on special subjects from central databases. In the information era it is no longer knowing about good specialist publications that counts, but rather keeping track of the quality and composition of a large number of databases in which the required data is stored without any gaps. The database guide will be appearing in many sectors, along with the telephone and fax book, reference works and restaurant guides. Dexterity on the information networks and familiarity with database contents will characterise the core skills of our contemporaries in the age of information.

The industrial-age media of today have for some time ceased to be purely information carriers, but are instead increasingly becoming information filters, albeit important ones. These affect a selection of the information which remains to be mastered in a meaningful way by the individual. The selection criteria may be based on politics, specialist/technical or commercial factors. Through direct access to information from world-wide sources and the specific search for information on the part of the individual, the choice of information and the dominance of the existing mass media in creating trends, fashion or atmosphere will be relativised. It is not surprising that the new media are attracting more than a modicum of attention from the press, radio and television because of their topicality. On the other hand, the critical comments are increasing. In the information age the position enjoyed by the mass media will no longer be so strong. No wonder, then, that observers are keenly following the developments in the Internet sector and the resulting comments are deceitful.

Every move forward has its corresponding retrograde step. Modern telematics offer themselves as a way out of the information dilemma described. The working tempo, which has up to now been fast anyway, will accelerate once more in the information society. A letter sent by post is already frequently superseded on its way to its recipient and the hectic stream of business correspondence is dictated by the fax. The speed of remote data transmission as in electronic mail with the option of multimedia data exchange will promote the 'five-to-twelve-mentality' even more strongly and will all too quickly obscure the fact that the decisive factor is not the transmission of data but its appropriate mental processing.

Communication technology – more shadow or more light?

Taking into account these new developments in communication technology, the question of sense and nonsense, usage and risks once more presents itself.

1. What will be the level of acceptance of these technologies on the part of the consumer?
2. What economic and social changes will come with the extensive spread of these technologies?

In the USA, home of the networking world, 96% of private households currently fail to make use of the data services, although 24% could do so if they wished. The sceptics' forecast, that a considerable proportion of services offered on the network will be left to sort themselves out due to a lack of demand, could be correct for the consumer sector. Their argument is: 'Who on earth wants to read his daily paper off the screen? Who wants to sit at his desk and order his new car based on a gaudy multimedia demonstration? How many people even want to put together their own individual television programme at the desired time from a well-nigh endless catalogue of television menus, film presentations and pre-recorded canned transmis-

sions? The end user in the consumer sector will play around for a time with such
superfluities and then, disillusioned, turn back to his habitual and more rewarding
distractions'. For hesitants and sceptics the beautiful new network world is largely
no more than a mega-modern plaything with an ultra-short absorption time. However, even they are agreed that the essential importance of the information highway
lies in the business, scientific and – maybe at the same time – in the political sector.

The optimists are convinced that, within a few years, much that is either personal or commercial will take place on the network. They argue that the cyber
world is absolutely capable of competing with reality. The playful applications of
cyber technology today, which enable us to move about within the virtual world,
will open up completely new vistas. The leap in development from the character-
orientated contents of the screen which characterised earlier mainframe consoles,
to today's Windows screen on the personal computer, illustrates the massive contrast between future possibilities and present-day applications. With the release of
contact with the virtual world from the confines of the mouse finger and its development into the audio-visual cyber helmet, the virtual world has gained
undreamed-of opportunities within the consumer sector. There is no need to move
out of the house for a spot of excitement. The only prerequisite will be having the
right equipment to connect to the cyber world. A few technical challenges must
first be overcome in order to enable broad-based application. The bottleneck will,
for a long time, be the data transmission capacity of the telecommunications networks. The transmission of a colour picture still takes several minutes on a present-
day analogue network. A few years will have to roll by before real-time happenings
in the cyber world can be transmitted.

Television: an Innovation Becomes an Antique

Modern-day television is a medium which is pushing up against its borders more
quickly than even its hardest critics expected. The great number of private channels
has not increased the multiplicity of programmes. The increasingly hysterical pursuit of viewing figures laden with advertising capital ends with triumph of the
alleged taste of the masses in the shape of infinitely interchangeable programme
series. The battle for industry's advertising budget – rather than for the favour of
the public – is constantly giving rise to new media competitors who, with the same
old recipes lacking in imagination, haggle to the tune of increasing stagnation over
their share of the advertising cake. They are driven by the myth that the injection of
adequate capital and not that of creativity will guarantee attractive programmes;
that it is sufficient to lure away a few public magnets who have been spoiled by
publicity and who are hopelessly overpaid, and to simply dish up the old show
hash under the guise of new programme titles.

Television today is well on the way to becoming outdated, not in terms of its
consistently high market presence but its demand to be taken seriously. The viewer
switches on – but more out of habit than in the expectation of finding cultured
entertainment or even of being informed. TV is becoming a permanent background

feature – the modern equivalent of the camp-fire, flickering away in the back-ground practically unnoticed.

If this state of affairs is approached bearing in mind the options offerered by digital, interactive TV but nevertheless applying our present-day understanding, the TV makers will try to stir up the tired television consumer. From one-way, purely receptive communication, the aim will be to create a two-way, parallel process. However, the 'active' participation of the viewer, his influence on the pro-gramme, remains limited. He may select the programme he wishes to watch from the schedules of a network provider and call it up at a time that suits him.

Interactive television should be called TI – Tele-Interaction – rather than TV. Interactive television will have to take over very many of the current options in on-line networks in order to be attractive. Viewed from this perspective, television is set to undergo a complete renewal in the future.

The network satisfies almost perfectly the primeval human characteristic of curiosity. Computers and modern networks have an extraordinary potential for addiction. It takes so little to be a part of the whole: an interactive television set or a PC with a modem and telephone connection, as well as the readiness to make use of them.

The social consequences of modern communication paths will be decided by the twin questions: what use will the consumer make of the new media; to what extent will he accept them? He can gain time, rationalise research, save resources or hope-lessly forget himself in the virtual reality of modern networks, which is the ideal of many providers.

The network world of the cyber age is an artificial, virtual reality.[8] Its reality is not something to be found in real life but rather in the endless meanderings of the network. Stealthily and almost unnoticed, another life may evolve out of searching for information in this medium. The freshly baked cybernaut is received as a novice into the fascinating, beautiful new world of the network, he switches playfully from meeting to meeting, database to databank, forum to forum, lingering here and there, losing himself in the endlessness of the data highway, then realising at some stage to his amazement that he has spent several hours of his life far away from any normal, interpersonal communication. The cybernaut is not so much the operator as the tool of his PC and the options which it offers and, not least, the poorer by a not inconsiderable amount in terms of usage and connection charges. The addiction potential of the virtual world is considerable. The addiction curve of a cyberholic is very different when compared, say, to alcohol dependence; this is a gradual process which takes time. A cyberholic goes down into the 'digital under-world' along with his PC, but may, on his first encounter with the network, sud-denly succumb to the fascination and fall victim to the addiction.[9]

Internet – the Embryonic Vessel of Virtual Reality

The international networking of individual computers is already breaking all the bounds of communication hitherto known. In 1969 scientists from four American universities, supported by the Defense Department, started the first (non-commercial) computer network, to which further stations were quickly connected. The original 'Internet', which was used purely for research purposes, today boasts 35 to 60 million participants.[10] There are a number of other commercial network providers competing with the Internet. For an access charge, data can be transmitted via a telephone line between the users connected so as to exchange texts, pictures, sounds or, using special software, telephone calls can be made world-wide for the price of a local call. Connected to the system are news agencies, book and newspaper publishers, libraries, museums, archives and commercial information suppliers who all feed in the information available to them.

CompuServe, the largest private provider, has been 'on-line' since 1979. It is a gigantic business supplying information to (currently) 3.8 million subscribers for a monthly basic fee of (currently) around US$12. CompuServe alone enables its users to access more than 2000 databases and thus provides access to an enormous spectrum of knowledge made up of collections of information from the most diverse special interest groups right down to general reference works, 700 specialist publications and newspapers, which can be called up at any time as complete text, including German Press Agency items.[11]

The operating system MS-DOS and Windows 3.1 from Microsoft are used on 80% of all the computers in use world-wide. The dominant software giant is offering, along with its operating system Windows 95 which came out in September 1995, and in association with other leading companies within the communications sector, a further international data network. The 'Microsoft Network' is automatically accessible to any Windows user who has a suitable modem.

Surely the most fascinating aspect of the Internet is 'freedom': freedom of knowledge, freedom of information, freedom to exchange opinions. Today the Internet is conceivably the most open and democratic communication system in existence – guaranteeing a wide diversity of opinion. The network operator provides only the supply network, the carrier, against payment of a fee. On the other hand, the information and opinions on offer in the network are determined by the users alone. The traditional suppliers of information and entertainment also participate in the network, but they determine the content of only a relatively small part of the whole in each case. They cannot exercise any specific influence on the basic diversity of opinions and information available on the network.

In terms of its composition the network is egalitarian, it cannot be regulated or controlled, it is decentralised to a high degree and has – so to speak – an anarchical structure. This structure makes the network as interesting as it is, not least of all for social minorities, who would go under in the mainstream. Important ideas can migrate more quickly from the peripheral areas into the spotlight of public awareness. For many the network offers the only remaining means of working in a self-determined manner, rather than simply being a recipient of orders from institutions, governments or companies. They wish to personally exert influence on what is taking place around them, they are self-possessed and removed from the control of the power moguls.

Some say it is a matter of guaranteeing the free flow of ideas in this medium, especially in the political sector. Then the computer network will, simultaneously and decisively, enrich our social, political and private lives. Others, of which there are not a few authorities and specific interest groups, are highly alarmed. The Internet is a constantly growing sub-culture of gigantic size, uncontrollable, impossible to monitor. Senders and recipients of messages remain, at least partially, anonymous; messages can be encrypted and thus illegible as far as the security services are concerned. The Internet also offers extremists – fundamentalists or neo-Nazis – a wide forum which stretches beyond any national borders.

Inevitably, the question of censure raises itself. Who is to prevent the network from being flooded with low-grade ideology or other forms of data refuse? Should a film or computer game which promotes violence, pornographic material, or a blinkered political view be banned in a particular country, then all that one has to do is to call it up from abroad via the network on to the PC.

Telepolis – a virtual workplace

Telepolis is the vision of a society which has, through telecommunication, discovered a new way of living together and organising work.

The cyber world will revolutionise our working lives, our working culture and the international employment market. Computers and telecommunications work to a major extent in a decentralised manner. Work migrates from factories and open plan offices to the home environment. It no longer has to be carried out in a few industrial population centres. Work is drawn to wherever the employee is domiciled and not vice versa, at the same time having a beneficial effect on traffic as far as travel to and from the workplace is concerned. The employee works increasingly at home on his own PC and sends the results of his activities down the line to his employer (teleworking or telecommuting).[12] Today there are already eight million employees in the USA working at home, at least in part.[13] Anyone who cannot work a PC will, in the long term, have little chance of employment.

Telecommuting allows the barriers between private and business life to become blurred. Working time does not necessarily become shorter, for the PC and the modem are constantly present and available. A primary consideration for teleworkaholics, when choosing their flights and hotels, is whether there is a modem connection available or else they are dreaming of a mobile phone with access to the Internet.

A start has already been made on this. A new generation of 'tradesmen' has already established itself on the network. In particular, those offering advice on the Internet, programmers, specialists in multimedia and other services necessary to create the cyber world will from now on be posting individual offers in their kiosks on the data highway. In the long term, large international companies will endeavour to extend their already established dominance in the same way to the data highway.

Telepolis – virtual entertainment centre

The network will make any information or entertainment in any conceivable shape or form available on your desk, in the kitchen, in bed or anywhere else.[14] All ideas which exist in tangible form, our entire cultural inheritance, any stored texts, illustrations or sounds will one day be available in digital form and can then be called up, viewed, transmitted or printed within seconds via the telecommunications network by any individual participant connected anywhere in the world. The network represents the final elimination of spatial and time-based barriers to accessing the outcome of intellectual activity.[15] Internet Relay Chat (IRC) enables real time conversations to take place via the keyboard. This generates a social network between the participants made up of artificial identities and within a common context generating fun and the opportunity to exchange ideas right through to flirting.[16]

Conclusion: the Information Era as the Generator of New Paradigms

The personal mobility of the industrial era is enhanced in the information era by intellectual mobility generated by the ability to access information via the network link. This heightening of individuality is also demonstrated in the massive increase in the opportunities available to individuals, to communicate with others by means of the electronic network, regardless of time-based limitations or geographical borders.

The supporting and driving force of the TIME industry in the information era is re-shaping itself and, in so doing, is drawing on telecommunications, the information sector and the media and entertainments sectors. The relevant branches of industry have, along with their present-day infrastructures such as telephone, computer networks – like the Internet – as well as satellite and cable television, embarked on a powerful competitive struggle to gain control of the global information highways. This competitive struggle takes place on several different levels at once. Politically speaking, the deregulation of the communications monopolies outside the USA, but also education policy and efforts to build up national information infrastructures on the part of individual states, are discernible. As far as technology is concerned, there is the telecommunications industry's concern to bring telephone networks and communications centres, as well as terminal equipment, up to digital level so that it is at least receptive to multimedia. The media and entertainments industry is taking steps towards digital technology with high resolution television and interactive TV. The computer industry, along with the Internet, is leading the way as regards the move into the information society.

In this competitive situation it is not the equipment, the hardware, which is the decisive factor but the software which will make the various modes of communication possible. The developmental quality of software is directly decided by capable individuals, i.e. the brainware, of the relevant companies or states.

The newly created economic setting which makes possible direct communication between companies, as well as individual persons and thus consumers, at very low cost, is the basis for new business patterns.

These patterns can be identified from the existing options offered by information technology and can therefore be formulated for marketing activities.

2 THE REVOLUTION IN MARKETING: FROM THE MASSES TO THE INDIVIDUAL

Marketing Changes in Different Social Epochs

'How much of a run-up do you need to jump further than you would just from a standing position?' This question was asked by the Zurich intellectual Adrien Turel on the subject of perspectives, unfolding a view of the future. Marketing as a business activity was not born yesterday, but is in fact considerably older. Over the course of time the marketing function has been re-defined in its different stages and has developed by means of adaptations to its current level. Definition of the marketing role was at the same time to a major extent dependent on the development of the product/market relationship. The development of marketing can be classified in four stages.[17]

First stage – local uniqueness

In the first and longest stage people did not go in for actual marketing. This premarketing period is also called the Robinson Crusoe Epoch by some authors.[18] For hundreds of years people have traded by bartering goods. There was no established currency and therefore no established precondition for a free exchange of goods on an established market. The fact that mobility was relatively restricted was a further limiting factor – products and services were bought from the neighbours. Anyone who could make anything, plant and harvest corn, stitch shoes, break horses or make a form of lighting could operate a business; every product was unique. Taking up an economic activity was comparatively easy. The only condition was – and this still applies today as far as commercial activities are concerned – there had to be customers for the service. In this sense it was easy to be successful.

The regional, national and continental trade, however, was in the hands of a small community, the élite of the time. If a consumer in Switzerland today buys even simple foodstuffs from a wholesale distributor he will be amazed at the wide diversity of countries of origin. Several continents may be present at a substantial breakfast in Switzerland: coffee from South America, sugar from Asia, milk from the home country, bread made with cereals from the USA or Canada, butter from an EU country such as Germany, Holland, France or perhaps Denmark. The yoghurt contains fruit concentrates from South Africa. The list is endless. In this sense not only the Swiss, but also many households throughout Europe, enjoy a global diet.

Second stage – mass production through industrialisation

The second stage began with specialised production and thus with the drawing of a definite line of demarcation between producers and consumers. It may be equated with the commencement of industrialisation and the mass production that this made possible. With it grew the requirement to bring suppliers and customers together in order to enable them to transact goods and money. Marketing in this sense creates transparency between potential buyers and sellers and enables them to make contact.

The first chains of shops were opened. This meant that a product was available not only in a single local outlet, but throughout the country in all branches of the same shop. Although initially, society was still locally orientated, there was an increasing consumption of products from unknown production workshops. So consumer orientation changed. Sales were requirement-orientated. Incomes increased and, with them, the requirements of the customers. Alongside general development, communication media such as telegraph, newspapers and post also improved. At this market stage, it was possible for a successful product to generate millions in terms of profit.

Several power shifts took place during this phase. Whilst producers were initially very strong, trading houses and distributor chains were gaining increasing influence. They were the ones who determined the range to be carried and what would ultimately be offered to the customer. The individual customer lost his influence on product generation and distribution.

Third and current stage – differentiated products

The post-war years mark the beginning of this stage, which is characterised by localised mass communication and the systematic implementation of marketing. With the introduction of improved means of communication after the Second World War and by means of radio and, not long after, television advertising too, producers found that they were able to centralise their markets and, for example, address parts of or even the whole of the USA. Marketing became increasingly systematised and at the same time established in the universities as a division of the economic sciences. The primary aim of marketing communication was to draw attention to a particular brandname. Mass marketing raised the entry thresholds for new entrants to the market by an enormous amount. It became very difficult for individuals or small companies to build up a new enterprise in established sectors. The means of mass production provided the largest producers with enormous progressive cost reductions. The profit margins thus achieved made it possible to extend market power and to keep new competitors at bay.

Consumers were not regarded as individuals but addressed as a uniform customer profile. This stage did not recognise any products differentiated according to customer groups. The competition was between the individual goods. This means that the struggle was for priority in terms of the items budgeted for within a house-hold: 'Shall we get the fridge first or a new washing machine first or should it be a car?'

Global competition

The increasing globalisation of markets and, in conjunction with this, the world-wide presence of individual companies, called for a re-think in terms of product presentation and market communication. At the same time various changes, par-ticularly in terms of purchasing power within the markets of developed countries, brought about a change in consumer habits. Differentiated products needed to be offered on an increasingly globalised and centralised market. The most remarkable example comes from the automobile sector.

The dominance of the American car manufacturers, which was still based on the thinking patterns of the third stage, was broken by the Japanese making over-tures to the individual consumer at the lower end of the market. When building up the infrastructure, the Japanese had not contented themselves with simply produc-ing cheap goods, but at the same time they achieved product differentiation in many different sectors. They turned the heterogeneity of customer requirements to their advantage and supplied appropriate products. In this era, marketing acquired a new function, namely, in addition to segmenting customers and/or the market, to define the requirements of this target group and to give guidelines for product adaptation. It is not the engineers or manufacturers who make the product, but the marketing people. At the same time, communication with the market segments had to be ensured and the distribution channels finely tuned. Marketing acquired the role which you can read up today in any text book. This recipe for success was in force from the 1970s onwards.

Now the different product categories were no longer in competition with one another. The struggle for the consumer's shopping basket took place at the level of individual products such as dishwashing liquid or pet food. As products with iden-tical coverage in terms of demand will be in competition, market communication must extol the virtues of further values and contents. These values are intended to reach the appropriate segments and stimulate them to buy. In many branches it is still possible to work very well with the media that characterise this stage, i.e. mail-ings, press advertising, cinema audiences, radio and TV, promotion at the point of sale or PR activity.

Although customers today have highly diverse and manifest preferences, mar-keting still frequently uses market research media, abstracting the requirement pro-file by means of statistics. Communication with the individual target groups is at the most carried out on the basis of a personalised approach to the recipient, but not by means of a highly detailed customer profile. If a major part of the informa-tion were available from the customer the service demanded could be carried out by the producer in direct relationship with the customer.

Fourth and future stage – customer individuality in the global market

The fourth stage came about with entry into the information era. The infrastructure consists of computer networks, fax machines, reliable telephone networks, computer equipment with appropriate software and cable networks for television or, more generally, pictures, sound and film. These technologies will completely change the marketing landscape in the highly developed markets and with regard to more up-market products in all segments.

This development will take place in three stages.

1. Direct marketing

This is the use of information technology to communicate directly with the customer. Technical media are mailings generated by the use of databases, the use of fax and data carriers such as CD-ROM with multimedia. At this level the customer is not directly connected to the supplier electronically. Many companies are currently implementing such approaches. The concept of direct marketing comes closest to this situation. Despite the partial use of information technology aids – these are often termed 'electronic marketing media' – this 'direct to customer' approach is off-line. This means that there is no dialogue. A further characteristic distinguishes this approach from electronic marketing: it is the supplier who takes the initiative. The customer, prospective buyer or, more generally, the market, is confronted with the message, the offer or the information.

2. On-line marketing

On-line Marketing is the second phase. This section has only got underway during the last 20 months. On-line marketing is set to continue its development and will be regarded for approximately another three years as the new marketing front. This time window is technology-based. On-line marketing in its initial and current form only became possible due to platforms such as the WWW (World Wide Web), which have been available for around two years for accessing the Internet. It was this software that first enabled laymen to access the existing world-wide network of connected computers relatively easily. At the same time the decision a decade ago to deregulate the telecommunications market and the efforts to do away with state monopolies are having consequences for consumers today. It is this opening that enables electronic markets to be created in the first place. In on-line marketing the customer is not himself in the system, but is present as a user at the other end of the line and this factor brings about fundamental changes to the perception of customer relations.

Today we have for the first time the necessary infrastructures and services which make the enigmas of choice, comparison, distribution, payment and the performance of services, and supply of software via the network possible for millions of customers on site. Direct communication can take place on-line.

3. Cyber marketing

The already existing technology and infrastructure of the telecommunications networks, computer networks and interactive TV networks will converge to form the third phase, that of cyber marketing. In this phase, the network terminal will become the vehicle by which consumers and customers enter virtual reality and establish contact with suppliers over the networks. The encounter will take place in cyber space, the layman will not be able to distinguish whether this virtual world exists physically in his terminal or somewhere else. He perceives a reality which does not have to exist as such. The form of this virtual reality is based on concepts such as multimedia and a number of other items of terminal equipment, such as cyber helmets and spectacles for audio-visual perception of the virtual environment as well as speech control, checking and navigating equipment, but also on aids which are coupled with our normal sense of reality.

Electronic markets

Various sectors – banks, tourism and distribution – are already familiar with electronic markets. One high-profile example is that of electronic stock-markets. Stock-market computerisation was introduced some years ago. Examples include the electronic stockmarket LSE (London Stock Exchange) in London and SOFFEX or EBS in Switzerland. Electronic markets are telematic systems which help to carry out the process of exchanging services between the different economic subjects – individuals, families, companies and state organisations up to and including entire group structures. Every day, financial transactions worth an average of 2,300 billion dollars are performed via electronic networks.[19]

Electronic markets were primarily created to make the exchange of information simpler and to clarify exactly what is on offer. The initial step in a purchase (which is always at the same time a sale and therefore a commercial transaction) consists of sifting through the possible offers and comparing them. This process is generally exclusively information-based. Marketing in this phase concentrates on communicating the advantages of the product and its performance characteristics and establishing those points which distinguish it from competitive items. Once the supplier and the customer have found each other, the agreement phase follows. The supplier's prices and his terms and conditions must be accepted by the purchaser or be defined by both parties. In this phase, the basis is established for dealing with the transaction which takes place in the third stage.[20]

The first two phases can be implemented almost exclusively on the basis of a pure exchange of information. The last phase is physical – products or physical services are exchanged, but this phase is always an exchange of information too: order, delivery notes and invoicing. Where bank business is concerned, such as in the purchase and sale of securities or debt instruments, transactions on the market are linked solely to information. It is for this reason, together with the highly

advanced standardisation of syndicate activity in attendance stock markets, that
the electronisation of this market activity has taken place.

By comparison to commercial activity via the Internet, these electronic markets,
as is, for example, the case with electronic stock markets, are regulated in the sense
that clear agreements and regulations governing the handling of the exchange of
services exist. Electronic stock markets may also be termed closed markets, since
all business is transacted by a defined group of banks or stock exchange dealers.

Certain reservations systems operated by airline companies provide an example
of an open, regulated electronic market. The SABRE reservation system can be
directly operated by users of CompuServe, albeit with limited functions. The sole
prerequisite is clear identification of the user prior to initial use. The main users of
SABRE are airlines, first and foremost American Airlines, as well as a large number
of travel agencies and booking offices. The system not only provides information
about flights, but also gives information on hotels, rent-a-car companies, shipping
companies and other information of use to the travel and tourism sector.

The exchange of data for payment purposes between banks is already handled
globally by means of the SWIFT system. Industrial enterprises communicate with
one another by means of EDI (Electronic Data Interchange) and send each other
not only invoices but also complete specifications for technical items.[21] Back in
1995, 43% of manufacturing companies in the USA were already exchanging
data.[22] These electronic systems are, however, not actual electronic markets.

So what's new? The Internet is an approach which may form the basis for an
open and non-regulated electronic market. However, what is currently lacking for
complete operation is an integrated facility which enables financial transactions to
take place to a major extent via the Internet. The inception of banking activities in
virtual reality is already a fact. 1994 saw the establishment of First Virtual Holdings Inc. in California, which has been active since 1995.[23]

Electronic markets are attractive to both suppliers and customers, because
information relating to supply and demand is more intelligible and the cost of the
sales/purchase transaction is less than in the real world; in addition, the transaction
can be made more quickly and without geographical impediments.

The sale of differentiated market performance items in highly differentiated
markets is one outcome of the information era. Market performance is frequently
no longer simply a product, but a service or replicable knowledge contained in
software besides. The supplier can identify individual customers and, using two-
way communication, adapt the specific product or service on-line and supply it
without delay. At this stage, marketing adopts the role of a purveyor of information, ensuring the flow of communication between the different partners. Marketing manages and nurtures the relationship. Moreover, we often talk about 'relationship management'. In this book the term 'on-line marketing' is also used for
this. This concept already incorporates the relationship within itself and attention
is drawn to a totally new function, namely, to enable communication to take place
without delay and without third party intervention.

If direct communication exists between the customer and the producer, then the
customer's requirements become the product specification. The border between

manufacturer and customer thus becomes blurred. The producer certainly supplies the goods or service, but the customer is responsible for designing ideas for the product. As far as the supplier is concerned, this means that he has to construct his offer in a highly modular fashion, but should nevertheless make the choice very easy for the customer.

In this marketing era, the role of the middleman is also being re-defined. It is easy to see that long-term success is being achieved in terms of direct contact through an on-line relationship with the customer. The role of marketing channels will also be re-defined. Cyber marketing will also bring about changes with regard to organisation and company size. If, over the past five decades, the principle has applied that larger means more powerful, this no longer applies in the information era. Here, power lies with whoever is capable of shaping communication effectively and efficiently and of making good and decisive use of his familiarity with the customer. It is not knowledge that is power, but knowing how to deal with it. This is not a matter of the size of an organisation. Dealing with information is not a question related to the quantity of resources, but solely a matter of quality.[24]

In the information era, companies will find themselves increasingly confronted with the same questions as organisations today in the software manufacturing sector. The underlying perceptions in this sector as well as the experiences of today's direct marketing people represent the core knowledge of future marketing personnel.

Old and new market barriers

In the information era, newcomers will stand a good chance in the race for future markets. As the paradigm changes, the rules of the game become completely different. Larger organisations are often very sluggish and only recognise new potential and opportunities for earning once these have developed into a visible form. At the beginning of the information era, capital therefore can, to a certain extent, be substituted for know-how in the IT sector.

The barriers are education and individual know-how. The information era will markedly speed up the already emerging trend of a two-class society.[25] It is the numbers of people who are neither educated nor trained, who have nothing to counter the dominance of the educational élite. The demands are becoming so great that subsequent further education will only provide small opportunities. The basis for a person's professional future is increasingly being laid in the first years at school.

The greatest impediment to rapid growth lies in existing customer relationships in satiated markets. Anyone who knows anything about using front line communication in order to win customers is clearly at an advantage. And it is no longer sufficient to offer a favourable quotation or a discount in order to entice customers who have already signified their allegiance elsewhere. If the relationship is being managed well as far as the customer is concerned, he will have no reason to change.

Far-sighted marketing professionals and clever business people quickly recognise this. They are already starting to set up cyber marketing. The aim of this book is to give them the necessary stimulus and ideas.

Resourceful users of new technologies and those who see through the new principles of the information era, will very quickly discern many opportunities to earn
money and ensure an income or to build up a profitable organisaiton. If solid on-
line relationships are established today these can become crucial in terms of success
over a long period.

With this the future of marketing will also change. We mentioned above that, in
highly developed economic markets, the fourth stage will apply to the decentralised
marketing of differentiated products and, overall, with regard to the marketing of
information technology globally. This will therefore be the case, as, even in markets that are not highly developed, the relevate éites will be participating in the
global composite.

Changing Paradigms

Paradigms are conscious or unconscious thought patterns which control actions.
Concentrating the paradigms in the information era on one point explicitly
means – doing business with anyone, at any time, nowhere. The specific paradigm
of the cyber world also runs – don't confront customers and don't just interact with
them but, as a supplier, rather integrate them into your own world.

Business means – exchange of market performance for payment. A business
transaction is a materialised dialogue, an exchange of information, goods and
counter-procedure. Marketing is the preparation for this transaction which also
includes any necessary clarifications. The cyber age makes it possible for marketing, based on the exchange of information, to prepare fully for this transaction in
every detail and to co-ordinate performance. It does not mean that the business is a
standard product or a routine service. There is no longer any possibility of marketing a product à la Ford Model T in the information era, unless this mass approach
is made within a market which is still a seller's market and is yet to become a buyer's market. But even in those regions of the world which are not highly developed,
these markets are dying out. The fact that suppliers and customers are both communicating with each other easily and at low cost, makes it possible to deal with
the wishes and requirements of the customer in a highly differentiated manner.

Doing business with anyone does not only mean that, potentially, anyone can be
acquired as a customer. This means at the same time that the customer does not
have to feel tied down by the exchange of information. The market situation of airlines is a very good example. Existing overcapacity in terms of supply makes the
customer relatively powerful. On the other hand, human beings tend to be creatures of habit. Particularly good experience of a supplier is a major impediment to
becoming involved with a new brand or supplier. The mechanisms are sufficiently
well-known. The status of brandnames and companies rests on the loyalty or
habits of customers.

'Any time' means 24 hours, seven days a week, every week of the year, year in,
year out. Opening times will disappear from our vocabulary in the information era.
Not to be available is fatal. This paradigm challenges organisational talent and will

provoke a radical revision of attitudes to working time and free time within companies. In the industrial era, business was possible with individuals at defined times and in certain locations only. This thought pattern no longer applies.

In future, business will be done nowhere. Nowhere, that is, in the geographical sense. If someone from Vienna orders a book in New York which is delivered by courier – where is the order placed? You can forget geographical references. Origin is more important than geographical position. The customer's action pattern is determined by his personal history, his origin and experiences and not by the place where he is currently staying and from which he communicates. All that matters regarding the encounter in a location in the virtual world which cannot be defined geographically, are the origin and intention of the two parties meeting.

The change of paradigm has a major effect on the current view of market strategies, for instance, regarding basic strategy in terms of cost management and differentiation. The strategic approach in the industrial era, of establishing a dominant position in a market by means of cost management, is set to give way. It is gradually being replaced by the approach of providing a service to meet the customer's requirements precisely and in accordance with his conditions, naturally at an appropriate price. The costs are not the only determining factor here.

The effect of the change of paradigm on the strategic approach can also be seen in product differentiation. In the present-day view, differentiated products are a bundle with a limited number of modified core products which are geared to special requirements. The manner of differentiation is critical as far as success is concerned. However, the methodology of differentiation in terms of current marketing theory is solely related to the marketing mix. The main differentiations in market performance are based on product, service, innovation, quality image or application. The cyber world knows no distances, no geography, and for this reason, the idea that a product, once introduced on to a national market, can be launched as an innovation on a market in another continent does not apply. The practically simultaneous spread of information within the global communications system torpedoes this differentiating approach. The fact that a prospective buyer is not in possession of certain information does not mean that he has no access to it and therefore is as yet unable to bring himself up to the same level of knowledge as other participants in the market.

Major differences based on distribution, such as direct sales, special marketing channels, selected sales locations or manufacturing locations, need to be examined. In nearly all of these differentiative modes communication is the decisive factor. Thus, any distinction in terms of market performance based solely on language or region which is successful today, may fail completely in the future. For, in practically every case, it is only the label on a product which makes it different from another or the name and the language in which the instructions for use are printed on the label. Medicines – for example – are marketed under various names and at very different prices due to the diversity of state regulations. Once purchasers in the individual markets become aware that different forms of presentation are being used to conceal products which all come from the same production centre, then it is simply a question of time until protests and intervention on the part of consumer organisations and the Monopolies Commission make this kind of differentiation by the manufacturer impossible. In general we can say that differentiation of this kind, built up on asymmetry of information, will increasingly fail. Asymmetries in terms of information are caused or exist naturally due to differences in language, mentality or culture. They are created by marketing, by consciously or unconsciously established or specifically communicated differences in the price, presentation and distribution of a product or a service for different markets or *vis-à-vis* certain competitors.

How then can asymmetries of information be disclosed? If we assume that the consumer can and does help himself to all the information that is available from each and every supplier on which to base his decision, complete clarity will come about. All the information necessary to enable the best possible market decision to be made will never be totally at hand, but it will be there to a much greater extent than it is today. The decisive factor in such a competitive situation will then not just be the formal relationship with the customer, but equally the emotional link. The emotional relationship with the customer is determined by the overall chain of common interaction, not just by a single meeting.

What does this mean? Someone has decided to buy a certain product – let's say a personal computer. He has the money and just one question. He rings up a large firm with a good reputation and tells them that he would like to place an order for a personal computer once he has clarified a certain small point with them. He wishes to have an assured delivery date, because he is going to be away for the next two weeks and is planning to start work with the equipment immediately on his return. He rings up. The lady on the switchboard is very helpful but has to pass him on to someone else. The music which plays while he is waiting to be connected is just right for his mood and he is in the best of humour. Someone else picks up the telephone, listens to his request and informs him that he will have to put him through to another colleague. More beautiful music. Another voice answers and he repeats his request. Having listened, the person explains to him why he will have to speak to yet another person. Somewhere along the line, this customer loses patience – his inclination to buy disappears and he hangs up. He is seriously looking for alternatives. His emotions are not determined by these individual conversations but rather by the chain of interaction.

There must be no let-up in concern for the person and the customer, if customer relationships are to be kept intact, and this must be nurtured to ensure repeatable business. The central element of cyber marketing is the solid building up of customer relations so that these can survive even in difficult situations – such as in a series of telephone calls.

New paradigms in marketing

The current change in paradigms is reflected particularly within the marketing sector. No other sector of responsibility within an enterprise, except for the function of a CEO or overall company manager, is so intensively concerned with the changes to the environment and the market. Based on their combined responsibility for the longer-term development of the enterprise, successful marketing bosses are characterised by a marked awareness of how to trigger impulses that unerringly point the way ahead for changing products and services, and to pass on to the organisation objective information in this regard. The anticipative role of marketing demands that those responsible within the sector recognise, interpret and understand the signs of the new age as early as possible. In the current period of upheaval leading up to the information era, unique chances of a strategic nature are, on the one hand, opening up. Marketing options and methods in the information era will, on the other hand, undergo massive expansion and renewal. This clearly indicates that, in the short term, we will not see a complete substitution of the existing marketing instruments and communication media by new ones. But it is precisely for these changing markets that new opportunities are being offered.

Companies and their customers are communicating directly with one another more and more and the costs involved are increasingly being reduced, which means that these are in fact relatively low. Concepts such as '1:1 marketing' or 'relationship marketing' take account of this factor. Thus, companies are increasingly acquiring highly detailed customer information. With this additional data, new opportunities arise for dealing with prospective buyers, possible buyers, customers and others in the market place – such as consultants, special interest groups or even the media – in a more direct manner than ever before. This fact is mirrored by catch-phrases such as 'individual marketing' or 'micro-marketing'. Thirdly, commercial transactions between buyer and supplier can proceed independent of location and freely as regards the choice of time. Transactions in this context include the exchange of information or the transacting of business, thus information, services or goods in addition to money.

The swift circulation of realtime information is one of the important aspects of the information era. CNN illustrates this in an exemplary manner. There is no time lapse from the point where the information emerges in the form of a report at the location where the incident occurs, and its transmission. Processing of the information, transmission and consumption take place simultaneously. Any viewer may make direct contact with CNN via Internet and state his views. If all those involved are on-line at the same time, there will be direct communication, otherwise the statements are received and exchanged via the electronic postal system (e-mail).

On-line banking provides a further example. In many cities of the world, customers communicate with their bank via cash dispensers. Account holders can call up statements of account, withdraw cash and frequently perform other transactions. In the case of the EC card these networks are international.

From individual to customer base

Today, the name of the game is to define a customer segment within the overall market and to clearly establish its needs and preferences, then use communication to approach the target group. Expressed in more general terms, a sub-group is established by means of a process of elimination and this is then worked on. Using this approach, one encounters a practical problem of principle. On the one hand a synthetic customer profile is abstracted, which, on the other hand, never applies in real terms or in terms of contact with actual individual prospective buyers within this segment. Even the extent to which this synthetic requirement profile is blurred is not known in advance.

In a number of companies this fuels the daily clashes between marketing heads and those responsible for sales. The marketing people plan very carefully, harnessing further resources to support their activities. These may be advertising, PR, event marketing, sponsoring as well as all kinds of others. All these activities are geared towards a group of uniform phantom customers. The marketing people have in-depth knowledge of the concept of their enemy, the competitor, and of the customer as a target segment. By contrast to this very clear, but abstract interpretation, the sales front generally breaks down. The marketing people reproach the sales and distribution side with their supposed ignorance and lack of knowledge.

Those responsible for front line sales are in contact with the real customers and know their needs and problems. They blame the marketing people for being theorists and out of touch with reality.

Attempts to defuse the animosity give rise in-house to periodic changes in structural hierarchy. One day, marketing is part of sales, then both functions are put on the same level, then distribution is incorporated into marketing. This does nothing to eliminate the basic problem, but the motives underlying the relevant arguments are redefined. In an attempt to help with bridging this gulf the concept of customer proximity was introduced and marketing obliged to recognise that the real customer does not correspond to the target group profile. This kindles the debate about the 'real' customer. Customer proximity cannot be accepted as a new concept by the sales people, as sales departments always have been forced to work with budgets based on their success with 'real' customers.

The paradigm of cyber marketing goes from the individual customer to the customer group. A customer is serviced in terms of his needs. Marketing and sales go hand in hand here. Sales are responsible for meeting his requirements, whilst marketing to a certain extent gets to know the customer, abstracts his requirements and then has to deduct further interests from them. This does not only apply to commercial customers in the capital goods sector, but equally to the individual consumer. Marketing means winning a customer with all his potential. Examples are customer bonding programmes operated by airlines and the bonus clubs run by branded goods manufacturers.

What does 'winning the customer with all his potential' mean? What is share of customershare of customer?[26] A holiday travel organiser examines two of his customers – a family and a retired married couple. During the past five years the family has regularly booked two weeks off each year, as has the retired couple. Turnover was approximately the same for both clients. The retired couple made more expensive arrangements. What is share of customershare of customer? In the course of his investigations the organiser established that the family booked only these two weeks' holiday and a maximum of one weekend city break flight per year. On the other hand, the retired couple were very active and, on average, had six weeks' holiday per year. Share of customer for the family was about 85%, but for the retired couple it was only about one-third. As a rule, it is easier to achieve extra turnover with existing customers. It would be desirable to get the entire customer turnover. This calls for clarity about why full share of customer is not being achieved. A supplier can only find this out if he is in dialogue with the customer and thus knows the trend of inclinations and preferences. The criterion for measurement here is not primarily that of market share, but of share of customershare of customer. Market share as a management criterion carries, to a greater or lesser extent, a degree of weight in different market phases.[27] Which is better, a market share of 50% and, as far as these particular customers are concerned, a share of 10%, or a market share of 25% with a share of customershare of customer of 80%? The answer is two-fold. Firstly, it is more cost-effective to acquire only 25% of the customers. We know that, for a given business transaction, the costs arising in respect of dealing with a new customer, depending on the sector, are higher by a factor of between 5 and 20 than would be the case with an existing customer. And, secondly, the mathematical product in the first instance is 5% and in the second 20%.

The new view of this paradigm has a further, highly positive effect. The argument of increasing share of customershare of customer calls for an excellent understanding of needs and procurement patterns. This means extending core performance, justified by real needs.

'From individual to customer base' is a lesson for existing companies who already service a certain number of customers. The new entrepreneur is very much aware of this uniquely possible development in terms of growth. He knows that success, especially in the beginning, can only be achieved with each customer as an individual, and on a step-by-step basis. As the customer base increases, there tends to be a decline in the value placed by staff and those responsible in many companies on the individual customer.

From passive to interactive

Esteem is conveyed by communication. Marketing communication using the means available in the industrial era, such as television or direct mail is, however, confrontative information. The customer is forced into a passive role and tries to defend himself against the flood of advertising paperwork by sticking 'no ads please' stickers on his letterbox. He switches over to another TV channel as soon as the advertisements come on. Communication means: both partners are talking and listening. Esteem can only be built up by using this kind of communication. Esteem also means respecting the customer's private sphere.

From observation to absorption

The cyber world makes it possible to conduct communication not only with an observer at the other end, but to create an intrinsic reality for this communication. The customer becomes a partner, absorbed in this world. This approach can achieve very strong emotional bonding as far as the customer is concerned.

From word to world

The concept of Corporate Identity, away from words and graphics, i.e. Corporate Design, is set to undergo a massive expansion. In the virtual world, a form of Corporate Identity with a totally new character can be created. The need for this three-dimensionality as regards identity is evident to some extent and may occur repeatedly or spontaneously at fairs and exhibitions. In hotels, restaurants, snack bars, filling stations, bank counters, car hire centres and airline companies, the need to establish a global identity is already the norm.

In this context, a company is also presenting itself 'away from home'. Corporate Identity, i.e. designing a company's locality, for instance that of an insurance company, in a manner which is both identifiable and unmistakable, is often carried out at a single site but not in all subsidiary locations. In this case we are not talking about logos or changing sales promotions, but about an unmistakable zone which the customer enters within the virtual world, and which he finds again in his home reality.

Corporate Identity within the virtual world gives rise to dealing with questions relating to Corporate Sound and Corporate Thought. How should the company decide in terms of the audio sense, hearing? What sound sequences should the company use to identify itself? The symbolic power of sound can emotionalise an appearance. We see examples of this every day on television: without background music, very many scenes from mediocre or lower-grade films would be thoroughly unenjoyable. Corporate Sound, which helps to shape the overall acoustic appearance of a company, at the same time embraces Corporate Music. Corporate Music could already feature today in telephone connection queues by way of a musical 'signature tune' for the company.

A further important aspect: what level of intelligence do I ascribe to my customer? The negotiation of virtual sales may be too difficult and too incomprehensible for the beginner whilst the experienced cybernaut develops negative emotions because, for him, the way the company is represented, its market performance, is too trivial.

The use of hypermedia techniques leaves behind comprehensible thought patterns – consciously or unconsiously. This, from today's viewpoint, gives rise to a completely new opportunity of establishing oneself in an even more intimate position directly in the thoughts of prospective buyers and customers. The virtual world demands a Corporate Reality.

The Priorities for Success in the Information Era

Cyber marketing incorporates its own intrinsic features. The basis for this is formed, however, by information technology. We are all swamped with information. Our main concern is to recognise the essentials, retain what we can use and find important information quickly.

Despite these enormous opportunities, many individuals are dissatisfied or even insecure. The extensive availability of information, the breadth of opportunity in having access to opinions, theses and beliefs is surely one of the main reasons. If people are exposed to a large number of such aspects, they will be forced to come to grips with them. This may, at the simplest level, take place by declining to take them on board, forgetting them or suppressing them. Individuals must adopt their own opinions, their own views, in order to be able to deal with the information with which they come into contact with in a meaningful way.

Basically, existence is determined locally, but consciousness is determined globally. In this sense, a number of suppression processes take place. Although close by a war may be raging and doctors are endeavouring, albeit with scant means, to ensure the survival of the victims, the other half of humankind is only bothered about the beauty of their fingernails. Evidence of this almost schizophrenic behaviour can easily be found in any illustrated magazine. On the left-hand page, there is a model, pretty as a picture, using her erotic charms to advertise nail polish; and on the right-hand page, there are pictures of war in Yugoslavia or Chechnya.

The incidence of such contradictions within a single horizon is set to increase in the future. It also asks for our ability to cope with conflict situations of this kind. People will try to build a world which is homogeneous and peaceful, whilst the realities on television and in other media present them with a totally different form of realism.

Every society makes use of the technologies available, but also reflects it in its values. Up to a decade ago, this meant the tools of the industrial revolution, namely, technologies to reduce human input in the workplace and to induce mass production. Division of labour became necessary. Initially thought and work were separated. The refinement of this principle meant that companies were blessed with a caste of managers in production, research, distribution and accounts. However, since the economic success of the Japanese and the prosperity which they have achieved in scarcely half a century, this Western attitude with its roots in industrial development is being questioned. There has been a resurgence of teamwork and communication, but this is only the beginning of a completely new trend. The traditional forms of technology still exist, but substitution is a question of time, or, more precisely, dependent on the build-up of the appropriate communication structure.

Whereas, in the industrial era, company size and the amount of capital investment were the most significant success factors, in the information era, new key conditions apply. The ability to learn, not only on the part of the individual but also on the part of the entire organisation, is paramount, speed and the ability to anticipate customer requirements or to point out new opportunities to prospective buyers is essential. In the industrial era a great number of market mechanisms were regulated and the particular details, shop opening times, working hours, etc., were laid down in a number of decrees and laws. There is, however, no closing time when it comes to videotext or a bookshop on the network. Instead it's 'open all hours'.

Marketing means learning. It is not an activity which can be made repetitive. It calls for thinking and reacting. The basis for it is information. Thus, for example, companies who have already acquired this insight, are no longer assigning responsibility for information technology to the finance/control sector but to marketing. In this way, they ensure that the information systems are geared to the purchasers and thus to the future, whilst also performing the basic function of coping with the past. What is book-keeping other than a special way of writing the history of the company? It is no longer sufficient to simply create products. Besides this, companies need to approach marketing directly for, in the future, this will be taking place on-line and directly with the customer. Hence, new aspects of marketing will become important and these will need to be reflected in management awareness. The unfolding technology of telematics can be used to maintain or promote awareness of information and the success of the enterprise.

The seven principles of information awareness

In terms of information awareness, the following perceptions are of paramount importance when it comes to making business decisions.

1. *Information must incorporate all business activities*

This principle is easy to comprehend. People set great store every day by the correctness of the information they receive or they make great efforts to acquire information for themselves because they realise that it will enable them to make more informed decisions. This also applies to purchasing decisions. Nevertheless, such decisions are not only based on rational thought – in fact, they hardly ever are. For a human being, only those things of which he has knowledge actually exist. Human beings can only achieve that which they can imagine. Compliance with human feelings can only be achieved by means of communication which, consciously or unconsciously, targets human emotion.

2. *The more directly and solidly market performance is conditioned by source information, the greater the possible and achievable profit margin will be*

All market performance is based on information, on knowledge. Every product has its origin inside the human head, and we human beings use our knowledge to create product items. Source information is, in this sense, primordial information which cannot be distributed as such and is not communicated. Source information may be

recognised market needs or a new technological concept from the R&D department. Patents and protected inventions are examples of source information or
knowledge of this kind. The directness of information is a statement about the temporal and qualitative transformation of knowledge into an appropriate product. If
information on a new form of technology is available, but is only transformed partly instead of completely into a new product, then this information will not fully condition market performance. If, between recognising a market need and doing something about it, a relatively lengthy period of time elapses, the advantage of the direct
approach will be lost. During this time, the need may subside or be met by a compe-
titior. 'Solid' means the proportion of source information in market performance.
The greater the original share, the greater the level of innovation will be.

It is only when information is successfully transformed into market performance which is then successfully marketed, that a profit margin becomes possible.
The profit margin is not determined by market performance alone, but just as
much by the prevailing market conditions. These are determined by acute need and
the possible alternatives available to satisfy this need, whilst at the same time, the
available alternatives are, in turn, a function of the existing information.

*3. With performing services which are based exclusively on information, it is
not production, but development, which is crucial as far as possible margins
are concerned*

Software production is the most popular example of this. Another example is a
very well known brand name. Establishing the brand name in the heads of consumers is far more expensive than producing individual cigarettes or mineral water.

4. Time is no barrier to competition

In the Middle Ages, no information from Paris ever reached the Bay of San Francisco. Three hundred years ago, information would be travelling for months. At the
beginning of this century, it was reaching its destination within a matter of a few
days. Today, it takes just tenths of a second to get from A to B.

Decades ago, it took a very long time to reproduce an item of equipment. These
days, the individual components can be obtained very quickly on the world market. The barrier of time is being broken down as information structures are extended and will be very small in cyber space. Building on the time advantage is becoming an increasingly less secure concept.

As far as straight market performance is concerned in the information age, such
as software, it is solely copyright that is significant. It takes practically no time at
all to copy or communicate information or software.

A further aspect of time relates to the reference to earlier competitive successes.
In a period when paradigms are breaking up, a glorious past is no guarantee with a
view to the future. The fact that a company has been successful in the past, today
no longer means that this success will last for the following day and into the future.

5. The critical factor is not the number of employees – it is the quality of their thinking which matters

This fact is most familiar in software development. When it comes to complex problems, a large number of people is no decisive factor, it is the right mind that will make success possible.

6. The ability to communicate determines market success

A company's success is decided by its ability to gain access to the minds of its customers and its ability to establish itself positively in their emotions.

7. As far as communication is concerned, contemporary attractiveness goes before quality

For the customer, 'contemporary' means 'interesting, attractive at this moment in time' – market performance and the cost of the service performed, meet the customer's requirements. In communication, quality is too often determined by the professional communicators. Such standards are not, however, geared to the customer, but rather to communication itself.

Market performance

What does 'market performance' actually mean? Suppliers make products which are bought by customers. Popularly speaking, this is true. However, in the future, more differentiation will be required. With the information era, a third type of market performance has come along, in addition to the industrial product and the well-known range of services – and that is software.

The product – hardware

The traditional product is physical, it may be an item of goods or a piece of equipment. It has a product life cycle which incorporates the phases of development, production and usage. Examples include all kinds of consumer or utility goods.

The service – brainware

A further market performance category encompasses all kinds of services, including insurances, transport and medical care. The service as such is something which marketing theory only discovered at a late stage. The most significant difference between a service and a product is that services cannot be stored. Services are normally performed as soon as they are demanded. 'Offering services' means setting aside capacity to service demand. If these services are not used, costs will nevertheless arise, but will not be offset by yields.

The software

Software is the third type of market performance. This market performance characterises the information era. Software is knowledge portrayed in a replicable manner. High level market performance very often consists of all three: products, services and software.

All three types are subject to quite different laws of development, manufacture and distribution. This applies to cost structure as well as to the marketing of this product or service. Market performance may feature in different phases during the life of a market. Depending on whether the market is emerging, growing, in its mature phase or even in regression, the requirements regarding the marketing of products or services will be different. The phases in the life of a market do, furthermore, demonstrate unequal earnings potential. It is only during the growth phase that the main weight of effort is placed on gaining market share. All three remaining phases will only be mastered with any degree of success, when costs and prices are right and performance differentiates to increase share of customershare of customer.

A company wins share of customershare of customer by being able to record, for any given customer, the major part or even the whole of his outgoings in this sector in the company's books. This is very often successful, whilst the actual performance is augmented by services or software. The original performance, the core performance, is extended.

In one dimension, the planning of market performance takes into account the level of the market and, in another, the type of market performance. It is on this that the fine tuning of overall market performance is based. Throughout all these fundamentally diverse marketing situations, the information era keeps further challenges up its sleeve.

Range and diversity

Practically every market is dominated by demand and no longer by suppliers. The range available to customers is infinite. Forget about what you have to offer being unique and special; it simply isn't true. Behind every item offered, there are dozens of alternative options which are just waiting to be called up. Like pearls on a string, the customer in the cyber world suddenly finds that they have become organised and easy to find, look at and compare. Whereas nationality formerly was a natural barrier because information scarcely penetrated from one country to another, today we find that this has not been the case for some time. Your offer on the Internet will be competing with everyone else's – world-wide. Setting different prices in different countries for the same product is now only possible to a limited extent.

Personal computers, for example, are as alike as two peas in a pod. When you purchased your last PC, you had hundreds of brands to choose from with very finely tuned price differences. These days it is easier to buy a car. On the one hand, there are fewer brands on offer, on the other, cars seem to be more easily distinguishable one from the other. PC novices can find hardly any differences in a computer rack. With the exception of a very small number of examples, they are all grey. They can be ordered in any country and are delivered anywhere by courier. Our lives are becoming more and more diverse. This goes for practically every sector. Ten years ago, there were several dozen television stations, nowadays there is a multitude. There are two reasons for this: on the one hand, more stations have been set up in the same sector, namely the numerous private stations. On the other hand, transmitters today have a wider range and this means a more extensive reception area. In addition, there are more networks and satellite television sets. The same goes for radio stations, contraceptives, breakfast juices, music titles, clothing, aeroplane manufacturers and practically all other private consumer sectors and the investment goods industries.

The wide range of different products, goods and services means stronger competition but, equally, diversity. The number of actively spoken languages in practically every developed country has multiplied in the last three decades. Social structure has become fragmented. Within the metropolitan environment it is possible, all over the world, to identify linguistic and cultural quarters which represent a microcosm of what was formerly a well-ordered world and its peoples.

Speed

These days, nobody seems to have any time any more. We can be contacted by pagers and mobile telephones, fax and other communication devices. Within the context of this accessibility, we are more open to what goes on on the fax or in the e-mail box than to what is happening next door. Communication is no longer an arm's-length affair in the direct presence of our correspondent but rather a long-distance undertaking involving equipment for the transmission of sound, the written word and pictures – total digitalisation.

Simultaneousness

Modern means of communiction allow us to participate simultaneously in whatever is happening. Simultaneous discussions between several individuals separated by enormous distances are possible in a forum on the Internet, all of which formerly took place sequentially due to the lack of speed in communication. Simultaneousness means that a customer is able to inspect the full range of what is offered at any time. It is justifiably arguable, whether the options available in terms of communication and the speed which goes with them bring about simultaneousness or vice versa. As regards communication in particular, working with selection and sequence is no longer possible. If something is communicated, we must assume that the message can arrive at different places at the same time. Thus, important messages within an enterprise can be distributed in seconds or depending on the transfer rate of the electronic postal systems. Given this simultaneousness, customers can indeed react very rapidly and check the truth of the information. This happens not least of all due to the physical and intellectual mobility of those who live in the information era.

Mobility

Finally, communication is not all that has become faster and more omnipresent. Whereas a hundred years ago, people were still rooted in their native soil, today they are mobile, both in terms of their environment and equally in terms of their powers of comprehension. As a society, we are more mobile and, at the same time, more open.

Rules of thumb in cyber marketing

TD – Think digital

The basic innovations of the information era have already been implemented. Technology is digitally based. Future developments will certainly incorporate changes but these will all be digital and electronic. This means seeing digitally – no more photographs on negatives and paper, instead they will be on disks which can be read directly into the computer; no sound carriers that cannot be directly connected digitally to the multimedia machine; no pictures on film, but instead digital on video disks; no communication using the old technology, instead it will be digital; no faxes on paper, they will go direct into the computer instead. Information is valuable if it reaches the correct recipient in time, for relevance to the present declines with every moment one spends processing information from various different media electronically. Therefore: think, see, speak and feel digitally. Throw away the ballast of dusty old media and bring in the standard of the information era. Only he who makes his start today will have the extra experience necessary and will have to convert fewer old media to digital in the future. Without exception, digital means significant cost savings, for media breaks mean loss of money.

Facts with fun instead of sentimentality

Hitherto marketing communication and advertising has been geared to emotions and desires. Every advertisement for washing powder uses sentimentality to mask inadequacy when it comes to explaining a cleaner. Instead of the mind, underlying emotions are being stirred and manipulated.

On the network, pure brainfood, clumsy with derisory excesses and overloaded with inaccuracies, will not be accepted. The consumers of network information drink in clean, entertaining facts and drain the vessel to the leas. They go out looking for information, select it and react. Up to now, advertisers have told consumers what they believed was important for sales. Attempts to hush up or gloss over things are pointless. Don't hide anything, be direct and genuine, this is what is being asked. Humour is an increasingly important feature, both for today and tomorrow, in order to raise the level of receptiveness above the sentimentality and to do this in a manner which is not ponderous but which is intellectually agile.

Data – digital gold

There is no point in collecting bits, for data are the building blocks of information relevant to a personal deepening of relations with and knowledge about the customer. Data are the rootstock of cyber marketing. To possess data also means having the option of locating changes and of implementing adaptations immediately and not merely in a matter of months. As is always the case in good management, care of data and information must be handed over to a single responsible person. In this case it is the person who is responsible for marketing. Responsibility for up-to-date, accurate data is a basic prerequisite in the information era. Experts pan the digital gold out of a number of individual encounters and melt the raw material down into a solid relationship with the individual customer.

Accessibility as a substitute for range

Range and distribution losses are criteria in the one-way communication pattern of the industrial marketing craft. What counts in the new media is accessibility for two-way communication. Both need to work together. The supplier targets the mind of the customer and, in return, opens up to him the body and soul of his own organisation. He does not want attention but time from his customer. Only time spent together is profitable time. This time should be used openly and the customer should enjoy it.

Ever ready

Customers are turning to the on-line media because they want to be able to buy, at any time, whenever they want to. For this reason, the supplier needs to be ever ready, whenever the customer wants information or whenever he wishes to place an order. Ever ready and whenever lasts for the same amount of time: 24 hours, seven days a week, every week of the year, year in … !

The customer as a pal

Customer telephone numbers can quickly be forgotten, fax numbers will be current for some time yet, the electronic postal address will be important in future. In the future, it will not only be messages to customers and other prospective buyers that are sent via electronic post but also photographs, films and detailed specifications, both in the form of pictures and sound. The supplier will be on familiar terms with his customer and will address him using his nickname. Thus, the supplier will obtain all the customer information he needs: his partner's preferences, his holiday plans, statistics information such as age, weight, salary, property, colour preferences, favourite foods and his preferred lifestyle, so as to be able to draw up individual offers for the customer and offer him a truly individual service.

Having fun is the best way to whet an appetite for information

New media can satisfy the customer's hunger for knowledge and information. Handling them should be fun – this helps to strengthen pleasure in the relationship and increase sales. Suppliers want their customer to linger with them and not just take a quick look at what they have to offer, and for this reason accessing should be simple. If it is easy, simple and larded with charm and enthusiasm, this will be rewarded by the customer coming back and by his loyalty. If the customer discloses information about himself this should be respected. At the same time, all the details should not be demanded right at the beginning by way of a prerequisite for dialogue. The accomplished use of dramatisation to establish a relationship with a customer is a digital romance, which becomes more intimate and familiar from one stage to the next.

Knowing the customer means storing good information about him. This is obtained by means of dialogue. Good dialogue is founded in mutual trust. Trust means respecting and being considerate. A dialogue comes about when two or more parties can and wish to participate in it. These are principles which one should always follow in database marketing.

Maintaining contact capacity

Direct relationships with customers come about through network media. This relationship is not buffered. When thousands of customers react to an offer, suppliers must be ready to accept the order straight away. They must be ready to process thousands of transactions in a very short time or to keep the option to transact open for several weeks, depending on how their zone of activity looks. Capacity dimensioning is, however, not a simple matter.

The customer is not the king, but the sovereign

Even in the information era the customer is still king. Or perhaps not any more? No – he is more. Democratisation imbues the customer with the power of the sovereign, the power of the people in a direct democracy. Managers are instilling into their company workforces that it is still the customer who makes the decisions and determines the future of the company.

Clarifying what valuable customers are

All company employees and all their customers must be clear about what criteria distinguish the individual customer as particularly valuable. Progressive firms communicate these criteria in the context of their partnership with the customer. They point out the advantages and privileges that their valuable customers receive from them. The company MCI has successfully introduced its 'Family & Friends' programme. Their customers enjoy special rates for telephone conversations held frequently with the same people, who may be from the family or simply good friends.

A valuable customer brings the company more business, and for this reason, he is rewarded and encouraged to remain a customer. One criterion is share of customershare of customer. The more share of customershare of customer a company obtains, the more important the customer. Cyber marketing takes these criteria as a theme within the enterprise. Which customers should be especially well looked-after and how? Which prospective buyers are set to become customers? Which purchasers are really prospective buyers?[28]

Conclusion: Marketing in the Information Era as Digital Relationship Management

Conditioned by techological development and social conditions, marketing as an activity has been subjected to changes. Whereas, in the industrial era, the emphasis was on mass marketing, marketing in the information era concentrates on individual customers. The change of paradigm states: instead of the struggle for market share, concern for share of customershare of customer is emerging; instead of confrontation, we have relationships emerging; instead of asymmetry of information we have dialogue. Within the network society, marketing is fundamentally digital, independent of space and time, interactive and dialogue-orientated, strongly fact-related and market performance directly geared to the customer.

These are the effects of far-reaching market transparency which will become established in stages on the basis of direct communication, on-line marketing and, finally, cyber marketing.

3 DATA – THE TERRAIN OF THE INFORMATION ERA

This chapter contains an overview of the principles and concepts which play a significant role in the information era. Knowledge of the differences between data, information and communication will assume an ever greater importance in the future. Awareness of how to handle information saves money and therefore time.

Information and Communication as a Fundamental Need

Communication is just as basic a need for a healthy human being as food, clothing and a roof over his head. The power of information is legendary but the expression is well-worn. However, what is a change of paradigm in the information sector? The collection, analysis, modelling and interpretation of data via market research have been features of marketing for decades. So what's new? Why should the ability to collect, disseminate, process, store, and analyse information as well as to derive decisions and activities from it decide the success or failure of a company in the future? What is new in the cyber era about 'information' as a concept when information in itself is something so old? As long ago as Rameses, hieroglyphics had ceased to be an innovation in the Nile Valley.

One thing is certain: information processing has established itself as an electronicised function conducted on the computer in practically every enterprise throughout the world and is as such light years away, technically speaking, from the inscriptions on the Egyptian pyramids. However, this fact alone does not account for the revolution which has occurred. After the business world, the households and private individuals of the highly industrialised countries have also kitted themselves out with personal computers. The first revolution is the amalgamation of all these information systems operated by suppliers as well as purchasers, i.e. to bring together all participants in the market by means of the electronic data networks.[29]

The second, far more drastic revolution will be the incorporation of users in this artifically created world. The current on-line relationship of the user in the man/machine interface divides the real world from the system world. The user is outside the system and he is conscious of it. He is an observing user. His position towards the system is just as externalised as it is when he is watching television, enjoying a film at the cinema or immersed in a picture or a painting. Even when playing a video sequence in which he himself figures, he assumes the position of an observer of a section of his own past.

The cyber world is far more revolutionary. The user is integrated into the system by means of appropriate system interfaces, such as, for example, the cyber spectacles. Through the cyber spectacles, the virtual world is conveyed directly via a miniature screen via the eyes into the conscious mind and the brain of the observer.[30] His real environment ceases to exist and he takes himself off into a new, artificially created world. The cybernaut may move through virtual space deliberately and in a self-determined manner, although he is sitting on a chair and physically immobile. The user is integrated within the virtual world and feels that he has an existence there. Instead of being simply an observer, he becomes a participant in virtual reality. Instead of visual perception, multimediality comes into play. He is no longer chasing abstract symbols such as letters or drawings, but is perceiving a photo-realistic world. The development of the cyber world exists today in embryo. The number of applications available is growing rapidly. In a few years' time the cyber shopping mall will be able to compete with the world of experience offered by a shopping centre. One suspects that, due to the high level of television addiction, very many of our contemporaries will be extremely susceptible to the adventures offered by the cyber world.

Many companies find the simple, civilised path to the cyber future barred for them by fossil EDP solutions. Whereas before, during the initial wave of in-company information processing, applications such as accounts and, with it, control, stood in the foreground, this has undergone a very marked change during the last decade.[31] Networks enable communication to take place within the enterprise and have immense coordination functions. Without telematics, it would be impossible to run the gigantic, global operation enterprises. The strategic importance of information has been recognised and is being transformed into sound commercial standing, added value and profits. However, there are a number of voices which deny the benefits of the information systems, or at least dispute the increase in productivity which has come about through the use of electronic information processing, or argue that progress in terms of productivity is not in proportion to the investments made.

A further page in the history of the information era can be seen in the way communication networks have emerged between the individual market participants. Whereas the closed and regulated electronic markets were the first to emerge, the next were open networks. In the same way as railway and road networks in the past were external signs of massive economic changes, the same goes today for the build-up of the information highway, with one major difference: the tracks and roads are visible to everyone, but not the electronic networks. They are hidden and not physically recognisable. Even less tangible is the traffic that travels along these new routes – information.

Basic definitions

The word 'information' has its roots in the Latin verb *informare* – to give shape or form to something. Or, in the transferred sense: to educate someone through instruction. Information, energy and matter are the most important factors in modern economic management along with landed property, capital and employees.

Information, however, by contrast to matter, raw materials or energy, displays quite different characteristics. Information knows no original, can be copied as often as you like and is not dependent on location. Information does not age and can be incorporated into almost infinite combinations. It is impossible to examine a piece of information to see whether its component parts belong to each other or not. An example of this is a picture with a short caption underneath it. This means manipulation is possible infinitely within the limits of reason. Moreover, this fact has also been used in advertising in very recent times. On television we see cows playing football advertising chocolate bars. Hence, in the same way, distortions and fragments of information rank as information. As information is used for processing information, and, in particular, itself, it can be analysed, thought about further, added to or otherwise processed further. It is with this that the problems of verification of correctness and completeness in relation to a particular context arise. Information is highly compressible, such as, for instance, in a picture.

A theoretic understanding treats information as a certain measure of order, as information excludes vagaries and uncertainties. One yardstick for order is negative entropy or 'negentropy'. This concept is represented in analogy to entropy in the theory of thermodynamics. In thermodynamics, entropy is a mathematically tangible magnitude of disorder. The quality of a piece of information lies in the magnitude of the probability that it will afford the user certainty in terms of his stated view.

Information as a concept is complex. Even today, we are still divided on precisely how the concept of information should be defined. Without astuteness, information can be perceived as a portrayal, an item of news, a message, a reply to an enquiry or something conveyed. Man obtains information himself directly, via other people or via information carriers such as newspapers, books, pictures, video cassettes, CD-ROMs, records or communication devices such as radio, television, fax, telephone or computer.

The semiotic characteristics of information

Before we can cope with the concept, we have to make a reduction. One way of understanding information is to divide the characteristics into a syntactic, significative, semantic and pragmatic piece of information. In language, syntax is part of grammar. The syntactic part can always be recognised. It describes the permitted building blocks which go to make up the information. When it comes to contemplating the syntax, i.e. the signs, science has hit on some good definitions, but not for the other, far more important semiotic characteristics.

Signmatics deals with the relationship of signs and objects. In this regard we also talk about 'objective knowledge'. Railway stations and airports are good examples. In these public places, signs and signals must be both compact and, at the same time, not dependent on any one language or culture. The pictograms used to designate telephone boxes, smoking areas, information desks or lockers, for example, are objectively defined knowledge.

The semantic part indicates the meaning contained in the signs. This mostly becomes evident indirectly from processing the information. From the meaning of the individual signs and their relationship with others latent knowledge – a message – emerges.

The fourth part is made up of the purpose of the information and the action hoped for; this is the pragmatic part. It remains mostly (and in IT practically always) hidden. This part is also termed 'effective knowledge'.

Information in the sense of information technology

The portrayal of letters, more generally known as characters, may take place in one of two different ways on the computer. The modern computer age is primarily familiar with character-orientated representation. The characters are portrayed on the screen in various typefaces and different written forms, such as underlined, bold or italic, something which does not, nevertheless, make it possible to reproduce drawings or even photographs on the screen. The image surface is divided up exactly into a box grid pattern with which 24 x 80 characters can be portrayed. For each box the computer makes a note of the appropriate character with the relevant specification. This type of character representation is less intensive in terms of storage than bit map representation.

In bit map representation, the screen is no longer defined in boxes but in dot matrix form. The number of points lies between some ten thousand and over a million. Together with the rate of picture element localisation, the number of picture elements determines the quality and hence the price of a monitor. The television works according to the same principle. The smallest unit is the picture element, also known as 'pixel' (from 'picture element'). The picture element is defined in terms of its colour and intensity and this makes exact colour portrayals possible, such as in a photograph.

By contrast to information, data can be objectified because it can be coded by means of signs, stored, transformed and, above all, transported. Information is, by nature, processable, liable to change, knowledge- and subject-related, the latter above all because a piece of information must always be understood in regard to a context. Something that may represent knowledge-changing information for one person does not have to be so for another. Probably the weightiest difference is that knowledge is understood as a magnitude of continued existence whilst information is construed as a flowing magnitude.

For representing information, information technology uses signals, information and messages. Signals are perceived as elementary and detectable changes such as a sound, a pictorial element, a line, a movement or an electrical impulse. Data is characters portrayed by means of digital conditions. In communications engineering, a sequence of signals including their spatial and temporal delegation is absorbed as news. From the point of view of communications engineering, the question was raised at an early stage as to how as much knowledge as possible can be incorporated in the signals. This is important for the achievement of short transmission times. The bit was determined as the unit of mass for information. The bit is an item of data expressed by means of 0 or 1. This data can be described by means of the simplest of signals, namely, a transfer between two conditions. An item of data as a sequence of characters must be built up in accordance with predetermined rules or syntax. Initially, data has no significance; it is only through subsequent processing or usage that the data acquires meaning. In everyday language we designate data which expresses the facts of a matter, serves a purpose, triggers action or which simply just extends knowledge, as an item of information. Therefore, data may become an item of infomation either through human interpretation or through the manner in which it is processed by computer programmes or stored in databases before being re-used. In the human sector, information responds to enquiries in respect of at least one of the questions, who? what? where? when? how? why? with whose help? to what end? Information is closely related to communication. Depending on a purpose or an aim, the correct information will develop as communication progresses. The pragmatic part of the information will then at least become identifiable.

Information – simply defined

In the following we apply a restricted meaning of the concept of information: information is an item of data which has its significance for the recipient. This meaning may lie in the fact that a recipient will give meaning to the data or the meaning can be inferred indirectly from the manner in which the data is subsequently processed. The meaning can also be deduced from the data. Information is generated, conveyed, stored and understood. If information is transferred unilaterally, this should be designated as 'informing'. Where there is a bilateral transfer of information, we should talk about 'communication'.

Collections of information are addresses in a personal address book, progressing via memory to the enormous collections of bytes in mammoth databases which are managed by high performance computers. We reproduce our own personal data over a typical day within our own memory in terms of examples of our own behaviour and that of others, information and emotions relating to our friends and undertakings or rules which we apply to deal with everyday matters.

Humankind has developed a natural framework for storing information in an organised fashion so as to be able to find it again easily and quickly. The classification of information can be categorised in five different ways. First of all, information is organised according to location. The information is related to a place – as in the country of origin of fruit or parts of the body in the event of illness. Secondly, an item of information may have a time relationship – time is a good organising principle for activities such as work, holiday or in many kinds of sport. Thirdly, mankind is familiar with alphabetical structuring – such as the telephone book. The fourth way of classifying information is by means of categories – trees are broad-leaved or conifers, the fir is a conifer. The fifth way is to divide up 'in continuum' – from the smallest to the largest, from the youngest to the oldest.

In the personal life of individuals, mental distance categories play a major part. The categories can be illustrated using a stratified ring model built up as follows. The smallest mental distance exists from information which concerns us personally. This is the central circle. This zone incorporates all the information that makes our life possible – from the cerebral system down to our own concepts of values. The first ring around us is information from direct conversations. This is the area where the formalised and informal exchange of information takes place. Very often too little attention is paid to this area – and the informal area in particular – but it nevertheless has a very great effect on us. The next ring contains reference information. Reference information is the basis for business activity, science or technology. We are confronted with reference information initially in school books and it accompanies us through our entire life in the form of telephone books, instruction handbooks or databases. The fourth sector consists of innovations and news. This is information on incidents, people and conditions which do not directly concern our personal life but nevertheless affect our opinions and behaviour.[32] The greatest mental distance is from information relating to culture, history, art, philosophy or belief.

Although we have so far been talking about communication in marketing, media advertising is not communication in the strict sense, as the advertising messages are without exception unilaterally directed by the advertising supplier to wholly or partially anonymous addressees. Real communication is, however, bilateral. This means in addition that the customer or prospective buyer is or should be at all times in a position to open up communication. For this purpose he must, however, be in a positon to find a contact person. Marketing communication will need to make this possible. Without a basic appreciation of the principles of information and communication, it will not be possible to cope with the tremendous task before us.

Information Value Chain

Information may be viewed from two operational perspectives: costs or value – as costs because procurement, storage and processing are conditional upon investment and generate costs. In value-orientated organisations, science and information technology are perceived as the ability to generate increased competitive advantages for the enterprise by means of information.

The information value chain is a model and a regulating principle within the context of this new awareness and serves as a bridge between data and information.[33] The information value chain contains five links: data recording and/or data generation and transfer, data management, information or data interpretation, models and decision-aid systems.

Naturally, the information value chain plays an important role in getting from data to information so as to enable us, in this way, to deepen our wisdom, extend our knowledge and ultimately to enable us to make decisions. If a chain is modelled, then its intended purpose must be known and formulated right at the beginning. The aims of information processing must be set in advance by establishing a 'transcending level', which, in this case, is the marketing contract which is subordinate to company targets. Company targets are always the same: to create objects of value to customers, market performance; as far as the employees are concerned, the work in their overall social and economic dimension; as far as the investors are concerned, yields as well as secure future investment. Management cannot and must not expect that decisions can be derived from information alone. They must be aware of what decisions they have to take, what knowledge they have to require before data is compiled and the preparation of the information can begin.

Recording and transferring data

The first element in the information value chain is the generation of data by collection and transmission. The start of the information revolution was marked by the use of technology to register, store, retrieve and transmit raw data. At that time this data was practically equated with figures. The opportunities offered by multimedia have been responsible for a tremendous increase in the forms of data. Certainly applications such as the recording and processing of POS (point of sale) data on networks between retail shops and central warehouses with linked-up storage and distribution systems are still in the majority. Electronic sales ledgers will register the sales made by an establishment at branch level by means of electronic POS systems and transmit the details daily, if not even without losing any time. In the further stages of information processing, details of consumer reactions and local needs and traits are obtained. In the case of videotext systems, a shopping record is developing as an auxiliary product to on-line shopping.

Clearly, recording raw data today is fundamentally different from previously, when representatives from market panel companies such as Nielsen used to count products on the shelves in shops personally, using a pencil to write the data down on a notepad. Computers and telecommunication have massively reduced the costs of data recording and data transacting. This change has paved the way for the marketing information revolution.

Data management

The increase in raw data has assumed proportions that threaten to overwhelm the users. This applies to the amount of data as well as to the speed at which data can be recorded. Once the data is recorded, the second level in the information value chain comes into play: that of data management. Without efficient means of managing, ordering, sorting, extracting, compiling and finding the data again, the first step in the value chain would be futile. The majority state that they have great trouble managing data. In many cases the further use of the data is not specifically defined so that it acquires a value for the user. In company-speak we talk about 'generic data'. One example is the retail sector, where phenomenal quantities of electronic POS data regularly accrue. Very few firms make use of their data, partly because they are not in a position to convert the data into pregnant and useful statements. Recorded data is only kept so that it can be called up quickly for a relatively short period of time. This is because of the cost and complexity of making the data available on-line. For this reason it is very important to refine the data into a condensed and expressive form.

Information – interpreted data

As far as the majority of users are concerned, 'information' is raw data which has been interpreted in a form which makes sense to the recipient. Information in the form of interpreted data is the third link in the information value chain. Database management tools help to organise the data. The full value of data is based on the ability to interpret data.

Several techniques have been developed for making the transition from raw data to meaningful information for the users. In addition to conventional commercial data interpretation systems, the artificial intelligence sector tackled the problems in detail some years ago in an effort to learn from data and extract information. Unfortunately results have not come up to expectations.

Today there are good prospects that neuronal networks will provide a method of extracting relevant information from vast masses of data.

Models

Modelling information is the next step in the chain. Large quantities of data can be reduced by using statistical methods. This is the way turnover and sales statistics used to be worked out. Today, however, information gained from the statistical models can be transferred to simulation models, thus enabling the decision makers to develop a far deeper insight into business and the surrounding world.

In addition to trend analyses taking into account seasonal characteristics, information of this kind is used for planning and decision-making in the production sector. In the retail sector aids such as price simulators and promotion models are used to project decisions. These means are often more accurate and give rise to better profit margins, as those responsible in each case do not have to resort to relying on their own gut feelings.

Decision systems

The aim of every link in the information value chain is to increase the value of the data. In the final analysis, information and data are only of any value if they improve decision making or, more generally, increase the real net output of the company.

Information Content

Within the value chain the data is enriched with value at every level. This view is process-orientated and may serve as a model for almost all the activities within a company. However, this approach does not do full justice to the information work. Whereas in a production operation the raw materials are procured as input and the product, made to market requirements, is supplied as output, the procedure is not so simple when it comes to information processing.

Steel sheets used in car bodywork are very different from the mould in which they are manufactured. Information, as we know, does not know the difference between the original and a copy.

Major inefficiency in information work is rooted in the habit, when dealing with information, of applying the behavioural patterns which characterise the physical world. Awareness of the major differences could actually lead to a better appreciation of our real world as well as to greater skill with information.

Within the context of information and information technology it is no longer sufficient to make the investment and then continue to use this new medium in the traditional way. Many PC users even today are still printing all the information from a computer out and filing the paper copy away separately, even though the information is available on the hard disk as well as on a separate back-up copy. People are reluctant to give up their old habits. A somewhat different way of looking at information emerges when the semantic aspect of information is considered.

The content of the information is what is ultimately decisive, and not so much the form, the medium, on which information is available or the amount of information. Contents may vary widely. One example:

1. Three.
2. Three half pumped up balls.
3. The juggler's three half pumped up balls.
4. Three of the juggler's half pumped up balls fall.
5. Three of the juggler's half pumped up balls will fall if he does not hold them immediately.

1 to 5 are, from the point of view of content, levels of understanding which are increasing in terms of quality. In terms of the technology of present-day company information systems, the levels in examples 1 to 3 are relatively simple to illustrate. It is very time-consuming and expensive to make a data-based representation of the progression of the balls as they are thrown. To illustrate the pragmatic aspect in information systems is a major challenge.

Levels of understanding

In any discussion about the role and power of information, it is important to examine what kind of information it is that we are dealing with. Information with relevance for companies can actually be split up into five categories. The categories, which are clearly distinguishable, are information relating to content, form, conduct, relationships and action. Up to now the category relating to content has been used in commerce in a systematic and simple way. Generating or maintaining the others is something which has only become possible at all in the last few years. Working with them is one of the keys to the future.

Object information

Information regarding the composition of an object is already providing a basis for the modern company. This information gives details of quantities, times, places, number and other quantitative magnitudes. A library management programme, for example, permits an overview of the stock of books, location and entries giving information on the content of the works. Personal files also provide an example. The data contains, in addition to addresses, insurance information, salary history and further personal details relating to the employee. Companies maintain detailed ordering records plus details of credit-worthiness and information on their contacts.

In its very nature, contents information is mostly historical; it gives details of when an individual was born, when and where an item was put away in the stores or when a customer placed orders. Typically, such information is to be found in the records, registers and filing cabinets of companies and official organisations. In the spring of the information era, this information was processed electronically by way of data on perforated cards.

Until the 1980s, the scene was dominated by the up and coming computer industry, which processed this information in enormous quantities. This was the great period of the commercial IBM computers.

Typical object information in marketing may include the price, dimension or weight of a product. This means that object information, in this sense, alone does not provide any information on the value of a product. In order to enable the purchaser to identify the value of a product, further types of information are used in marketing communication.

Object information must always be included in offers. It should provide a means of defining the position of a product as far as prospective buyers are concerned.

Attribute information

Attribute information describes the form and composition of an object. In contrast to object information, this category may encompass a wide range of data. An object is specified by means of attribute information and, through it, may even become identifiable as a single object in terms of individuality.

This may happen, for example, in a PC system through the indication of clock frequency, hard disk size, screen size and type as well as printer details. But even with this attribute information, it is not yet clear whether the system is an IBM-compatible DOS Windows system or a Macintosh Apple system. This point will only be clarified when details of the drive system are to hand. Attribute information is extremely important in the progression from general statements to specific information. At the same time it is very important to know how and what individual data, in the right compilation, will provide a specific item of information. This data was stored for a very long time in character form but, with the introduction of picture, sound and film processing, the attribute information will be increasingly available in multimedia form also.

These techniques became possible because data carriers were discovered which were capable of storing millions of bytes and processors are available today which are capable of processing these quantities of data within an acceptable period of time. The time needed to double storage capacity, with no change in the cost of storage chips and storage media, has, during the short life of information technology, averaged around 9 months.

Strictly speaking, construction plans, development and production documents are all attributes information. Just like computers, refrigerators and cars, mankind also has this attributes information. In contrast to industrial objects, attributes information is, in nature, held decentrally in all parts of living beings and plants within their DNA structure.

The object information describes the past and the attributes information best describes the present, which means that the problem of compiling information on the future is still with us. The information value chain is a model which sustains major growth in terms of value by enabling information about the future to be compiled.

Relationships information

Information on the relationship between objects is essential in order to be able to portray the network in relation to dependence and influences. Statements on the future can also be made together with the information outlined above and the following type of information.

Information on behaviour

Behavioural information is based on object information and calls for major resources in terms of computer capacity. Simulation of the behaviour of physical objects calls for them to be portrayed three-dimensionally and also for portrayal of the time axis.

Simulations of molecular processes or population growth are examples of such information. They are essentially rules which determine what has to take place and under what conditions. Systems which forecast the weather are built up in this way; these require enormous computer power and storage capacities.

Using reliable simulations it is often possible to build a fault-free and generally dependable device straight off. The prototype is no longer available actually but only virtually. All simulations are carried out on this virtual object.

Based on this idea, Boeing is building its largest commercial aeroplane, the Boeing 777, initially just on the computer. It is the largest project of this kind that has ever been commenced and has cost almost US$5 billion. Using more than half a dozen mainframe computers, thousands of specialists and hundreds of development teams are linked together by means of workstations. The aircraft is being developed, tested and put together in this virtual world, long before any item of material is touched in conjunction with its realisation. Behavioural information will make statements possible in the future. Behavioural information is used to characterise the benefits of market performance for customers.

Action-triggering information

The information revolution is not only aimed at building up the virtual world, but likewise the interaction of the scientific world with the real world. Once decisions have been made, conversion to reality can take place. Information about converting to highly specific actions is therefore necessary. As computer systems become steadily cheaper, it will be possible not only to extract information from data but also, by means of information, to bring about actions triggered by information.

Simple machines of this kind have been in use for years, whether they are dishwashing machines or very complicated control systems for power stations or for industrial robots. Although these systems have been used in what have, up to now, been relatively primitive conditions, very many more of them will be used in the future. Information processing has been an extremely laborious procedure hitherto. For instance, where robot technology has been used it has been necessary to programme every movement minutely. These movements will be copied by the new techniques of virtual processing. A person's movements will be directly captured using sensor techniques and it will subsequently be possible for them to be called up again and adjusted appropriately.

Communication

Communication is a concept with several levels of understanding. Communication in the technical sense means the transfer of data from one party to another and, in a broader sense, the exchange of information. The quality of understanding of communication is to a major extent, although not exclusively, characterised by the grade of the levels of understanding regarding the content. In addition to the content, the context of communication plays just as important a part. The situation in which communication takes place is very often the prerequisite for the correct evaluation of this communication. Content can be ambiguous or vague. Take the words: 'Put away?' These words take on a completely different meaning depending on whether you are in the police station or on the golf course.

In advertising, ambiguities are assuming an increasing role as, by using a clever combination of content and context, it is possible to achieve a new breakthrough and hence capture a higher level of attention.

Information technology today only conveys the contents of information. The context as far as the user is concerned is formed by his own imagination or individual reality. Communication in marketing by means of on-line technology is therefore based on content. The context plays a subordinate role in the sense that certain tacit pre-conditions are assumed.

Communication in cyber marketing goes one important step further. In the cyber world, it is not only that content is conveyed, but context is also created. The user is no longer standing outside in his own context but plunges into the system and thus into an artificially created environment which, as context, helps to shape communication.

The possibility of creating such a cyber world so realistically that it is interchangeable with reality, or can no longer be distinguished from it, is already to hand and is being used primarily in the entertainment industry. The film *Jurassic Park* is a very good example of this. The rapid development and increased functionality of software to generate cyber worlds that are true to reality is enough to take your breath away.

The availability of software to create cyber worlds quickly and true to reality will come about sooner than companies are ready and have the infrastructure available to make full use of the new possibilities offered by cyber marketing.

Virtual Reality Information Systems

The processing of data and information content is carried out using electronic systems, or computers, which then store the information and are used for its onward transmission. The development of information technology is not predictable and progress to date has been on a perfectly smooth evolutionary basis. For this reason, in very many companies these days, there are technologies at various stages of development. Migration to current technology, which would allow more efficient handling of data and information, cannot be achieved without upheaval. In almost all cases a new beginning is called for. In addition to this, there is the fact that market leaders within the IT sector have implemented a product and marketing strategy which has actually chained customers to the relevant products.

Above and beyond all the technological leaps made by commercialised systems, one aspect had remained constant until two years ago: the systems were used to reproduce existing reality as a model. Up to then reality had been portrayed in its different aspects. One example is computer integrated manufacturing (CIM). This envisages integration of the planning and control data generated in the office into business management functions, technical production and distribution. In order to master the various operational functions, a data processing system was implemented with a common database. Although CIM was very extensively propagated by manufacturers and specialists, it had only limited success. The reasons for this are four fold.

Firstly, different operational functions, such as the operation of numerically controlled machines, stations for budgeting and pricing individual parts or for communication by means of electronic mail, are best served by different system architectures. The incompatibility which this presupposes is not easy to overcome.

Secondly, an area of tension exists between already existing ideas about processes and information requirements and those which are introduced within a standard software context. However, every organisation has its own rules and specific requirements which can be attributed to the relevant activity, the products and the people involved in it. The area of tension between existing organisation and the model portrayed in the software can be defused by outgrowth, i.e. bringing reality closer to the system and by means of individual extensions and adaptations.

Thirdly, the information system is mostly static in relation to the development of the real environment. If operational reality is characterised by marked changes, then its portrayal in the information system cannot be adapted quickly enough.

Finally, the development of information and communication technology is so rapid that existing generations of products for the functions to be performed are regularly being replaced by others, giving more output and functions at less cost.

The following rules may therefore be drawn up for the implementation and use of telematics:

1. The company needs to be familiar with the perspectives which apply to the use of telematic systems and formulate and implement a valid policy based on them.
2. Insist on the openness of the systems used. Systems should be capable of being linked to one another by means of communication. Tasks should be capable of being distributed on the system platforms: certain system components, such as operating systems or databases, must be compatible between the different platforms.
3. The portrayal of the functions in the software should be neutral in terms of operation. One example of software which is to a major extent neutral in terms of its operation is word processing.
4. Any universal introduction of information systems should be divided up into separate technology modules which are nevertheless capable of communication. This will permit the overall system to be renewed in blocks.

The common basis is database marketing. Marketing databases can be built up in companies using existing data. The basis for this is provided by the principles of data warehousing. CD-ROM, fax, videotext and the Internet will connect to database marketing. A further base technology for shaping content is multimedia.

For the past two years a second possibility for using information systems has been available. Whereas systems had hitherto been image-related, the possibility was now emerging of giving them some kind of form. No longer is it solely a matter of reproducing the model of external actuality, but a new virtual reality is being fashioned and communicated. At the same time, virtual reality may be similar to physical actuality to the extent that we may confuse the two, or the world of our thoughts may be confronted with a completely new notion, that of cyber reality. This fact and the opportunity of communicating, distributing and participating in the cyber world globally constitutes the enormous revolution which will not only change marketing but also the whole of the commercial world as well as society in the years to come.

The Productivity Paradox

Successful business activity pre-supposes knowing how to make the best use of information. A great deal of information is packed away in computer files and databases as well as in employees' heads. People are not only storers of information, we also generate information. As managers, we use information to organise and control the actions of others. All human economic activity is based on the generation of information. Take an average working day in a medium-sized town. An engineer produces drawings based on calculations which contain coded information on which part is to be produced. Production specialists draw up information defining the manner of the manufacturing process. An architect creates, with the outline of a building, only the information needed to realise it. An investment consultant provides his clients with analyses relating to the behaviour of and possible trends in the market. On these will be based the decisions relating to the purchase and sale of individual securities and currencies. People in far-flung parts of the service sectors are trafficking in, manipulating and generating information.

When we look at the work done by lawyers, accountants, advertisers, bank managers, newspaper reporters and thousands of other people employed in the service sector, what strikes us is the extent to which the activity is information-related. Towards the end of the twentieth century and in only four decades of the computer era, the core of commercial business is becoming increasingly transparent. Many employees in many a company are engaged in collecting information, generating or modifying it. In a typical company of today with an automised industrial operation, fewer than 5% of the workers are engaged in physical work in the actual sense of the word. And, even within this small percentage, information has completely revised the content of the work.

In banks and insurance companies, information, as far as practically all the employees are concerned, means work content. The understanding of work has changed completely over the past 50 years. Even as far as airlines are concerned, the greater part of the employees are engaged in planning, checking, reserving, informing and other activities. The work content of these people consists to a major extent in dealing with information systems. They work with database applications, programmes, computers, terminals, printers and other system components.

An American study of the 100 fastest growing companies showed that the greater part of the employees are engaged in converting data into information. Marketing is the dominant activity and management the dominating function.

Obviously the ability to process information and to draw benefit from it is an important, even if it is not simultaneously the sole pre-requisite for company success. Despite this fact, there is a powerful discussion going on about the proportion to which the use of information systems increases productivity. The American economy invested US$750 billion in information technology (IT) structures during the 1980s and almost as many billions in software and services before it was even possible to operate the equipment at all. The use of information technology per employee has almost doubled since 1980. 85% of IT investments was in the service sector. Despite this, this sector never achieved more than an average growth in productivity of 0.7% in the same period.[34]

The critics of information systems latch on to these facts as a basis for their arguments. They comment very cynically that the population of computers has increased massively, but productivity has not gone up. The other side in this debate counters this with: 'It is not enough to pump technology into a company and then to try to deal with the work in the same way as it has been done for years'. This argument seems to be right. The massive interest and the numerous projects of business re-engineering are sufficient proof of this. Hence, and for one further reason, the productivity paradox should resolve itself in the future and disappear as a subject for discussion.

Costs represent one viewpoint and information as value is the other way of looking at things. The productivity paradox clearly originates with those who like to nit-pick and separate out costs. Where this mental attitude prevails there will never be a pay-out from investing in information systems; costs in respect of the infrastructure to promote more efficient information handling cannot be justified economically. In order to be able to survive in the future knowledge-orientated society, companies and their managements need to complete the change from the nit-picking mentality to awareness of the bit.

Conclusion: Cyber Communication as a Means of Communicating Content and Context

Modern-day information technology offers scant opportunities when it comes to handling data. Many company systems are restricted to the level of object and attributes data. The possibilities of easily portraying further levels of understanding with regard to relationships, behaviour and actions are relatively limited. For this reason electronic communication is restricted to content.

Cyber space is a wholly artificially structured reality. It is capable of reproducing physical actuality in a way that is very true to reality or it offers the possibility of creating new realities. Communication and dialogue in this virtual reality are therefore not determined solely by the content but also by the context in which the person addressed is no longer standing outside but is an incorporated participant. This factor, after letterpress printing, the telephone, the television and the Internet, represents the greatest change that has taken place with regard to human communication.

In the industrial era, information content was beamed out to the addressees via the mass media; the information era, with its digital networks, creates the pre-conditions for direct contact dialogue; this dialogue is reinforced in cyber space by the artificially created context of the virtual world. The ability to convey content as well as context by means of cyber communication is a revolutionary first.

The information value chain with its component links – data recording, data management, interpretation of data to provide information – creates the necessary pre-conditions for communication. Through cyber marketing, database technology incorporates the most significant implementation of activities in the information value chain.

II – Perspectives, the What

4 DATABASE MARKETING

Databases today already offer a basis for marketing activity to a certain extent and will in the future offer a complete basis for such activity. Whether working with databases in the marketing department and approaching the customer by means of databases is one day termed database-marketing, database-based marketing or information-based marketing, has no effect on this development. However, marketing does not only need a database with customer details. Marketing as an activity calls for an abundance of further information presented in such a way that it is clear and easily accessible. The three main sectors are customers, market performance and competitors. These need to be split into further categories. The customer sector will embrace prospective buyers, customers and 'entitlement' groups. The entitlement group can be sub-divided into press, shareholders, financial analysts, consumer organisations, branch associations, official organisations, consultants, free agents, suppliers and employees. The competitors' sector may comprise customers, market performance and organisation with details relating to personnel, representatives and branch offices. The market performance sector can be subdivided into all the relevant areas of information which are important for the particular user both externally, internally and as far as customers are concerned.

In the following we shall be concentrating on the aspects of those databases and information carriers in marketing which strive to achieve increased customer bonding.

Databases: the Basics

To present market performance to the customer by using telematics, to sell and thereby to strengthen one's position towards one's competitors in relation to a particular customer, is the aim of the concepts described in this book. Only the constant achievement of market performance will maintain the level of customer bonding. This is the basis for tightening the bonds that bind the customer. This realisation is not new. What is new is the enormous costs that accrue every time this fact is carelessly ignored. Depending on the branch, the costs involved in winning business with a new customer are higher by a factor of 3 to 15 than the costs involved in servicing an existing customer relationship and, because of this factor, of performing the same transaction. The direct consequence of this state of affairs is that any increase in customer satisfaction feeds through directly and disproportionately into profit.

The correct use of information technology in on-line marketing increases marketing effectivity. This is conditional upon actual customer understanding and the use of the medium within the context of serving the customer. Results will show themselves in terms of improved accounting results when the new thought patterns go hand in hand with the use of on-line marketing and these are geared to the paradigms of cyber marketing. This is a completely direct approach to database marketing. Database marketing aimed at gaining market share means, furthermore, going with the flow in mass marketing and recording increasingly negative results. Using new technologies with an out-dated marketing mentality will never satisfy the future market conditions of the information era. The use of technology under the premisses of cyber marketing cannot endeavour to make any improvements as far as yesterday is concerned, for cyber marketing is a new dimension and it is on-line marketing that enables access to it.

How must today's direct marketing change? The first stage is database marketing. To be successful – to really grow in the current decade – does not mean using database media alone, but individualising marketing at the highest level with a very large number of customers. Database marketing is the instrument which is used to identify customers precisely and to address them in a highly individual manner. With the help of the database, market performance needs to be efficiently implemented. Real on-line marketing initially offers customers a dialogue and then market performance. Cyber marketing deepens the dialogue into an individual relationship. The dialogue has loyalty and faithfulness as its aims. These are not clichés or lip service such as were formerly a feature of mass marketing. Faithfulness and loyalty are values which should be consciously aspired to in all aspects of on-line marketing.

Four steps – identify, address, perform the service, maintain the relationship – are not only or initially targeted at gaining market share, but at increasing share of customershare of customer. Even frequent studies of the long lists of commercial customers will be misleading if only the name of the company is recorded. Companies belonging to the 1000 largest in the world, of a particular continent or country, such as Nestlé, ABB, Citibank, Sony or Daimler-Benz, may mean either a tiny or an enormous amount of share of customershare of customer. It is not only the number of companies which is significant but rather the number of contacts and business transactions with individuals within the organisation, i.e. share of customer or links with a large corporate client.

Firstly, through good database marketing, more should be sold to the existing customer. And, secondly, database marketing today in mature markets is directed at increasing share of customer rather than market share. The increased profitability of this approach can be illustrated by means of the Lorenz curve. A company will achieve 90% of its sales with approximately 10% of its customers. What can be more natural than to develop a more intensive concern for these 10% of customers and, at the same time, to pursue the growth of the absolute figure with these 10% of customers in terms of sales and profits?

Certainly some companies record losses with their strongest customers – time for a fundamental change in business practices. Customer orientation should not be the best kept secret in the marketing department but should rather be cultivated throughout the entire company. An absolute necessity in this culture is an accounting system which will supply the company management with figures regarding the contribution made by the individual customer to profit. A transparency in terms of costs which will permit the individual customer to be observed.

Database marketing is not only an on-line marketing method for giant companies. No, a tobacconist's shop with a superior range of tobacco goods for pipe smokers and cigarette smokers can operate database marketing just as well as large mail order companies or airlines. The effect on sales figures will be highly stimulating if every customer regularly receives a birthday card from his tobacconist and service in the shop is very personal. Is the customer of this small outlet any the less pleased than he would be to receive a card from a multi-national concern? Often the person addressed does not know who in the giant concern he really has to thank for the greeting. The signature is printed, he does not recognise the name of the person sending the greetings and, when he tries to proffer his thanks, a typist answers his call who has never even heard his name before. Without going into this further, the effect of such incidents is well known. Who is more genuine? Who is more honest? With which of them will the customer feel like a human being? In which situation will they be sure to come back and buy again?

The example shows that opportunities today with a properly used PC are absolutely comparable to those offered by a large system. A significant change in the paradigm of size is being brought about by the information revolution. Larger no longer automatically means really stronger and better. In the industrial era, the size of a company was a significant factor in terms of dominating market share and being able to raise financial investments so as to maintain this in the long term. Today this is no longer the case. Genuineness and astuteness are toppling size.

Every customer represents a niche in the market

The notion of database marketing is as old as EDP. Databases have been in use for some time. What company does not have a customer database with addresses for sending out customer information such as mailings, catalogues, information brochures and invitations to events? So is everything the same as it ever was? No – in the meantime the playing field has been completely transformed. Whereas it was formerly still a matter of standard products because, in the boom years, it was hardly possible to keep up with demand, the situation has changed considerably over the past ten years.

The 1980s saw a massive break-through in the demand for standard products. Customers had become used to being able to choose from a broad range of goods and so to wallow in a feeling of individuality. The number of new products began to grow a tremendous amount faster than the number of new purchasers. Today a supermarket carries a range of something like 20,000 products, at least ten times more than the corner shops of yesteryear. The number of drinks offered in a shop alone has multiplied. The same applies to other sectors too: in the music shop the number of available titles has grown and the good old gramophone record has given way to the cassette tape, the CD and the laser disc. Although the number of new media on offer is exploding, the number of new books is still increasing every year.

At the Frankfurt Book Fair, the electronic media had increased by 80% in 1995 by comparison to the previous year, the purely electronic book products by 180% even, nevertheless 93,000 new book titles were presented. The number of suppliers and markets for the product 'jeans' is practically infinite. Jeans are an example of a further trend. Products have not only become more diverse but have been extended to cover classes with different purchasing power. Whereas jeans used to be the characteristic garb of the working classes, suppliers of brand names are now offering trousers with a designer label at a price for which one could very easily buy a smart suit.

In addition to the growing number of products there is a further important development which is still active today. The erstwhile media are becoming fragmented. This can be seen very clearly in the print media sector (newspapers, gazettes and journals) although regional daily papers are disappearing. But, in their place, we now have printed products for special interest groups, such as model railways, wind surfing, fencing, dog breeding and much more. Instead of the regionally-orientated media, particular specialisations have become established. This trend will become even more accentuated in the information era. People will increasingly become world citizens with distinct and individual tendencies. Consumer goods marketing is defining new lifestyle profiles. Whereas this kind of segmentation is still visible externally when it comes to the youngsters, the kids, clear allocation is much more difficult when it comes to the higher age categories. In the information era, the markets will be segmented in accordance with information practice. This is already happening today through special television channels such as MTV and CNN. Whereas marketing strategists in the 1970s were able to benefit from an enormous range of operation on three television channels, it is difficult today to reach an assured number of interested people on one specialist channel.

The demise of the broadly orientated mass media does, however, also have its advantages: by using intelligence it is possible to reach practically all the special segments. Why waste time and money trying to reach those who are, in the final analysis, not interested or interesting?

Practically every item of market performance, regardless of its enormous popularity, will ultimately find itself with niches of customers who find the product or service irresistable. How many customers are there in a niche? The response to this question is not orientated exclusively towards market realities but towards the earnings potential of a given niche in the market. Marketing expenditure incurred in realising the potential of a market niche formerly exercised an overwhelming influence on earnings potential. This meant a definite minimum number of customers. Lower communications costs and attention focused on share of customer today define a single customer as a niche. The database is the one possibility of keeping control over the various individual customers. Maintaining contact with the different customers in the right context in each case can only be done by a database. It is only this that reliably charts the history of contact and dialogue with the customer.

How much does it cost to make contact?

An analogy may be drawn between mass marketing and taking a net to catch a goldfish, instead of being intelligent and using a hook. Nevertheless, if only the one fish that needs to be caught is there in the water, then it will pay to use the net. But this is not the case in the sea – that is, in the actual market. Computations show that, last year, the average consumer was bombarded with more than 5000 advertising messages. Obviously he will ignore and forget the majority of them. Immunity to mass advertising has grown in harmony with the avalanche of mass advertising. Think back to the last television advertisement you personally saw. What was being advertised? If you are like the majority of viewers, you will not remember and will state in a totally noncommittal way: washing powder and shampoo. But which brands? There is bound to be one or other advertising spot which you still remember because of its originality. But did you buy the product? – probably not. For, if an advertising spot is truly *perceived*, something interesting happens: the spot takes on a life of its own. It exists within the conscious mind of the consumer, not so much the product but the advertising slogan or a defined sequence of scenes. He remembers it. If the product name or the company name is not in the slogan – then it's hard luck on the advertising strategist. Moreover, the efficacy of advertising depends solely on how the advertisement is presented and not on the market performance which is to be sold.

More than ever it makes sense for companies to cement existing customer relationships than to waste time and money on acquiring new customers. Granted, consumer articles in daily use are subject to the rules as regards levels of familiarity. But this marketing rule no longer applies exclusively to motor cars, PCs and other major budget items. All products, all services which not only trigger a purchase but also a period of use with guarantee commitments and service possibilities are, ultimately, chances to mould long-term customer relationships.

The strategy of customer bonding is anathema as far as old school style marketing is concerned. The costs of customer bonding and customer acquisition are in a ratio of 1:5 or, for the cost of gaining one new customer, five existing customers could be serviced.[35] At senior management level in many companies, it is only the market share figures that are discussed. Those responsible for marketing present the percentages in terms of changes to market share, market growth, range fluctuations and much more in the quarterly inquisitions held by their regional managers. The presentation is always along the same lines: market share, media presence, scale of economies, costs, return – with everything standardised in terms of percentage figures.

Without having recourse to the mass media for sales orientation purposes, many of these economies of scale are no longer so important. Products in small batches, which can be fully absorbed by target customers, are more profitable than large quantities for a disinterested mass market.

In addition, marketing professionals see themselves confronted by a new and rapidly spreading scepticism. Long years of overkill in terms of advertising, poor service and seedy product quality, compared with awakened expectations, have made consumers distrustful of new products. Customers search and make very precise selections before they make their choice. They prefer to rely on people and companies whom they trust to find the products that they require.

Share of customer is therefore becoming more and more crucial and, in relation to market share, has assumed a poll position. How much turnover is it possible to generate from a dearly won customer? This is the controlling question if, for instance, a small kiosk by the petrol pump can sell drinks, snacks, newspapers and magazines, car accessories and other goods, and all with practically no advertising costs.

If the customer relationship achieved by means of so much input is extended into a relationship of trust, this will be very profitable. However, the rules in this intimate customer relationship are quite different to what they were in the marketing mentality of the mass era. The customer is no longer a statistical, sales-generating entity in a media campaign.

Reaching the individual

Database marketing extends, differentiates and specifies market segmentation and the marketing mix which is geared to it. The four classic Ps in the marketing mix, namely Price, Place, Promotion and Product, are in good company with the four Ts:

- TARGETING.
- TAILORING.
- TYING.
- TAPPING.

Targeting

Targeting is well illustrated by the term micromarketing. It is not a matter of crude market segementing but of fine tuning and aligning one's sights on the target public. This is not achieved using the wide angle lens of an artilleryman but by means of the sharply selective eye looking through a telescopic sight. Targeting frequently does not suceed at the first attempt but is a process which eventually evens itself out.

Tailoring

Tailoring is the adaptation of the offer to suit the purchaser. However, before the offer can be drawn up there has to be communication. Communication is successful when the exchange of information takes place in a situation where the supplier has good knowledge of his customer. The database creates the basis for this. Database marketing is the art of knowing the individual customer better than he knows himself. This means collecting and evaluating information which will promote the business and, primarily, customer bonding.

Tying

Tying means 'linking up with' the customer. We very often hear talk of 'customer control'. This expression is rooted in a mentality which, in the new era, gives no further hope of any permanent customer relationships. Exercising control is a matter of a position of power. This used to be taken for granted in some supplier markets. It was so, for instance, during the 1980s in the computer sector. However, this situation has undergone a tremendous change. Within this branch there are currently very few monopolies that exercise real control, as for instance Microsoft. As in the case of IBM, this dominance may become an organisation's undoing. As soon as an alternative presents itself to the customer, he will unload his frustration in a change of supplier. Customers cannot be controlled. But a relationship of trust can be maintained with the customer. This relationship essentially consists of trust and satisfaction. Winning trust is a critical point in database marketing in general. In the majority of countries there is data protection legislation in force. There is a high level of both public and individual criticism as regards the possible misuse of the data. We shall be dealing with this aspect in more detail in due course. It would then seem to be clear that database marketing is less of a technical problem than one of trustworthiness. Good products are offered by many companies, but the companies who do the best business are those who foster good relationships of trust with their individual customers.

Tapping

Tapping, the fourth point, expresses the fact that sales and thus at the same time profits, if the supplier has made the right calculations, will flow from a good relationship. At the same time, a source can be tapped to give further profits by using the customers as references for prospective buyers. The best advertisement for anything is a satisfied customer. Reference-based acquisition is therefore mostly successful because the customer is typically bound into a social network which is, in terms of requirement, to a major extent homogeneous. This also applies in the case of business customers.

The subtle use of database marketing is highly effective and the following is a relatively graphic example. The Hotel La Trémoille in Paris has for a number of years maintained a customer card index and today has a database which gives information about the requirements and preferences of its guests. Hence, on making his reservation, the guest receives the very room that he normally occupies if this is even remotely possible. Naturally, all the extras are also covered, such as preferences as regards newspapers, breakfast or details of possible diets. The guests are very faithful to the Trémoille. A business friend of mine said: 'I do a lot of travelling. Everywhere customs are different. But what I have become accustomed to and really like I hardly ever get or have to expressly order it every time – and that's tiring. At the Trémoille I feel as though I'm at home. There they know what I need'. Other top hotels also operate databases of this kind. If a regular visitor orders his nightcap he gets his Ovaltine served at the correct temperature and an apricot yogurt without having to ask for it. His allergies to particular flowers are as well known to the hotel management as the instructions for dry-cleaning his clothes.

Hospitality has a great deal to do with people knowing the individual guest. This is something which is held in high esteem primarily by people who, due to their trade or profession, spend more nights in strange beds than they do at home. This kind of hospitality used often, in the old days, to be found in very small hotels which were operated as family businesses. But these operations, the prototypes of 1:1 marketing, have now disappeared to a major extent. The information which used to be in the heads of the *'patrons'* is today supplied by the database. How to use this information in dealings with the customer is a question of training and the business climate. Unlike the days of the family operations this information is, however, not locally but globally accessible. The use of database marketing in a hotel chain is very efficient. For, in contrast to currency from country to country, the habits of travellers hardly practically change. 'Tapping' at the level of this marketing concept means finding out at the same time what other destinations are more often frequented by customers. Activities can then be extended taking into account these standpoints. The example of La Trémoille may become a yardstick when it comes to competition in future. Hotels are in a position to influence the way rooms are fitted out, the rooms themselves, the room service, the friendliness of the staff. Nevertheless, an intimate relationship with a customer is only established when a host has due regard for his guest's minor idiosyncrasies, which each of us has, and makes it possible for us to give full expression to these – it is on this that the strongest kind of customer bonding is based.

Car hire companies also discovered the advantages of more intimate customer relations some time ago. Companies such as Hertz and AVIS offer special customer deals for their best customers. Their preferences as regards the type of car are held, for each category, along with all other data on a globally available database so as to ensure that collection of the vehicle, for example, at an airport, takes place very soon after arrival and without too much paperwork. The personal customer card is the crucial item.

Customer programmes and good customer relations also serve the companies in that they enable them to extend their range and adapt to requirements. Customers represent the best sources for innovation. For who is in a position to give better information on market performance and further requirements than those customers who frequently and regularly order market performance items?

Database Marketing on the Advance

The following law applies in every sphere of commercial activity: it is a relatively small percentage of customers who generate the major part of a company's turnover. This is certainly true of a medium sized retailer in Milwaukee. Ed Caroll, Vicepresident – Sales, Promotion and Marketing, at Carson Pririe Scott, states: 'We have found that 50% of credit card business makes up 90% of card volume. Some customers are clearly much more equal than others. We reckon that, over the next five years, the 70% promotional expenditure will be reduced to 55% and loyalty will increase from 15% to 55%'.

A study carried out in 1995 by Deloitte & Touch in the USA for the American DMA (Direct Marketing Association), shows that two-thirds of the largest retailers are already making use of database marketing and 40% of the remaining third are planning a programme and intending to set up a customer database in an initial step towards this. The reasons put forward by those companies which are not yet using database marketing are diverse. In the case of 26% of a total number of 81 companies it was suggested that this was due to the necessary expertise not yet being available for developing and implementing a marketing instrument of this kind. 17% indicated that the costs involved were not justified. 11% felt that they had enough data material in their possession to cover marketing requirements. 10% were not convinced that a programme of this kind would increase marketing performance. 5% gave lack of support from top management, whilst 7% said that they had too little knowledge (hardware and software) to be able to make a decision in favour of such activities. Finally, 6% were unable to calculate the return on investment. Various other reasons accounted for 4% of the 249 companies asked.

Mallory Weil, a specialist in direct marketing, commenting on this scepticism, said: 'Since the birth of my child I have received mountains of post from direct marketing companies who are active within the baby and child sector. But I have, to date, had absolutely nothing from the shops in which I made my purchases for my son'.

Interesting conclusions can be drawn from this. Some companies are lacking in a full appreciation of the basic concepts of database marketing; they are, therefore, uncertain about its advantages. Some companies are experimenting with database marketing in small-scale tests but without having previously formulated a marketing strategy or success factors. However, those firms who are using database marketing are finding that customer loyalty is increasing, marketing efficiency is increased, costs are reduced and profit margins become wider. The stumbling blocks as far as the use of database marketing is concerned lie in technical affairs, the development of long-term expectations in terms of the outcome of finding an internal champion who will push activities further and guarantee the synergies between different distribution channels. Interestingly, only 4% of the companies cited reservations on the part of their customers in respect of data protection considerations as a hindrance to a database marketing programme. In many companies, the change of paradigms had already been carried out. Instead of 'We produce it – you consume it' in mass marketing the motto is now: 'We serve you in the way you want to be served.'

However, the implementation of a database marketing programme is no simple matter and it cannot always be mastered quickly. The example of the warehousing giant Sears Roebuck demonstrates this. In 1989, Sears had a huge number of different databases. 'They were neither integrable nor were they really usable' said the Director responsible for customer analyses. 'The chain even had trouble with the old mass marketing mentality. There were many who opposed the use of the databases because their range was too limited, too much work was involved in looking after them and their use was shrouded in mystery. Arguments about technical complexity were brought in. Then a fundamental change in opinion was announced. Sears was uniquely positioned to make use of database marketing. Out of the approximately 91 million households in the USA, around 71 million had an existing relationship with Sears, either through the shops, mail order or through other activities on the part of Sears subsidiaries'. Sears standardised the databases and today is able to reach customers directly and in a personalised manner. This made communication relevant to business. Loyal customers are pinpointed and, for management, measurable targets can be established. Thus, for instance, in 1993, database marketing was used in a test aimed at increasing sales of appliances. Customers who had purchased tools in the past received a thank you letter together with a comprehensive catalogue of the tools and a coupon offer. On average these mailings achieved an almost 30% sales increase in the test departments. A further programme was concentrated on top flight customers with the aim of increasing bonding; this resulted in more frequent and, on average, higher levels of purchase. They were rewarded with special discounts and early notification of clearance sales.

The number of companies in a survey of 148 conducted in the USA who are already making use of database marketing is encouraging.[36]

These figures show one thing very clearly: database marketing is red-hot, not only because of improved yields achieved through profit-generating customer relations, but also thanks to the efficient canvassing of new clients and valuable information on purchasing trends in terms of both products and services.

Perceived growth due to database marketing in the past twelve months:

Considerable increase	41%
Slight increase	40%
No change	17%
Slight decline	0%
Massive decline	1%

Growth expectations over the coming 12 months:

Massive increase	59%
Slight increase	34%
No increase	7%
Slight decrease	0%
Massive decrease	0%

Advantages of Marketing Databases

Not all companies draw the same benefits from database marketing. There is evidence of such benefit where one or more of the following conditions exists:

- Narrow, precisely defined market niches.
- Competition-intensive markets, for example, due to their being mature or recessive.
- Diverse distribution channels.
- Local purchasing habits and changes are significant in terms of logistics and production.
- One-off purchasers are to be reactivated.
- Actual acquisition costs are increasing.
- The profitability of each individual customer should be known.

It can be clearly seen from the examples already put forward that the database is not, in itself, a solution, but a tool. The database is a collection of data relating to customers, prospective buyers and possible purchasers. The database contains individual data elements which together can be condensed into meaningful information. The data elements come from different sources, both internal and external; they are easy to manipulate and sort. Access must be simple and meaningful.

Key information on customers

Data content should be capable of supplying key information on affinity, frequency, 'recency', amounts expended and share of customer. This information serves to record the customer's purchasing patterns.

Affinity

Affinity describes habitual behaviour, i.e. product and service consumption to date – within the framework of a customer's particular personal preferences – which represents an indicator as far as future requirements are concerned. In banking, customers with high levels of savings are not a good target group for credit business. Companies with a large number of company cars to insure are, however, potentially good customers for other vehicle leasing deals.

Frequency

Frequency expresses the following fact: the more business is carried out with a business customer or a private consumer, the higher the probability is of increasing that business in the future. What is more important, increased frequency reduces the costs of doing business. Airline companies, car hire companies and telephone companies have developed easy to use frequency programmes to bond customers to themselves.

The inclination to buy

The inclination to buy is linked to the length of time for which an activity has been taking place and differs depending on market performance. This factor is called 'recency'. If a customer asks at the beginning of the year for summer holiday brochures and rings up again in the spring to check up on prices, then, with every month that goes by without further interaction, it becomes less likely that he will in fact make a booking. A corporate customer who had been regularly sending in orders for office materials to his suppliers every six weeks but who has now failed to order for 10 weeks, may be lost as a customer. This probability increases with every week that passes without an order.

In cyber marketing, the difference between frequency and 'recency' is very important. Knowing the communication frequency in an individual customer relationship is of subordinate importance. The time which has elapsed since an incident such as initial enquiry or call for a quotation is the yardstick for the quality of the customer relationship and the inclination to purchase. These times differ from one another, depending on the customer, but move within a distribution framework which can be portrayed mathematically. The knowledge thus gained is used to determine the point in time at which contact needs to be resumed so that dialogue is not broken off, and to find out, by reference to the target, what is holding up simultaneous dialogue as far as the customer is concerned.

Total expenditure

The total expenditure is the total spent by a single customer in a specific requirement sector over a defined period of time, that is, in the case of consumers, expenditure on holidays, sports items, meat, video films inside a month, or, in the case of corporate customers, over the space of a year on raw materials, volume of investments or auxiliary goods. One important rule applies in the case of consumers as well as for corporate customers: the more powerful the customer's position is, the stronger the inclination to split market performance between a minimum of two suppliers. The top segment of private investment customers in private banking have divided their overall assets practically without exception between at least two investment institutions. Enterprises that operate globally have two suppliers in each sector and aim in this way to strengthen their negotiating position and minimise the risk of bottlenecks as far as procurement is concerned.

Share of customer

Share of customer gives information on a particular supplier's share in the appropriate expenditure. As already mentioned, customer groups exist where it is practically impossible to raise share of customer to around 100% as these customers operate a two-supplier policy.

Application

Benefit does not only depend on how the data is used, but just as much on how well the database has been designed and set up. Before an efficient database can be established, we need the answers to the following questions:

What will the database be used for?

What is the database's significance within the overall enterprise? What should the benefits of the database be? To formulate the answers to these questions, a multi-level development concept should be used. Once a database providing a major benefit has been set up, further functions can be added to it. This is a sensible procedure because it will provide more rapid availability as far as the basic functions are concerned. Nevertheless, any projected extensions should be incorporated at the design stage and this will simplify the addition of further functions.

Who will be using the database?

Within an enterprise, different functionaries have other concurrent needs. It is important to decide whether the database is going to be used solely by the marketing department or at the same time by other departments, such as, for example, sales, purchasing, logistics or product development. Much attention must be paid to the required level of know-how as far as users, or, quite simply, those who will benefit from the system are concerned.

How will the database be used?

Every user category should define how the database and the application envisaged for it should look. The more clearly and precisely the software application is specified, the more effective the database will be. The requirements clearly formulated at an earlier stage are reflected in the design and in the costs.

What data is available?

Data which is already available must be examined to ensure its reliability and usability. Usability is determined by the testimony of the data and the level to which it is relevant. In general, it is the relevance factor which should have the most attention paid to it. Certain personal information, such as date of birth, is in practice not time-sensitive – the customer can only be born once – but addresses, civil status and other attributes are liable to change. Usability is checked from two angles. The first approach should cover only that data which is necessary for the intended purpose; this is to avoid overloading the software application technologically and from the point of view of maintenance expenditure. The other is to endeavour to intercept any additional needs which may arise as early as possible in the application.

What further data is required?

Very often, the required data is either unusable or it is not available. The sources should be identified, whether these are internal or external. Certain data is publicly accessible, such as demographic details or other information such as statistics or level of income. Lifestyle and behavioural information needs to be collected internally and processed and assigned into information groups in accordance with the information value chain. Both the recording of the data as well as its further processing should be integrated into the maintenance of the database and be of as simple a structure as possible.

What information is required?

The majority of users expect to use the information in the form of an on-screen search or a printout. The compilation of indicative reports must be undertaken in conjunction with the users. The reports may be put together in different catagories: *ad hoc* enquiries, standard reports, reports for presentations. They should be graded appropriately in accordance with the quality of their portrayal. The periodicity of the reports should be borne in mind.

Who will be responsible for implementing the database?

The technical perspectives and the parameters imposed by any existing in-house information strategy are fundamental. It is in any event a matter of costs and risks whether a project of this kind is to be implemented using one's own resources or whether it is better to commission an outside contractor. The section that will subsequently be responsible for using it must be actively involved in the project to set it up. Chapter 8 contains fundamental points from a broad analysis of information technology projects which indicate how such projects can be implemented efficiently and primarily so that they incur minimum risk.

Prerequisites for Database Marketing

There is a great deal of data available in companies today – it is only the information which is lacking. This statement may appear contradictory but it is not. Each and every company possesses very many diverse computer applications. These applications can only exist on the basis of data. At the same time, the greater part of this data is not filed away in databases but in data files. The search for individual items of data, in order to gather information from it, will certainly be a nightmare in a data file organisation. Enterprises which have stored a major part of their data in databases are already better served. However, databases do lead an isolated existence and therefore data from one source cannot be processed with data from another. The really rational way to acquire information is through data warehousing.

Data warehousing

The basic notion of data warehousing is very simple. All historical data and customer information is stored under a common roof. The data warehouse is a gigantic data store, access to which has been optimised without affecting the working systems already installed. These can continue to run and fulfil their functions in the organisations. In the data warehouse, applications are used which are intended to serve new purposes, for example, to extract management information.[37]

In what way is this new? Data warehousing calls for massive address rooms and enormous general storage capacity. Whilst the information can certainly be stored on hard disks, processing has to take place in the main memories of computers as the time needed for access on disks leads to elongated processing times. These capacities are available with the latest generation of 64 bit chips.

Decision support systems

The key questions that companies ask are: Who are my customers? How profitable are the customers? What is the value of a customer for his overall life as such? How can the customer relationship be maintained efficiently and improved in terms of quality? Banks and insurance companies also ask themselves these questions.[38] Insurance companies employ armies of mathematicians to calculate the risk aspects and the portfolio for individual insurance categories. Banks and insurance companies possess an enormous quantity of data on their customers. Data warehousing offers a basis for a systematic approach to this material. In decision support systems (DSS), questions are so formulated as to provoke answers. The path of DSS development is strewn with mistakes.[39] Many cases of failure are to be found in a lack of understanding of the decision problem, formulated by Alan M. Turing in 1936 in his trail-blazing essay.[40] Turing, the spiritual father of the computer, clearly defined the limits and possibilities of computers on the mathematical deterministic basis of existing software.

By way of an example, for banks there are three areas which are very interesting when it comes to the practical application of DSS:

1. The acquisition of customers and maintenance of customer relations. DSS analyse the existing customer relations and identify possible requirements in terms of the bank's marketing performance. The current customer situation is changing. The relationship must follow the changing requirements. If a 25 year old university student needs credit for education then it may be assumed that he, depending on the stage of life at which he finds himself, will later avail himself of further services, e.g. when he opens his own practice or when he wishes to finance his own house or owner-occupied flat, and most certainly when it comes to matters of providing for old age and investing the assets which he has acquired.
2. In terms of customer relationship it is essential that the service is performed. Decisions and information are necessary for purposes of individualisation and rationalisation of services. The quality of the services can only be examined on the basis of the transaction which has occurred. The second sector deals with matters of quality, with the aim of improving services both overall and in individual cases.
3. Profitability cannot be measured in terms of services or customers alone. Rather the question is about where there is a potential for profit, depending on further aspects such as geography, type of business, specific transactions or service channel.

Decision support systems are, technically speaking, highly complex in terms of their implementation. However, one dimension of difficulty can be considerably reduced if very good guidelines exist whereby certain decisions need to be regarded as already taken. A DSS will only assume a decision once the decision framework is depicted within a system. This decision framework cannot be set up by information technologists but must originate from the relevant specialists.

Some Examples of Database Marketing

Telecom

In the deregulated telecommunications market, customer bonding is, commercially speaking, the decisive factor. Companies, as well as private individuals, will be offering each other different possibilities of communicating by telephone, fax or data transfer. Society's choice when it comes to long distance communication will be orientated towards the price offered and the additional services. As regards the various European Telecoms, a similar competitive situation will develop as is the case today in the USA.

A highly intimate level of customer bonding can be achieved by adapting the current uniform charges structure to customer requirements. This means, as far as a customer bonding programme like 'Family & Friends' which has been launched by MCI, that the internal structure for realising this marketing concept must be made available prior to its introduction. With 'Family & Friends', a private customer can communicate with his family under special price conditions. Information such as who uses the data lines, with whom and when, as well as using which tarifs, are required for this. These conditions are reproduced in a database and shown in the monthly statement.

Unisource, the subsidiary of the Telecom companies in Holland, Spain, Sweden and Switzerland, was commissioned by its shareholders in 1995 to create a software platform for this kind of customer bonding. The estimated duration of the project was more than two years.

In order to make this service possible, future application is based on data warehousing. Company customers should, at some point in the future, receive special price agreements from their telecom providers in respect of their communication requirements. As far as this example is concerned the details are less important than the fact that a marketing project of this kind takes several years from the moment of its implementation up to the point when it becomes a reality for the customer.

With the opening up of this market, all other competitors who are able to bring these marketing skills – supported by their information systems – to their customers have the advantage. In this case it will not be possible to take over an existing software system from companies which have been pushed into the background because the existing applications are non-compatible.

It is already possible to implement database marketing and the notion of customer bonding in very small companies or within a trade context. Frequently, expenditure on data technology is very small because the human being involved will assume a major part of the actual function.

Congratulations cards for good customers

A chain of jewellers' shops sends its customers a card on their birthdays. The gentlemen annually receive congratulations on their wedding anniversary. Men in particular tend to be targeted when it comes to congratulatory messages of this kind because it is they who are inclined to forget the date. Along with the card you will receive a dated discount coupon for a purchase above a defined amount. This brings the chain of shops additional business. The card can be sent by post, fax or fully electronically via the network.

A telephone call at the end of a holiday

A holiday company which offers its holidays solely via catalogue and telephone is able to provide its management with items of statistics. These give information on which customers have provided the strongest turnover over the past few years. This takes into consideration those individuals in particular who have been responsible for initiating holiday trips not only for themselves but also for other customers. These customers are regularly telephoned by the Managing Director once the holidays are over and asked about their experiences. The best customers already have the feeling that they belong to the company.

Telephone help free of charge

A specialist computer shop gives its customers, when they purchase hard- or soft-ware, a voucher which entitles them to the free use of the telephone customer advice service. This is valid for a certain period and depends on the level of accu-mulated purchase volume. The core of this is a suitable database which has details on how much time of free help still remains. At the same time, customers are informed about imminent new versions of the software they have bought. This type of service profiles the business in a market which is increasingly fighting over price alone. The business is popular with new subscribers and in this way a devoted cus-tomer base has been built up.

The Most Common Errors in Database Marketing

Relationship marketing, contact marketing, 1:1 marketing, frequency marketing, target group marketing is, in the last analysis, database marketing. These activities are often not beyond reproach. To identify the valuable and best customers, to improve the relationship with the top customers and through this to develop more business with them, and therefore in this way to increase share of customer, to win further customers by means of reference information and to increase market share – these steps are not always implemented in just the way the textbooks recom-mend. At the end of the day all customers are the same, but are not worth the same. What are the errors that are so often made?

1. The database is developed for future use without a clearly defined plan

The database may serve various purposes. On the one hand it exists to write to prospective buyers, on the other hand to sell on addresses, and then there is ulti-mately the intention of operating a database marketing system. For each purpose, the database must be different in terms of its design and realisation. Of equal importance is the concept governing management of the data, once the database exists and is capable of running. By comparison to looking after the database over a period of years, the cost of building up the database represents a relatively small expenditure. Which data and information are important and which not? The deci-sion on this calls for a clear targeting of the activity. The greater the uncertainty – as regards what is important and what not – the greater the expense. Only unequiv-ocal decisions will point to a way out of this dilemma. In the initial phase, it is important to ensure that targeting is reduced to the essentials. It is only in this way that expenditure can be kept at a justifiable level.

Since the database is a tool for achieving a target, commercial targeting must be determined *overall*. Without a corresponding marketing programme, database marketing should not be introduced. Only a properly worked out programme will define the necessary activities within the organisation and create the basis for achieving the desired attitude among those in the workforce who will be dealing with this instrument.

2. Trying to accomplish a highly complex solution by means of unachievable expectations

If, within a particular enterprise, different sectors of interest are represented when the database is set up, compromises are often arrived at aimed at optimising the database as an instrument for everyone concerned. This is an impossibility. The centuries old truth which says that things should be kept simple and uncomplicated is apposite here. The first step should be a straightforward one. Once the database has been introduced, additional complexity can be introduced in stages.

3. Thinking – as soon as the database is up and running – that database marketing has been introduced

Implementing the technical solution only means creating the tool. The real challenge lies in the application of the technology and anchoring it in the organisation, as well as in responding to customer reaction. Database marketing, as is the case with cyber marketing in general, is not principally a matter of technological implementation. What is important is the marketing-orientated implementation of procedures which allow customer relations and, hence, an expansion of the market to emerge, both of which will produce profit for the company.

What is important today may be irrelevant tomorrow as far as the customer is concerned. The customer's attitude will be shaped not only by his own performance but, at the same time and to a considerable extent, by the behaviour of his competitors. And good market players are characterised by a very distinctive feature: they are good for surprises. Frequency programmes, on the basis of which customers are awarded loyalty bonuses, are constantly being revised. If customer requirements in terms of the bonus programme cannot be quickly and genuinely met, this is just as damaging as poor service. By way of an example let us take the Frequent Traveller programmes operated by the airlines. These days the Frequent Traveller programme represents part of the overall assessment of what an airline is able to offer. The conditions under which free flights are available is just as much a factor as the in-flight services offered.

4. Implementing the marketing programme quickly and inexpensively

Buying an off-the-peg solution will not make database marketing any cheaper. The 1:1 approach to marketing is supposed to make the relationship with the customer more personal. To this end, a company needs a database solution tailored to its own requirements. This is very often based on the concept of data warehousing. This means that the relevant information from various databases within the company is centralised on a very powerful database – an actual data store – and periodically up-dated. Applications of this kind are very complex and have only been feasible for a short time in terms of cost.

5. Excessive targets

Once the programme is up and running some companies are intoxicated by the initial increases in sales and set themselves unattainable goals. Experience shows that, following introduction, there is first of all a leap in sales which, however, subsequently settles down and does not continue to increase at the same rate. The novelty effect evaporates with increased familiarity and usage.

6. No structures in place to monitor whether targets have been achieved

Without sufficiently clearly formulated structures or without any structures at all it is impossible to achieve all the targets set. If there are still no details available about frequencies or share of customer there are two ways of extracting this information. On the one hand, values drawn from past experience within the sector may be available or the values will have to be built up, something which takes time. Controlling the achievement of targets represents a target in itself and must be explicated as such.

7. The programme is not accepted within the organisation

Any programme can only be successful when the company's own organisation understands the intention and believes in it. If employees identify with the target and know what it is supposed to achieve, then the motivation necessary to convince customers will exist. The programme must first have been accepted internally before it makes sense to introduce it.

8. Waiting until your competitors have implemented the programme

Whoever is the first to bond his customers to him and whoever does this the most strongly will create an advantage for himself towards his remaining competitors. Stragglers will have to make great efforts to persuade customers to change, something which will only succeed with major financial input, more time and considerably more marketing flair.

9. Absurd loyalty bonuses

The ultimate aim is to increase frequency, customer bonding and share of customer. The loyalty bonuses, which, in the final analysis, no longer have anything to do with regular business, are in this sense absurd. The aim of a Frequent Traveller programme is to bond customers to an airline. In the end rewards such as, for instance, the free availability of hire cars, which have nothing to do with airline business, shoot wide of the target established by the basic idea.

10. Collecting information behind the client's back

The customer relationship is based on trust. If companies see database marketing solely as a high-tech mailing list, then the guiding principle can no longer be based on either trust or the relationship with the customer. Instead, information will be gathered from credit card companies, data services and other sources rather than through direct contact with the customer. Customers react extremely angrily when they discover that information has been collected behind their backs. Data collection strategies are divided into two customer groups; customers who opt in and customers who opt out.

Data Protection Legislation

Various countries have enacted legislation governing data protection, data processing and formalities governing the handling of personal data. Personal data always relates to natural persons, although it may also concern legal persons. The sphere of application is defined, as are the categories of legitimate data. Almost without exception, legitimate data covers a person's religious, ideological or political opinions and activities, health, private details and race. They also include administrative measures in the area of social assistance and records of criminal prosecution.

Data collection in particular and the proprietorship of data collections are regulated by law, as are the processing and dissemination of data. In certain European countries, very strict rules apply as regards the transfer of data to other countries. Even intra-group transfer of legitimate data is considered to be disclosure to third parties.

The regulatory framework must be observed without exception and the involvement of legal specialists is therefore highly advisable. A sense of awareness needs to be developed among staff within the organisation. The need to protect data must be understood from top management right down to the people in the front line as well as temporary staff. Data protection legislation within a company can only be put into practice through staff awareness.

It is advisable to protect data from access once it is no longer required. Technically, such protection can be achieved by setting up various storage systems and, administratively, through appropriate measures governing access to data. A risk scenario is a useful aid when it comes to formulating an effective protection policy. Input and transmission errors, hidden software errors, defective software functions, fraud, theft of software, misappropriation, theft or dissemination of data, logic sabotage or hacking into the network are all possible scenarios, as are support and maintenance failures by key staff or suppliers. Data protection policy should take the organisation's alternatives and requirements into account. The criteria of specific purpose, relativity and proportionality all have to be taken into consideration.

Minimum data protection standards are based on proven data safety methods which regulate the various features of data protection. Access by unauthorised persons to data-protected systems, whether internally, by physical entry or externally, through entering the network, should be controlled. The control of access via the network cannot be guaranteed by adopting unsophisticated measures, such as barring physical entry within the organisation. Access extends to all storage media not available in digital format, for example, paper, sound and optical records. Input entry control should be mandatory for each system. Automatic entry systems should be capable of *post hoc* audit or control as to who input what data and when. Control of storage, transfer and access must be assured, so that access for purposes of erasing, altering or copying data is impossible and is only available to authorised persons.

Management should define which staff members are responsible for introducing administration and supervision procedures. The periodical control of data security is highly advisable, as well as the execution and observance of data protection requirements.

It should be possible for customers to make enquiries about data protection. If required by individual customers, information on data protection guidelines and regulations should be supplied.

If a customer exercises the alternative of opting in, he gives written authorisation for the storage of his personal data. In Germany, he also has to confirm in writing that he wishes to receive direct advertising. Under the opt-in alternative, various companies leave it to the client to choose whether he wishes his personal data to be made available to other companies. Opponents of the pure opt-in alternative claim that the client should always have recourse to the possibility of opting out.

In principle, all customers should have the opportunity of opting out. Caution should be the order of the day. Customers often exchange details about themselves if they think this is not directly linked to a customer relations programme. If there is no such linkage and they are given the choice of refusal, they associate this with junk mail and waste-paper basket advertising. The opt-out alternative should therefore be used within the context of a customer transaction. For example, before a warranty expires, the supplier contacts the customer with an offer to extend the period of warranty or to conclude a service contract. The supplier is then targeting his personal data whilst at the same time giving him the option of cancelling such data. In this case the customer will recognise the innate value of the offer and is unlikely to make use of the opt-out alternative.

All information should be treated on a general and highly qualified basis. If the customer of the jewellery chain mentioned above is sent birthday congratulations, the text should be restricted to a simple birthday greeting; it should not read, for example, 'Congratulations on your 51st birthday'. Highly specific birthday greetings bring the client too close. Intimacy will cause him concern; he will feel he is being watched or even persecuted.

The enterprise should have a damage-limitation policy for contingencies such as this. It should never find itself unprepared when things go wrong; it should be able to call on some basic strategies so as to be able to deal with a number of such situations.

Conclusion: the Database as the Anchor of Cyber Marketing

The database is the anchor of cyber marketing. A proper appreciation of this statement, so that it becomes a pivot for actual as well as anticipated future exigencies is, together with a dialogue-orientated attitude towards the customer, vital if we are to secure a profitable position in marketing in the information era.

The contents of the database should include the individual customer's data as well as details about his usual methods and means of communication. The historical file should incorporate information about types and preferences. The database should facilitate customer dialogue and its contents should therefore be given a weighting. Cyber communication should be tailor-made to suit the customer's requirements.

Apart from the formal aspects of data communication, the basic way in which the database is used is highly critical. The customer relationship should be established on an individual basis and viewed as a long-term commitment. Databases can be structured for mass marketing but this is not the current trend. The change of the marketing target from market share to share of customer should not only be taken into consideration in terms of technology, but equally in terms of organisation.

The database will remain a central element, even if, in the course of future development, instruments of communication are extended and modified. The design and orientation of the database must take account of the certainty that, in future, massive changes will take place in on-line line instruments.

5 ELECTRONIC MARKETING

Marketing has been making use of electronic media ever since these first became available. The use of telephones and fax equipment is today called tele-marketing. Viewed in this way, these communication options are also marketing instruments in the broader sense.

The Value Added Chain within the TIME Industry

The availability of digitally-based marketing instruments within the information society will be created by the development of three inter-competitive industries: the mass media, the telecommunication and the computer industries. These three industries are growing closer together as their individual market performance is set to become so alike that it will not be possible to distinguish between them. The reason for this lies in the basic digital technology, the ability to bring multimedia interactively to the consumers or purchasers of communication media and the increasing importance of software in all three industries. The use of chip and processor technology as well as the cable as a principal transfer medium is an external feature of this increasing overlapping. All three industries will in the future be producing a value chain with the same functions arranged in an identical structure. The links in the chain are generation of content, integration, communication, platforms and terminal equipment.

The marketing relationship in the information era should be structured in the same way. Generation of content means setting up the communication content digitally. By way of example we might take a video film or pictures of products and customers or accounting details for a group of companies. The aim of a marketing programme may be the quotation of a group of companies' shares on the stock exchange or to keep possible front line investors informed about the future negotiable share title. The product is a form of title which, in the absence of any details about its past in the market statistics, calls for a high level of clarification.

Contents integration is achieved by editing digital content and the selection of different marketing instruments for each target group. This means that a video may be processed to provide a Web page for the Internet. Included will be information relating to market position, future prospects and financial details. In the same way the video may form the basis for a CD-ROM which is handed out to institutional investors following a presentation. The main advantage of the CD-ROM, however, lies in the large numbers of financial figures that it can accommodate, which enable an analysis of the group of companies to be carried out.

Communication describes the communication process or the sequence of communication involved in passing information from the supplier to the purchaser or between the two of them, in this case the Internet, the presentation event and the CD-ROM. It may well be that the first step to the stock exchange is initiated by means of newspaper advertising and television spots on a business channel so as to establish a basic level of familiarity. Here the print media and television also constitute links in the communication chain. In the majority of cases, marketing assumes platforms and terminals. Whilst it is hardly likely that a laptop will be supplied with the CD-ROM to enable a prospective buyer to conduct his own presentation, an item of software could be given away which would guarantee the prospective buyer access to Internet information and communication via e-mail.

Media and entertainments sector

The structure of the mass media and the entertainments industry may be briefly outlined as follows. Film studios are the producers of content. They employ scriptwriters, actors, musicians, camera crews and other specialists who are necessary for the production of a film. Music companies are other producers of content. The contemporary music business is blossoming. Without going into details, it is becoming clear that, from a time point of view, large amounts of content are being created predominantly by the entertainments industry. Television broadcasters and radio stations are incorporating these contents into a current programme. This even applies to news broadcasts. A major part of the picture material and the news is bought by the majority of television stations from agencies. The actual programme transmitted is, seen in abstract terms, a structured flow of information. Formerly, in the time of state monopolies, television and radio stations were also contents producers to a major extent but this role is now changing. Deregulation witnessed the emergence of a supplier industry for broadcasts in the television and radio landscape. Communication consists in disseminating up-to-date information.

Distribution takes place via satellites, radio or networks. Companies which offer satellite capacity or Net providers are the industries which have emerged here.

The platform manufacturers are the companies which supply the technology and equipment which make the activities possible, from generation of the content to the communication of information. This includes satellite manufacturers, camera manufacturers, manufacturers of audio and video equipment for professional use or producers of glass fibre cables. Terminal equipment producers are manufacturers of radio and television sets, satellite decoders, programme decoders and video recorders.

Telecommunication

The telecommunications industry is still somewhat less complicated in its structure. Contents producers in telephone conversations are generally individual people.

Integration takes place in the telephone exchanges, communication by means of wires, cables, radio or satellite. The terminal equipment is a telephone or fax machine.

The information industry

The complexity of the value chain in the computer industry is greater than that in telecommunication and somewhat lower than that in the media industry. The various contents suppliers are software companies with computer programmes, but at the same time individual persons using electronic mail. The technology and capacities available on the computer networks mean, however, that video pictures are being increasingly admitted and communicated as content. This further illustrates convergence into a media industry. The most important suppliers of content are active within the database sector. Economics, science and education databases in their thousands are filled with content and this information is accessed.

Distribution takes place via the computer networks which are linked together. Control over them varies, however. The local networks (LAN – local area network), for instance, are private. The networks within a larger location area (MAN – metropolitan area network) belong in part to private enterprise or to the Telecom organisations, which, in many European countries, have yet to be privatised. The extensive networks (WAN – wide area network) are operated entirely by suppliers from the telecommunications industry.

Terminal equipment in this industry is provided by personal computers and, to a minor extent only, by terminal stations. In 1995, 3 out of 10 inhabitants in the USA owned a PC; in Europe, Switzerland, with 22 PCs per 100 inhabitants and Norway with 17 PCs per 100 inhabitants were the leaders in this field. Japan registered only 8 PCs per 100 inhabitants. A further yardstick for the importance of this industry is the fact that, in 1994, sales of PCs in America exceeded the amount spent on television sets for the first time.[41] All three industries are, equally, converging as regards multimediality. Bearing in mind that telecommunications companies today are virtually restricted to transmitting the spoken word and data only (fax communication is in the last analysis data communication), they are now anxious to become multimedial. The television offers pictures, video and sound, and at the same time text, if you happen to have the vehicle of videotext, but, for the time being, it still lacks the function of interactive communication. The technology of the multimedia will, therefore, be examined in further detail.

Cyber marketing using which instrument of communication?

The key questions as far as companies are concerned are the following: 'Which of the three industries will be dominant in the future? How should the marketing department within a company set targets and make resources available so as to be sure of staying on the right track?'

One part of the answer is based on the importance of mutating from electronic marketing to cyber marketing. Ultimately, marketing has to meet various performance expectations within the framework of the various customer relationships and the range offered thus needs to be individually tailored. The ability to respond to customers individually is the crucial point in database marketing, as stated in the last chapter. It is here that the contents of dialogue are processed individually – always within the possible performance spectrum – and released as firm information in conjunction with the offer. The offer may be communicated, both today and in the future, by means of a variety of different communication options.

The starting point for communication is knowledge of customer profile. The use of this knowledge for an appropriate purpose is only possible by means of a database. The concept of instruments of communication must be flexible in terms of its structure. It is the only way not to lose sight of communication behaviour and customer preferences. The various alternative ways of using technology as a vehicle for communication are limited today, but perhaps not all the alternatives have been exhausted.

The following considers the pioneering future electronic opportunities in marketing from the point of view of their application. These instruments are currently in use within the direct marketing sector, both in terms of marketing practice and marketing jargon. Direct marketing is familiar with traditional instruments such as direct mail, coupons, catalogues and personal contact, whilst the telephone, telefax, view data and videotext, private radio, satellite and private television as well as video, video disks and CD-ROM are construed as the new media in direct marketing.

The direct marketing suppliers fraternity are fond of presenting these instruments as dialogue marketing or individual marketing, although there is, apart from telemarketing, no suitable media available to them when it comes to actual dialogue. In this context, individual marketing is practised as the only form of personal contact. The real, and hitherto only, type of dialogue marketing that is capable of responding to the individual customer, i.e. the network, such as the Internet, has not yet penetrated the conscious mind of every established direct marketing group.

The way to cyber marketing

In essence, the chain of activity comprises the generation, processing and communication of content in terms of electronic marketing. In cyber marketing, the context, the virtual environment, is created in addition. The way to cyber marketing is by way of electronic marketing.

The generation of content will always be digitally based. The processing of content is, ultimately, a question of which instrument is used for communication or for providing the information. Communication may take place by using a combination of different instruments, for instance, telemarketing, videotext/view data, CD-ROM or Internet. The combination of instruments may vary; for instance, we may have a CD-ROM catalogue which offers certain options for making contact with the sender – first of all, software which will exchange electronic mail by means of a self-installation mechanism using a commercial on-line service supplier such as CompuServe, automatically steering the customer towards the supplier's electronic bulletin board, as well as enabling the use of on-line facilities for an access period of (for example) four hours free of charge. In the second option, the CD-ROM generates a fax directly and sends it back to the sender. This takes place either directly from the PC via a modem or as a print-out via the standard paper facsimile machine. The third option is to send the paper print-out by post.

However, what is significant is not only communication of the content. In this phase of a communication landscape made up of highly diverse technological possibilities, the requirement is to actually put customers in a position where they can enter into a dialogue. In any event, the actual backbone of the relationship will be formed by the database, since it is at this location that all customer information needs to be available. Of course, this also includes knowledge of how the customer communicates and how we are to make contact with him.

In order to build up a long-term direct customer relationship, it is imperative to know which instruments are going to play a part in the future. This knowledge and the ability to develop different communication options for the different customer groups will be decisive in terms of success. It goes without saying that, in the introductory period, the new communication options will be communicated by means of the traditional media and instruments used hitherto. This means that, in future, a database will also need to offer the additional option of supplying a customer with products or information directly by post – a conventional form of communication pointing the way to the new opportunities in the virtual world.

The instruments discussed will play a part in the cyber age, not necessarily in their currrent form but in a more sophisticated form which has yet to be developed. For a period of two to five years yet, they will continue to form part of the repertoire of the budding cyber marketing specialist and, hopefully, be used successfully. The cost structure as regards electronic marketing is certainly set to become more interesting in the future. Lean marketing is also electronic marketing. The massive costs incurred in direct selling can only be countered by the consistent application of digital media. In practically every instance where companies have embarked upon the step-by-step introduction of electronically-based customer relationships the costs involved have been extensively reduced.

Telemarketing

Telemarketing signifies the systematic and sales-orientated application of the telecommunications infrastructure, telephone and telefax.[42] For some years now, Telecom companies have been running offers which provide useful options for marketing, such as the possibility of freephone numbers for customers and other prospective buyers, with different dialling codes depending on the country, but also higher rate numbers for chargeable services. One background development was voice mail and talking advertisements. The most resounding development was the facsimile machine, which opened up a further dimension to what had hitherto been the possibility of merely transferring speech down a telephone line. The combination of speech and fax transfer currently ranks as one of the most attractive media forms in the range offered by the telecommunications industry.

Certainly, progress in computer speech recognition and the conversion of language into text will further increase the attractiveness of the telephone in the future.

On a computer, the fax function can be directly integrated in the computer by means of appropriate software and no longer needs to operate via a separate fax machine. This, ultimately, will mean the transfer of information from the database directly on to the customer's fax machine in the network.

Passive telemarketing is often designated as 'inbound' and active telemarketing as 'outbound'. One example of an inbound marketing procedure is the free-of-charge breakdown assistance offered by many motor car manufacturers. Alfa Contact operate an entire network of breakdown companies in Europe who, if called out by an Alfa Romeo owner, will travel direct to site. They assist the owner and customer in any unfortunate situation, such as when someone has locked his keys in the car.

Sending out special quotations by fax in order to clear stock remaining in the warehouse is an example of an outbound measure. Telemarketing makes a completely new type of company possible. Dell Computer is an example of this. A combination of media campaigns, catalogues and telemarketing to market products for the discriminating customer is an alternative option to cost-intensive distribution via dealers or field personnel. Today, an average 70% of the sales recorded by the larger mail order companies are based on the use of telemarketing. Here the telephone and the fax machine serve as a vehicle for clarifying and submitting the order. In the banking sector, Citibank overall and, in Switzerland, Crédit Suisse are particular examples of companies who have assumed a leading role in telebanking.

Three possible ways of using fax technology in marketing

The fax machine has undergone a technological change since it was introduced on to the market. The greatest step has been the integration of fax functions within a computer, away from an individual machine, which, at best, is still combined with a telephone. With this there are several different options available:

1. Bulk despatch fax communications – outbound. A number of addressees are sent a personalised fax message. A limited number can be serviced by a telephone/fax machine. Using the computer makes it possible to service a larger number of recipients simultaneously. Dialling takes place automatically, as does re-dialling.[43]
2. Using fax messages sent from the computer makes it possible to operate database marketing in a highly practicable fashion. Individual items of information are compiled in bulk from databases and despatched individually and simultaneously.

3. Captured fax information – the 'inbound information path'.[44] Prospective buyers dial the target fax and call up the required documents on to their own fax machine. This can be combined with a chargeable number. Using this approach it is only possible to transfer entire documents complete, the user cannot view the information first and then access those sections which are of value to him. This problem can be alleviated by means of indexes and numbers which vary according to the sequence of contents.

The traditional fax machine is a very simple but useful marketing tool. The technology is rapid and can be understood without a knowledge of software. The possibility of migrating fax functions on to the personal computer or on to a special fax server and of making use of broader functions represents a natural development path. The basic marketing concept can be retained, although a technological leap is being achieved. Fax communication can be implemented at any time, in contrast to making contact by telephone. In this way you can service your customer with the desired information or support whenever he wants it, for, using the fax capture facility, the customer can choose the time when contact is made himself.

Fax communication is comparatively reasonably priced, especially where the customer is dialling your machine and choosing from among 100 different documents (this, of course, depends on the machine) before finally calling up the required documentation on to his own machine. In the case of documentation despatched from the computer's data files, it is possible to make changes at any time. Piles of old versions which have to be disposed of every time they are revised are a thing of the past.

Criticism is often levelled at the poor quality of fax documents. The quality of the document received is dependent on the model, the resolution and the printing process used by the fax equipment involved in the transmission of a document.

Fax capture combined with database

A computer offers the facility to store thousands of documents which can be captured specifically by a caller. Computer firms in particular have recognised fax capture as an extremely useful facility. For example, the technicians at Microsoft were overloaded for a long time because they could only be contacted by telephone. As in other sectors, a great many of the questions asked by users were the same. Microsoft replied in writing to some queries and made them available for fax capture. Thus they were able to ensure that customers no longer had to wait and technicians could use their time to deal with more complex enquiries. Side effect: increased customer satisfaction and reduced costs.

Even airlines have noticed this. Swissair use a combined speech and fax system in their Qualiflyer programme. Keeping track of every customer's air miles account and giving information on it at any time meant, when this customer-bonding programme was introduced, a great deal of additional expenditure in terms of time and money. This additional burden increased even further when the air miles coupons had to be processed by other partner airlines. However, these could very often not be automatically transferred via reservations and handling systems as credits to the customer's air miles accounts because, at certain airports in the world, a universal check-in system was not being operated. In addition, diverse systems such as Sabre, Galileo and Amadeus were being used. In order to free up staff from the most common enquiries, Swissair introduced the Qualiflyer Fastphone in the late summer of 1995. This makes it possible for a subscriber to call up his air miles account by telephone; additional air miles can be added and new additions to the programme and current promotional offers called up by fax. On telephoning, the customer is guided through the options by means of a female computer voice and communicates with the computer via the buttons on the telephone. Discretion as regards personal details is ensured by inputting the relevant Qualifyer number and a special PIN code. The Pin code can, in addition, be modified at any time by the customer via the telephone. This example clearly demonstrates that, for a service of this kind, it is essential to be in control of the data infrastructure. Naturally, it is possible for the customer, at any point in his dialogue with the machine, to express the wish to speak with a representative of Swissair. The customer will then be automatically put through to a human contact.

Fax capturing can be incorporated in advertising by way of a promotion. In this way the value of marketing communication is enriched. It is impossible to portray a product in detail in any advertisement. This particularly applies to equipment in the consumer or investment goods sector. In advertising it is possible to capture the attention of the public, but specific or in-depth information is not possible. The dialogue is introduced by asking prospective buyers to pick up any information of interest to them by communicating on the fax.

A further application example is to be found in the investment consultancy sector. The customer of a bank or an investment consultant can call up his portfolio at any time and monitor developments since his last statement. Customer portfolios are available on the system. The basic step is the link-up with a fax machine. In the banking services sector, there are even more possibilities available for setting oneself aside from one's competitors by offering additional services of this kind and for making cost savings.

There is practically no business sector which cannot profit from the use of fax marketing and with it reduce company costs and increase the quality of information.

At the moment this is particularly true for companies in the personal computer sector. Depending on which configuration a customer has purchased, the pattern of his requirements that is likely to ensue will be different. The customer will need information about equipping his machine and will obtain this information for himself. He may possibly approach a competitor if the supplier does not make use of his existing relationship. Customers who require modems, printers, scanners or other peripheral equipment also need highly comprehensive information in order to ensure that they can use the product they have bought on their system. Via fax it is possible to configure and quote for a complete computer system in accordance with the wishes of the prospective buyer without a single employee having to take this on board himself. The larger manufacturers have already known about computer system configurators for more than ten years. Using a marketing approach of this kind, the manufacturer can go directly to the end customer and this is particularly so in the hotly contested PC market. This has several advantages for him. In the first place, he gets to keep the middleman's margin or he can pass this on in part to the end customer by way of a loyalty discount. Secondly, he does not need to use expensive staff to deal with sales and quotation work, but instead he can make use of the fax system, thus saving costs. Thirdly, a system of this kind is relatively easy to adapt and use for different countries. Fourthly, the supplier has background information to hand which shows him which configurations have been requested and what the possible market trends may be. Fifthly, the contract specification can be very easily transferred into the extended information systems at the point of order. Sixthly, an active after-sales marketing policy can be operated. This is geared quantitively speaking to a wide circulation procedure and provides the customer with additional offers and extensions to his system. An important factor as far as Europe is concerned is that this service can be offered nationally, but, as soon as a customer expresses a wish to speak to a company representative, he can be put through to the head office.

Companies such as IBM make it possible for their customers in America to access a library of technical specifications. The same applies to Hewlett-Packard.

There are a great number of options within the tourism sector. Travel agents will give detailed information on individual travel packages. Hotels can be described very well and in detail, not just from the point of view of the number of rooms they have, but also as regards travel there, special entertainment programmes and adventure holidays. People letting holiday homes can send detailed pictures and floor plans as well as occupancy details to prospective buyers.

If a tourist office centralises the different attractions offered by a particular country or region and makes the information available to prospective buyers in different countries by means of a simple polling system, then it will be possible not only to give these attractions a high profile on the market in an efficacious and cost-efficient way, but, at the same time, additional facts and opportunities can be provided to extend the general tourist advertising spectrum.

Estate agents can offer property in the housing or landed property market by areas or postal codes. Documents relating to further education courses offered by a private institute or a specialised association establishment can be distributed by fax. Publishing houses can publish announcements of titles or excerpts from their publications. Today publishing houses are already offering indexes, short descriptions and reviews of books by fax and prospective buyers receive, along with the description, an order form which they fax or post back if they wish to order a volume.

Societies, consumer forums or special interest groups will find that various applications suggest themselves. They make the information available and members collect the news, bulletins, etc. that are of interest for them.

Within the marketing sector it is possible to conduct customer questionnaires. The marketing office sends out questionnaires on which recipients mark the answers by means of small crosses. The sheet can be faxed back. A software programme is used to evaluate the questionnaires and this sets up a schedule of results by means of a database or table calculation programme. In plain language this means that information from customers or orders can be evaluated electronically. Orders sent by post are scanned into the computer system before being processed further.

In one somewhat demanding application, a database – inevitably – will be combined with the fax function. This is a highly specialised form of fax polling. However, it is possible using this combination to develop a large number of dialogue activities. This link-up represents a preliminary stage of communicating with a customer by means of the Internet and, therefore, represents a sensible way of gradually introducing the marketing instruments. The database can be modified at any time and this makes a highly relevant form of communication possible.

Why fax marketing?

From a marketing viewpoint the greatest advantage offered by fax marketing is the simple way in which a customer relationship can be built up. In terms of application philosophy, fax information polling is identical to cyber marketing. By contrast to bulk mailing operations using a fax machine, cyber marketing leaves the initiative to the customer, in the same way as fax information polling. For this reason fax polling is highly suitable as a supplementary means of servicing those customer groups who are either not able to communicate on-line or who do not wish to. Offering the possibility of being able to send information actively to the customer, fax marketing is the sole instrument which can be used simultaneously for the old marketing approach of mass information and the new marketing philosophy of cyber marketing, always taking into account its limitations in not being capable of multimedia operation.[45]

The development of fax technology is closely allied to the renewal of telecommunications structures. The spread of ISDN (integrated services digital network) will make possible a quality of transmission in the latest generation of fax machines which a copy on normal paper will be hard put to surpass. It is for this reason that we often talk about 'remote copiers'. The incorporation of the fax function into computers will lead to fax communication representing in the long term a genuine alternative to e-mail (electronic mail), in particular when the other party either cannot be contacted on the system or when a physically visible message needs to be generated immediately. This is possible if the addressee has a standard fax machine which can be contacted at any time. The step from paperless faxing to the electronic transfer of data (EDI) is a small one. Whereas today EDI is an instrument of communication between large companies, this is set to change in the future. The fact that Microsoft make it possible for EDI to be used as a function on their network software (MSN for Microsoft Network) will help EDI achieve a very rapid breakthrough, even in medium-sized and small companies. This should assign a growing role to EDI within the business to business sector.

Modem marketing

We often hear talk of 'modem marketing'. Today the modem is an item of equipment which converts analogue signals from the telephone network into digital characters. All computers need a modem to enable them to communicate in an analogue manner via telephone lines. Modem marketing can therefore relate to fax communications despatched by PCs as well as to access to the Internet. In this form the concept is not sufficiently representional, neither is its content adequately characterised. A very special type of modem marketing is, however, the private electronic post box. Here the customer dials into the supplier's computer where he gives a password and collects information. This kind of communication can be propagated by marketing. Its use, however, will be focused chiefly on the service functions sector and not on procurement. Viewed at close quarters, this function may be seen as an instrument in the same way as inbound fax marketing, EDI or as a special type of electronic mail on the network.

Videotext

View data is still in existence, but it has, following major initial euphoria, never really played a significant role in many countries. Even its marginal dialogue capability will not be able to save view data (BTX) in the long term. The possibilities and functions which it offers have already been overtaken by the Internet. It is anticipated that there will be a revision of the services which view data offers. In Germany, Deutsche Telekom, with a view to acquiring a launching pad to enable it to offer on-line technology in the market place based on extended services such as access to the Internet and e-mail, re-named its BTX/Datex-Jim 'T-Online' in September 1995. This metamorphosis meant that, overnight, T-Online became the biggest network in Germany. The on-going introduction of ISDN and the extension of T-Online to incorporate multimedia capability will ensure the survival of the former BTX, albeit in modified form. These systems will then only have any chance of survival if a complete link-up with the Internet is successful; insofar as this is concerned, T-Online will go into the Internet as a private network.

The situation is similar as far as videotext is concerned. Videotext is an instrument in the hands of the support sector, the radio and the cable network industry. In 1995, videotext was a function which was still addressing the market exclusively via the medium of television. This is set to undergo a very marked change in the future. One aspect of the change is being determined technologically whilst the other is being determined structurally. The technological aspect is the digitalisation of the television sector. Using a digital television will give you better picture quality whilst digitalisation also lays the foundations for multimedia. Interactive TV teleshopping in simultaneous dialogue is becoming possible, although this calls for new television sets and suitable software applications. The structural aspect is emerging from the general problem areas experienced by suppliers in the mass media. The developments which are being introduced mean that what is on offer in terms of media is becoming even more widely spread than has already happened due to the liberalisation of the broadcasting market. Since market potential remains fairly constant, competition is being sharpened due to a battle to suppress the constantly increasing numbers of suppliers. On the market side, a more pronounced level of differentiation and individualisation is increasingly emerging. The contact quality of the mass advertising media is declining. Ultimately the way out can only be through the option of interactive TV and it is here that videotext will be able to assume the function of structuring the interactive option.

The organisations operating videotext in various countries are anxious to make the content of their medium accessible on the Internet too. This means that, by means of videotext, it will, on the one hand, be possible to address today's television consumer and, on the other, the pure personal computer user. It is already possible, with the appropriate equipment, to watch TV programmes on a personal computer using one application window whilst a further window is in use to communicate via the Internet.

Multimedia

In 1994, multimedia was a press event and enjoyed much media attention; no other technology was treated to publicity to the same extent or more deeply implanted into the minds of the general public. Multimedia was transformed from an exotic to a common concept. Today multimedia is accepted in the commercial world and is becoming increasingly more popular. Nevertheless, many decision makers are not clearly aware that multimedia is a technology and not a product in itself which makes possible a computer-based, interactive range of information from various media. This will be evident from its background.

Origins of multimedia

As we see it today, multimedia technology lies somewhere between desktop publishing and hypermedia. At the beginning of the 1990s, desktop publishing was regarded as a major breakthrough. The performance capability of the processors, bulk memories and the new software functions enabled every PC user to prepare camera-ready copy, type-set and complete with page proofs, himself electronically. Various layouts complete with pictures and text become easy to handle on the screen. The revolution which came about in printing and the graphic industry due to electronic publishing, which had initially become established within the newspaper and magazine sector, soon spread to encompass smaller companies manufacturing traditional in-house print products or who supplied trade outlets, associations and private individuals with printed matter. Desktop publishing made every man his own publisher, editor, graphic designer and printer.

Multimedia signifies the convergence of text and picture, as already familiar from a desktop publishing context, with sound and film. Multimedia systems are made up of hardware and software. They make it possible to produce multimedia products and to play them through. Because of the volume of data involved, multimedia applications are either read on site by CD-ROMs or called up on-line via a network.

Within the context of the transfer of information and for individual information handling purposes, multimedia offers itself as a leading technology. Multimedia is digital and can therefore be transported to the consumer via different carriers. Writing and pictures represent a fragile medium if we are to maximise appeal to the emotional sector. Emotionalised communication can be conducted almost only through video and audio, that is, sound. Within the context of learning, in particular, hearing, seeing and doing are regarded as a necessary combination to ensure an optimum learning sequence. Using multimedia all three requirements can be taken into account. Multimedia applications can be built up to be highly interactive. This means that the user can build up quasi-active communication with the system and be guided along learning paths by means of dialogue.

Computer-based training (CBT) is one of the new commercial benefits of multimedia. European Telecom enterprises set up a company in 1993 which devised a training programme based on these modern technologies. The following application example provides a good insight into it.

Carla is a postal officer in Poschiavo (an alpine valley in southern Switzerland). This morning the boss told her that one of her colleagues was to be absent as of immediately for an indefinite period and that Carla would now have to take over responsibility for personnel administration. The relevant IT application was on the colleague's PC. There were no courses for operating the application until the autumn and, in view of the fact that so many colleagues were on holiday, it was impossible to release her for a spell at a suitable centre. He suggested that she might investigate the possibilities using the recently advertised remote training facility via the computer.

Carla sat down at her PC and rang up GLOBAL TEACH. The first thing she discovered was that it was quite easy to talk to GLOBAL TEACH. She selected the language – Italian – from the catalogue, followed by the field – Personnel – whereupon the desired CBT title appeared. Under CBT Information Details Carla found a description of the learning programme as well as information on the time requirement and the necessary hardware and software. A click of the mouse later the CBT was remotely transferred on to her PC in Poschiavo – where it came from she didn't care. The important thing was that she could now start working on the material. And, because GLOBAL TEACH had also identified and started up the software platform for CBT there was nothing to stop her getting started .

Unseen by Carla, at the other end of the line, at the PTT Head Office in Bern, the GLOBAL TEACH server had made the desired information and the CBT available via the network; in addition, it had checked the available

*disk storage on Carla's PC prior to loading and then appended the user sta-
tistics. When Carla has finished her first lesson the server will save her work
so that next time she will log on in the correct place and complete with the
number of points which she collected in the first section. The name is fiction,
but all the rest is reality. The basic functions of GLOBAL TEACH are a
matter of fact.*

As regards the considerably public presence which has been accorded to multimedia there are also a few very critical voices. Certainly, the reality of multimedia
application will look different in the future to the way we see it today, something
which still does not prove that we are basically on the wrong track as far as our
ideas at this time are concerned. As is the case with a marketing programme, any
plan based on facts and assumptions will be overturned at some stage. Through its
implementation the plan is relativised and the ultimate form may well not bear any
resemblance to the original ideas. What is important is the process which can only
be consciously moulded using a plan or a vision. Shaping the future calls for an
appreciation of future possibilities and it is only in this way that proactive creation
will be possible.

Multimedia as a form of access technology

In this sense the multimedia scene is set to undergo massive changes and in the
future will exist as diversified branches. Multimedia at its current technical level
will be used where no interactivity is called for. In all sectors where communication
or interaction is to be effected between system users, multimedia will cease to be
used in its present-day form – it has already developed further into hypermedia.

Nevertheless, multimedia remains an important form of access technology
today. Multimedia is employed in sales marketing for purposes of advertising, presentation and selling; it is also used in other marketing activities, such as market
research, for purposes of research into customer preferences. Using multimedia it is
possible to put over product designs or services in a manner which is true to reality. Difficult to access or highly complex market services may be communicated at
different levels. Multimedia is well suited to the portrayal of dynamic situations
and statements. In addition, hypermediality conveys content-related information
relationships to a high and structured degree and this makes it easier for human
recipients to absorb these. Using appropriate software it is very easy to achieve a
highly individualised and dialogue-orientated presentation.

In terms of product development, multimedia is used for virtual prototyping; it
is also becoming possible to build up a virtual product range. The portrayal of
characteristics lends itself relatively well to visualising. United Glass provides us
with an example of this kind of application. The company is located in St Albans,
UK, and it produces glass containers for customers such as Nestlé SA, United Dis-
tillers plc and H.G. Heinz & Co. Every year approximately 1800 different glasses
are designed. United Glass uses a combination of different hardware and software

to design these in association with the customer interactively and at great distances. The design of the new glass can be viewed on the system, fitted with different labels as required. In order to test sales impact, the product is shown on a stand in the warehouse – in proximity to other products. A special software module makes it possible to visualise by means of simulation the behaviour of the items in a package under stress and with solid or liquid fillings in various transport situations. Once the design has been finalised, the data necessary to produce the glass is despatched direct to the model builder, the printer and the advertising companies. This kind of product development saves any duplication of activity and, ultimately, time and money.

Multimedia has rightly established a niche for itself in terms of sales and marketing presentations. Many more companies could make enormous advances in this regard. This shows the great number of companies that are currently offering multimedia services.

Multimedia makes a new type of product possible. Publishing companies such as Orell Füssli, NZZ, Birkhäuser and Springer are currently offering multimedia products such as classified directories, reference works or encyclopaedias. Certainly, the multimedia products sector looks set to undergo massive expansion and this is likely to happen predominantly within the learning and further education sectors.

Hypertext and hypermedia

Hypermedia is a concept related to multimedia products which makes possible links between individual content segments that go beyond the confines of the media themselves. Let us imagine a computer graphic or photo-realistic illustration showing information signs in an entrance hall to a media presentation. These signs point to the book, video film and audio products departments. We can enter the appropriate department by using the mouse to click on the signs. As soon as the operator clicks on the word 'video films' he finds himself in a shop with the selection of videos. He may then navigate further along the pre-set search paths, make his selection and view a video sequence on a trial basis.

The hyperlinks, the links which transcend the media, make more flexibility of movement possible in terms of screen portrayals than is the case where the user is guided hierarchically via a tree structure. Conventional texts, whether they are printed or in the form of a data file, are perceived by human beings successively and in clear sequence. This means that the arrangement of the information is defined in terms of a single linear progression. In a book these are words, sentences, paragraphs and chapters. The normal reader begins at the first page and finally finishes at the last. Hypertext is not sequential, as the reader has the choice of how he wishes to absorb the information. As the text progresses he may leave the text at specially marked points (mostly words) and call up a completely different page or paragraph and continue from there. An illustration of this application is a dictionary which explains concepts and refers the reader either to related or contrasting concepts.

Hypermedia is, in this sense, multimedia with hyperlinks. In hypermedia a link between the media and a change-over are both possible. Thus, it is possible not only to call up the description of a musical instrument under a particular heading, but also a picture by way of information as to how the instrument looks and a sound sequence which will reproduce the sound of the oboe, for example. Bearing this in mind it is not surprising that, since 1993, the electronic encyclopaedias in hypertext have outstripped the printed ones and a massive growth in sales has been recorded.

The first works published about hypertext go back to 1945, when the grandfather of hypermedia, Vannevar Bush (1890–1974) published an article in *Atlantic Monthly* entitled 'How we could be thinking'. Around 20 years later the term 'hypertext' was coined by Ted Nelson'.[46] After a further period of almost 20 years the first hypertext system was brought on to the market by Apple Computers in 1987. In 1990, the first global hypertext system was created in CERN – the World Wide Web (WWW). It was hypertext technology which first made access to the Internet of interest to the non-scientific user.

When should hyper-functionality be used?

The rules for using hypertext and hypermedia are as follows:

1. Comprehensive information exists, either in dispersed form and/or in different media.
2. The individual items of information are linked to one another in terms of content.
3. The user requires only an extract from the overall information in each case.
4. The user is working with a computer: hypermedia is digital.

Dictionaries, reference works with cross-referencing are, to a small extent, examples of this. From a global viewpoint, database information with similar content is structured in exactly the same way. It is only the point where the information is filed that is geographically different. Those with responsibility for staff within an enterprise can use hypermedia to record employees' particular abilities and knowledge. It frequently happens that a specialist office within an international group needs to pinpoint someone within the company who is in a position to fulfil a highly specific task. In cyber marketing, as is also the case in companies with a scientific base where work is carried out within specialist teams, it is crucial for the company management to know who possesses which abilities and special knowledge within their own organisation.

As far as Web surfing on the Internet is concerned, the conditions governing the use of hypertext are fulfilled. Web surfing is merely the portrayal of links between the information content of quite separate computers whose geographical position is immaterial and, in terms of information content, completely irrelevant to the search.

Application of hypertext

Hypertext applications are already in extensive use, for instance, in museums, where they are used to illustrate how mankind developed from a hunter into a tiller of fields. In libraries hypertext applications are used to make the grind of searching for particular title categories easier. Tourist guides for countries or towns which are mostly available on CD-ROMs make an individual journey of discovery possible. In the same way, language programmes are also available on CDs today. Using hypermedia, the user can make his selection from a range of several languages and pick up both oral expression and the written form. Within the interactive learning process entire pictures of objects or typical scenes can also be portrayed.

The application of mind mapping, which offers a system to improve the imprinting of interrelated events on the memory, is available for use on the PC and works in close conjunction with hypertext technology. Collections of legal texts are linked by means of hypertext, enabling the user to produce personal references from individual legal texts which he has identified by means of a full text search system.

Instructions for use, as in pharmacology, based on the linking of attribute information, can be clearly communicated. If the quantity of information is small or if it can only be presented as a whole if it is to be intelligible, the presentation should follow conventional lines. Information based on a large quantity of unrelated data is not suitable for hypertext, e.g. the telephone directory with numbers and names. A standard database is better for this.

Multimedia carriers carriers

Multimedia, like hypermedia, is a technology which only becomes manageable as far as the user is concerned in conjunction with software and computers. Very often the carrier of the digital information is confused with the technology and options offered by multimedia. The carriers are always digital. The most important carriers of multimedia applications are, on the one hand, the CD-ROM (in the future the video disk too) and, on the other, the network.

Although the use of multimedia is only limited by the power of the imagination, several different applications have already become established. Highly cost-efficient is the technology for POS kiosks and POS notices, electronic catalogues, sales presentations and in the sphere of exhibition information.

CD-ROM

If, however, multimedia on CD-ROM, regardless of the information content, is used as a substitute for traditional print media, then failure will be found to be pre-programmed into it. By contrast to traditional media, multimedia applications on CD-ROMs can and should be in interactive form and it is here that their greatest advantage over printed matter lies. On the one hand, users' questions are answered and, on the other, the user is able to select information very rapidly and specifically. The criteria for a sales catalogue may be price, model specifications or other product attributes. This function can be put to good use, particularly where there is a wide range of products available, to offer prospective buyers real help with decision-making. CD-ROMs can be very easily sent by post, are comparatively inexpensive to manufacture and can be updated quickly and easily. Up to an hour of music or video sequence can be stored on a standard CD-ROM with a 600 Mbyte data capacity.

Use of CD-ROMs

Using CD-ROMs because they create an innovative image on the market is not an adequate reason for using this carrier. In the initial phase of multimedia euphoria, CD-ROMs were used primarily for their image. Two-thirds of customers would hardly have noticed if they had received only an empty silver disk from such an innovative company. Business triggered by CD-ROMs was small-time in nature. The CD-ROMs handed out were boring and were often viewed incorrectly before being laid aside. Their attractiveness was essentially determined by information content and fun – facts and fun. CD-ROMs should only be used in an application in which they make sense – sense for the customer, that is – not for the producer.[47]

Networks

The possibility of communicating full multimedia capability via networks is a question of transmission capacity. Networks will be increasingly enriched by multimedia capability in the next few years. However, it will be a few more years yet before adequate transmission capacity for fully interactive multimedia capability, broadly spread, is available. Nevertheless, this is an important fundamental point when it comes to shaping the cyber world.

Multimedia terminals

A further type of carrier is the multimedia kiosk.[48] Electronic kiosks of this kind are often incorporated into POS concepts. Bank customers, for example, when interacting with cash dispensers, have their attention drawn at the same time to other bank products.[49] Cross-selling is a feature of mortgages, credit business or investment management services. In the case of banks, the kiosks are usually placed in counter halls or electronic banking centres and have simple graphical user guides. One example is 'La Caixa' (La Caja de Aborros y Pensiones de Barcelona), one of the largest banks in Spain. 400 of its 2300 branches have multimedia kiosks installed; these are fitted with touch-sensitive screens. Users are identified by their passport, user or credit card. These kiosks are designed for dealing with payments, drawing cash and calling up bank information. At the same time the user can also obtain tickets for the theatre or the cinema which are printed out directly. To enable the desired seat to be reserved, the various seating arrangements in stadiums, halls and other such entertainments centres can be viewed at a glance. Payment is by credit card or direct debit to the user's account. La Caixa, however, uses the kiosk to display vacancies in various companies and to advertise landed property and real estate for a number of estate agents. In this way La Caixa earns itself additional third-party income.

Further applications of multimedia terminals are fairs information systems at major exhibitions. At these electronic information desks it is not only possible to obtain a print-out of the desired information on paper, but also to compose the best route for an individually compiled visit to the fair.

Multimedia and database marketing

It is possible to link multimedia applications up to databases by way of text information and data. It is also possible to incorporate multimedia data. However, there is still a great deal of development work to do in this sector. Looking up particular photo subjects in display files or video files is not a particularly simple matter. Dealing with multimedia data in databases will still call for a degree of innovation. Nevertheless, the combination of hypertext applications and database marketing is a very appropriate one when it comes to achieving real progress in communication.

Multimedia applications

Multimedia systems are very often used by car firms in their sales rooms and in their dealers' display windows. In this context a distinction is drawn between moderated and non-moderated systems. Non-moderated applications run autonomously, i.e. as audio-visual information without the personal intervention of a consultant. The aim of these systems is primarily to draw the attention of potential customers to the point-of-sale and the products presented. Their effect lies in their content-related presentation and is generated in part using sound. Eye-catchers are used to build up contact with a reticent person with the aim of imparting information. Thus kiosks are very well placed to address people who shy away from making direct contact with a salesperson.

Experiences within the automobile sector

Multimedia kiosks in a display window are intended to build up sales contacts and ultimately to persuade the prospective buyer to enter the salesroom. The American motor car industry has been using kiosks in its showrooms for some time. Back in 1987, General Motors had more than 11,000 computer-controlled video disks in use in its sales outlets.

The strengths of multimedia can be demonstrated very well by reference to this application. The choice of model when purchasing a motor car is triggered primarily by emotional momentum. Prestige is not simply a matter of the correct choice of manufacturer, but also hinges on the choice of model from within a particular series as well as the type of vehicle in question and is determined by means of extras and special accessories. The diversity of colours, wheels with special tyres, the number of doors, sliding roof and various attachments to the bodywork can be portrayed very quickly and with no trouble in multimedia systems using graphics programmes. The entire range can be presented to prospective buyers without generating the enormous costs that are incurred when all the types, variations and extras are paraded on site. The emotional link is, however, not forged by the vehicle alone, but also by the surroundings in which the car is presented. Technical details, such as improvements to individual parts systems, can be portrayed in a way which is easily remembered as well as intelligible. Driving features can be put over very realistically by means of extracts from films, in attractive surroundings and at different times of the year.

The multimedia systems on site at the dealer's premises will considerably enhance adventure-value. A system of this kind also provides an ideal way of filling in the waiting time for people who are interested in a particular vehicle. At the same time multimedia systems are used on site for market research purposes. These systems record which criteria have been selected by the prospective buyer and called up by way of information. These aspects of information behaviour shed light on customer preferences and decision criteria related to car purchase.

Moderated systems will support a sales consultant in his dialogue with the customer. Systems of this kind were introduced at the premises of 170 VAG dealers by Volkswagen AG in 1988. The system chiefly served as an audio-visual support for sales discussions. The technology was based on video disks which contained basic information on the models available. By means of a BTX connection, data on the network was fully updated daily. However, due to the relatively high procurement costs for video disk technology at the time, this system was not implemented by all dealers. But the degree to which dealers, even in 1992, were finding the system useful and the extent to which it had been accepted still varied. Around 45% rejected this kind of sales support. One-quarter reported that they frequently used it and had had good experiences with it. The rest indicated that they used the system often. Eventually Volkswagen gave up the system – due to the high cost of the necessary annual renewal of video disks which was many times in excess of expenditure on present-day CD-ROMs.

In 1993, BMW developed a multimedia workplace for salesmen in their appointed dealerships. This was, however, not devised for end customers as certain information was not intended for the market. It featured eight modules covering different sales areas, e.g. information regarding selection of the type of vehicle and its accessories with relevant sales prices. This corresponds to a configuration and offer function. A collection of economic arguments responds in concrete terms to questions that might possibly be posed by prospective buyers in respect of costs and permits a performance analysis to be made. Further information as regards the range of offers available in the leasing, credit and maintenance sectors is available. A customer card index enables the seller to identify and service his customers. A calendar and survey of activities form the basis for notes related to personal time and activity planning. The dealer's fleet can be managed and models marketed on site. The reporting procedure between the dealer and BMW is also standardised.

Mercedes have set up a customer advice system within the service vehicles sector. This matches the criteria of need, chassis selection, technical structural calculations and evaluation of driving performance to a usage profile. Based on this it is possible to portray an economic viability calculation for the customer, taking into account individual customer data such as staff costs, tax, insurance, performance in operation, service life, minimum return and different financing methods. A quotation is drawn up using graphic representations of the vehicle together with its special structures and based on information which has emerged during the sales discussions.

A CD-ROM from Opel in Germany targets pure advertising very much more specifically. The European subsidiary of General Motors availed itself of modern multimedia technology when, in 1995, it used an interactive journey to advertise its new model, the Opel 'Tigra'. The CD starts with the user landing in the main menu on the first level. There the observer collects advertising films, photographs and brief information. A single click on the video window above the user bar starts a longish advertising film by means of hyperlink. A further chapter, 'Coupés', displays the family tree of the 'Tigra'. The ancestors of the Opel-Coupé are illustrated by means of old advertising spots.

The section entitled 'Environment' shows the Opel advertising spot, 'What a Wonderful World' from two years ago. This thematises the environment aspect and contains further information on the catalytic converter, fuel consumption, engine technology, solvent-free paint and other environmental themes. The 'Tigra-Show' incorporates what the title promises: pictures of the cars and extracts zoom in on the screen.

The second level provides more detailed information on design, safety, technology and service and contains a few goodies in terms of interactive product presentation. Under 'Design', for example, we find information about the boot area: the observer can use the mouse to load a mountain of luggage into an open 'Tigra', thus experiencing the boot, if not exactly physically, certainly in a far more impressive way than if he were reading about the car's capacity in litres in the brochure. The Tigra CD-ROM is a very impressive example of interactive information in the consumer sector.

Nevertheless, the competitors of General Motors are not asleep. In 1994, Volvo USA took an advertising page on the Internet. With this advertisement Volvo succeeded in polishing up its old-fashioned image to a major extent using hi-tech. Similarly, Chrysler can also be contacted at its virtual showroom along the information highway. Here you will find models of Plymouths, Dodges, Jeeps and Eagles. In 1995, European manufacturers were still something of a rarity on the Internet. Only Fiat advertised its follow-up to the Tipo there – the 'Brava'. At the same time

Fiat thematised the new communication instrument very cleverly in both the print and the mass media. The advertisements were based on Windows technology as were the TV spots.

Management reports in multimedia

Management reports on CD-ROM are already current practice. In 1994, IBM published its management report on CD-ROM. The City of Zurich has indulged in multimedia advertising for Zurich as a commercial location with a CD entitled 'Zurich Greater Area'. The CD gives succinct and target-seeking information on Zurich as a commercial location and was commissioned by the real estate companies ABB and Goehner Merkur, as well as the World Trade Center.

Marketing programmes in multimedia

The planning of marketing programmes can be carried out in hypermedia, e.g. the introduction or re-positioning of a new product in a continental or global dimension. Ultimately it is not only the architects of the marketing programme who will be involved in its implementation but, in many cases, a large number of the employees in every country and every branch office. Instead of sending product handbooks and introductory literature along to branch offices in thick and hefty tomes, this can now be done by CD-ROM. Certain sections can be marked up in the Contents section in order to make it clear that this information can be called up at any time on-line on the network and is therefore up-to-date at all times.

Distributing information in this way has the advantage that certain information can be copied from the CD-ROM and modified for the current market conditions. Product roll-outs in Europe call for each and every manufacturer to come to grips with the various different languages in use across the continent. In many cases each individual country translates its own version from the original text. If these tasks are taken care of by the head office of the company involved, the task of field marketing will be made considerably easier. Control may, for instance, be exercised in terms of a requirement for all translations to be published locally on the network or sent to the head office, where they are then made available to everyone. The same applies to photographic material, video clips and other information which originates locally. If the marketing programme is managed over the network and if the existing possibilities are fully utilised, a company which is already established in this area will save itself the costs which this new type of communication inevitably brings with it. Using new technologies oneself is, in addition, the best way to find out how these can best be used as an instrument in the market place.

Multimedia represents an important base tenet for cyber marketing. The shaping of virtual space and the message of adventure which it incorporates is effected by way of information via all media but these media must, basically, be consistently available in digital form. The most important prerequisite for the step-up to cyber marketing is, therefore, an immediate switch to digital information carriers as far as pictures, videos, text, data or sound are concerned.

From product catalogue to virtual market performance

Extensive numbers of product catalogues are subject to the four rules for hypermedia and are suitable for multimedia applications. Here the margin and/or the price level of the goods or services offered as well as market acceptance is crucial as far as cost efficiency is concerned. The product catalogues must, in their interactive form, give the user a real advantage over the printed word. It is only then that it will be possible to use this instrument profitably, e.g. by means of a configuration aid or an electronic order form which will process the order so that it is ready for communication. The order can then be put into the network by modem as electronic post, transmitted directly from the computer network as a fax or printed out and manually faxed or sent by post.

Virtual market performance conveys a service or a physical product which exists by way of an offer to the interested party before this service or product has in fact been created. The market specifications and functions, the concept and all the data necessary to bring about performance are stored in various computers and people's heads. The purely virtual product will never exist as a certain part of the product must already be to hand in a real way. Only a service which is materialised in part can, as a rule, be supplied to a purchaser within the desired time. Undoubtedly, companies will be anxious in the future to create an almost completely virtual product.

Japanese car manufacturers are endeavouring to implement this approach. Production is to be virtualised to the extent that a customised order can be delivered ex works within three working days.

Building up market supply, for instance, with the help of hypermedia, can be the first step towards virtualising a company. At the same time this virtualisation is being built up logically with the customer in mind. This means that all the processes which are not only production-dependent will need to be contracted time-wise. Virtual enterprises are masters when it comes to time-based competition.

Multimedia costs

Multimedia does not come cheap. Typically, around half the costs should be budgeted for in the video filming sector. The entire expenditure incurred in making a video production will be taken up by shooting video clips, i.e. preparations using a script, technical infrastructure, actors and subsequent processing in the studio. Multimedia productions without video are, therefore, very much more favourably priced, and for this reason multimedia applications are often only provided with pictures, sound and texts. The remaining 50% of the overall production costs go on analysis, VDU and graphics development (6% each) and the remainder on developing applications, project management and integration.

Cyber media or virtual reality

What are the perspectives offered by multimedia? These are certainly virtual reality. It is achieved by means of photo-realistic portrayal and simulations. Before he can step up into the cyber world the cybernaut needs to have other items of equipment to hand to enable him to do so.

Cyber media makes a completely new dimension possible in terms of the transmission of information or reality. In all applications such as hypermedia, videos, multimedia or simple software applications, the end user remains outside the medium. The user is aware that he is only an observer. This changes in virtual reality. Here the end user is, as an object, incorporated into the application as a creative participant.

There are five steps to building up virtual reality. First of all, a scene or an object is modelled in virtual space by means of a photo-realistic portrayal, followed by the behaviour of the objects. These relationships are represented visually. Then the interaction equipment is put in and, finally, the scene-dependent real time is actualised.

The cyber era is bringing about the following paradigm changes in terms of digital representation and the transmission of information content:

1. *From abstract symbolism to photo-reality.* The transfer of information, by videotext for example, is communication by means of characters. Virtual space can be photo-realistic. Whether virtual space eventually reaches the consumer via interactive TV or a personal computer is of secondary importance. Companies should, therefore, not only be worrying about the corporate identity of the abstract symbolism of their company logo, but also about their own corporate reality in cyber space.

2. *From object to space.* Communication is, in addition to content, also context. Is the contrast made between the desert and one of its original inhabitants and a new motor car in a television spot a conscious one aimed at capturing the attention of the viewer at the outset? Can a desert-like cyber landscape awaken very unpleasant associations? With space atmosphere is evoked. Virtual space has such a tremendously potent effect because it assumes the place of normal reality. Opportunities in cyber space are only limited by the imagination.

3. *From visualisation to multimedia realisation.* A journey through music is conceivable; depending on his posture, the cybernaut may be a different instrument; depending on the text, spoken various sound sequences may be generated. The hypothetical speed of movement corresponds to the rhythm of the sound sequences. Instead of the visualised object, multimedial experiences occur.

4. *From observer to participant.* The cybernaut immerses himself in virtual reality. He is no longer merely an observer of content but has the opportunity of shaping this himself.

5. *From man – machine interface to man – machine involvement.* Mankind experiences a new feeling when dealing with the virtual world because the interfaces are extended and a smooth integration of the chief senses of seeing, hearing and feeling is possible.

Conclusion: the TIME Industry's Offer of Multimedia as a Basis for Cyber Marketing

The TIME industry (Telecommunication, Information, Media and Entertainment) which is poised to dominate the information era will base its communication services on multimedia. The current electronic marketing instruments are being tooled up by the relevant suppliers to cope with multimediality. Nevertheless, instruments such as fax, interactive versions of videotext and the physical distribution of digital data carriers, such as, for example, CD-ROM today, will continue in existence for some time yet and, in some market segments, will retain their importance because of customer preference.

Certainly, the skilled use of multimedia and hypermedia is a pre-condition for making full use of the opportunities offered by cyber marketing. The Internet already offers minimum multimedia capability and the pre-conditions for the use of hypertext. This is one of the reasons why the Internet and, in particular, the World Wide Web (WWW) rank as a prototype for the implementation of virtual realities within the global information society.

6 THE INTERNET – LIFEBLOOD OF VIRTUAL REALITY

The Internet is a development which is currently being promoted primarily by the computer industry but which grew to maturity within an academic context. It is not the highly acclaimed 'information highway', neither is it the 'Global Information Infrastructure' (GII) but, in its simplest form, the prototype, a pattern for them both. The way forward lies through the cyber world. Viewed from this perspective, the Internet is not merely a fashion phenomenon, but rather the base which will provide the foundation for virtual reality. A large number of adaptations and modifications still remain to be carried out before this can be achieved. However – and here all the experts agree – the Internet is the lifeblood of the information society, even if it is still in its infancy.

Essentially, the Internet is a communication system which represents an equivalent to the telephone system. Even as far as the use of standards is concerned, it ranks as one of the rare exceptions within the computer industry, an industry which, in terms of its historical development, has produced hardly any standards that are truly public or generally accessible. Nevertheless, the standards which make communication on the Internet possible are freely available, public and not the protected property of individual companies. This makes the Internet independent of the manufacturing sector in terms of both software and hardware. As far as the telecommunications industry is concerned, representatives of which banded together at an early stage to form the Geneva-based ITU (International Telecommuniction Union), there is nothing trail-blazing about the world-wide use of standards.

The Internet is not a recent innovation, but rather it represents for scientists a tried and tested method of communicating with one another. Following the discovery of the Internet by the commercial business world, which was already starting to take place in 1995, and taking into account increased interest on the part of commercial enterprises, it is set to undergo some sizeable changes. The potential for earnings associated with the further development of the Internet is providing a huge stimulus as far as the interests of the three primary industries are concerned, something which, in turn, is having a marked effect on the Internet itself.

As far as the business world is concerned, the first commandment is how to understand the network and not how the Internet is used. The key to successful marketing lies not only in understanding the instruments alone, but in understanding the environment in which they are used. As far as the user is concerned, the Internet is a form of technology, a tool, a world of its own, a specific cult.

From a technical point of view, the Internet represents the interlinking of distributed and open systems. 'Distributed' means that there is no central station with a control function. 'Open' means that the basic rules are freely publicised and accessible to everyone. Every user has the opportunity to shape the network and thus to make his or her own contribution towards its further development.

The new technological possibilities on offer – completely unrestricted global communication – form the basis for the Internet culture. There is a strong link between the range of applications possible and the discipline which applies to all forms of interchange on the system. Therefore, just as technology is public, global and distributed, the disciplines prevalent on the Internet are likewise public and unwritten. Central control may not be tolerated, but any violation of the fixed, unwritten rules on the part of a single user will be mercilessly punished by every other user. Internet is the first technological phenomenon to successfully bring about a global change in terms of the interpersonal approach. There may, in the past, have been centralised control of the mass communication media, but this is no longer the case as far as the Internet is concerned.

The Internet Today

In order to appreciate the present-day situation as far as the Internet is concerned, we need to know how the Internet came about. It was in 1969 that work started on a crisis- and bombproof computer network for the American Defence Ministry. The ARPAnet (Advanced Research Projects Agency network) which existed at the time provided a means of linking various military stations and research institutes. Primarily, the ARPAnet served as a research project aimed at setting up stable and robust computer networks. A further function of the network was to guarantee communication, even in the wake of a nuclear exchange. As far as the realisation of these aims was concerned, the main technical problem lay in the fact that the various computers available from different manufacturers were incompatible. The computer systems available all used different operating software and this made communication between individual computers impossible. Before any thought at all could be given to establishing a network of computers, there needed to be a common base, something which presupposed the definition of a generally binding protocol for the different computers to use to communicate with one another. The TCP/IP (transmission control protocol/Internet protocol) became a standard which is still in force today.

During the course of the late 1980s, the original ARPAnet was split and, on the scientific side, the NSF (National Science Foundation) network developed.[50] This network still exists and is operated via the advanced network system (ANS). By incorporating other systems it has proved possible to devise a network of computer systems, each of which communicates with other networks via its own network, i.e. it is 'inter-netted', hence giving rise to the name 'Internet'. The Internet is really a medley of different computer networks, some smaller, some larger, which is based on bridgehead functions and not an 'international network', as might suggest itself at first glance to the observer. The DNS (domain name service) was created to enable users to find the different organisations and their users on the network.

A link was forged between the scientific networks of universities and colleges in every country in the world. Researchers use the Internet primarily for exchanging personal information by means of electronic post (e-mail). Electronic mail is the most frequently used function on the Internet. For information on the progress of projects within specific interest groups whose members are able to communicate with each other simultaneously by way of text, the Usenet News group was created. The FTP (file transfer protocol) function enables software to be transmitted throughout the network. Of course, this also gives rise to the possibility as far as users are concerned of mutual access to the scientific databases and gathering information in digital form. The Internet in this form was not designed for commercial activities. Access to the network was a simple matter, but a high level of knowledge was called for to be able to find one's way around the different functions and the clamour of the network.

Who operates the Internet? Actually – nobody. The Internet belongs to nobody and is not centrally operated by any company, organisation or state. The Internet emerged on the intellectual soil of mutual understanding and cooperation in the scientific sector. There is no central authority to decree conditions. Based on this initial position, opinions on the future of the Internet are split into two camps. One camp is of the opinion that the network will have to be globally regulated between states. The other feels that the Internet in a non-regulated state reflects the real world with all its diversity of opinion and conflicting views. If the network were to be regulated and interstate supervision introduced, it would mean the death of free speech and with it entry into an Orwell-esque era of total control.

Which view will gain the upper hand and which side will ultimately succeed with the most convincing arguments is probably a matter of how the network and the data highway are handled.

The breakthrough within the non-academic world could only take place once user guidance and access to the Internet had been greatly simplified. User-friendly connection to the network was a development which, for once, was not engendered in Silicon Valley, USA, but, amazingly, was born on Lake Geneva in Switzerland.

The World Wide Web (WWW)

The World Wide Web (WWW), also known as W3 or, simply, 'the Web', originated in the CERN (European Centre for Nuclear Research) in Geneva. In 1989, Tim Berners-Lee and Robert Cailliau put forward an information system to be based on hypertext. In 1990, the first browser was written.[51] A browser is a software programme which enables a link to the Web to be created from a local PC. Inside the Web, the opposite of the browser, the server, makes the connection with the local PC possible and maintains it. The term 'server' designates a computer and a software programme within the network. The server responds to the enquiries made by the browser and delivers a Web document on to the computer of the enquiring user who is using the browser. This may consist of a single page (Web page) or a multipage digital document. The communication link between the browser and the server is regulated by the HTTP (Hyper-Text Transfer Protocol). The Web pages are written chiefly in HTML (Hyper-Text Mark-up Language). HTML demonstrates radical limitations which is leading to work being carried out on new languages for programming Web pages.[52] One of the trail-blazing programming languages and logical concepts as regards the use of resources on the Internet is being developed by the Sun Microsystems company. 'Java' is set to establish itself in the future as a standard for software applications in network operation.

In 1991, the original browser was extended by CERN to enable it to be used on a series of different platforms. 'Platform' in this context is the term used to designate the hardware and the operating system used by the relevant computer installation. The advantages of the CERN browser gave impetus to a very wide dissemination. In 1993, there were 50 Web servers world-wide. In May of the same year, the US National Center for Supercomputing Applications (NCSA) issued a browser by the name of 'X-Mosaic'.[53] Mosaic was created by a 22-year-old post graduate student called Marc Andreessen. This browser permits the portrayal of colours and graphics. X-Mosaic was free of charge and available for Apple Macintosh and Microsoft Windows, which caused it to spread at a meteoric rate. There was an immediate increase in the number of Web servers and only two years later, it reached 50,000.

1994 was the actual Year of the Web. In May, the first global WWW Conference took place at CERN in Geneva. 400 developers participated in this conference which was also dubbed 'The Woodstock of the Web'. In October, the second WWW Conference was held in the USA. 1300 people attended this conference which was organised by NASA. At the end of 1994, the Web had 10,000 servers, 2,000 of which were being commercially used, and already 10 million users. Data transactions were of similar magnitude, as if the entire works of Shakespeare were being simultaneously transmitted every second. By 1995, the Internet was attracting phenomenal attention in all media around the world. This is primarily due to the WWW, which enabled the ordinary PC user to gain access relatively easily to the world of the Internet. The Web is an example of how auxiliary activities within the context of basic research can generate progress in a completely unintentional way.

Through the development of WWW the positive aspects of the Internet were brought even more prominently into the foreground and on to the user's screen in a simple and straightforward manner. Access to an enormous number of the most diverse databases is an ideal basis for building up knowledge. With WWW the Internet became a global medium for the distribution and exchange of information. Today it is a speedy and cost-effective vehicle for world-wide communication. The Internet is enjoying increased acceptance and thus incredible growth.

The downside of the positive aspects lies in the fact that contact can only be made by means of direct addressing: a complete and up-to-date directory of subscribers, such as the telephone directory, does not exist. There is no actual structuring of the search facilities available on the Internet. For the individual user this means that he has to spend a great deal of time looking for a piece of highly specific information. The expression 'surfing' on the Web is a graphic way of underlining the fact that there is no clear path when it comes to searching for information, but the user moves on, as it were, over the piles of interrelated search concepts. Hunting for subscribers or content is inefficient. And the explosion and increase in user numbers and the information brought in by them in the form of Web pages is extending the existing chaos. John Naisbitt, a researcher into trends and author of a number of mega-trend works, estimates that the number of Internet users will be a billion by the year 2000. In July 1995, there were already 25 million Internet users and 60,000 networks and, in September 1995, some 6 million servers.[54] In February 1995, electronic mail could be sent to 154 countries. The pioneer of Internet and co-founder of TCP/IP, Vinton Cerf, currently MCI Vice President, estimates that the number of users world-wide will be 200 million by the year 2000.

The WWW as one aspect of the Internet

When people talk about the Internet, they are almost always referring simply to the Web. The World Wide Web is the linking of information which is presented to the accessing user in the form of Web sites and the contents of which are linked together by means of hyperlinks. At the same time, the relevant information is strewn world-wide over the entire network. The actual impact of the Internet is sustained by companies setting up their own Web sites.

Modern companies mark out their image as leading enterprises by being present on the Internet in the form of a Web site. If they are really clever, they combine their presence on the Internet with their presence on the networks of commercial on-line suppliers. The product and the customers are the crucial factors in this combination.

The transition from purely being present on the Web to cyber marketing is, however, a very lengthy process. As in the real world in a pulsating bazaar, business can only be concluded if an energetic seller is present. In the case of the Internet, this means offering a prospective buyer the opportunity of an electronic dialogue. In the case of cyber marketing, it is matter of the ability to service the individual customer relationship.

With the massive spread of Web clients who make access possible to the World Wide Web, the taboo on the commercial use of the Internet was broken. Even if marketing in the WWW is acceptable today, the Web page should nevertheless be based on information and not just be an advertisement. Visitors to the Web site should be able to learn something. The Internet is still very densely populated by information gatherers asking about facts and graphics. If the market performance to be put over is not itself information, then the way in which the products are portrayed and put over must be entertaining and informative, even an interactive experience. The visitor should be asked to communicate his views, opinions and requirements via e-mail. This step will open the door to a dialogue. The Web page should be frequently freshened up with new information to ensure that it retains its attraction. Regular visitors expect new information periodically and, if this does not happen, they will stay away and the Web site will be ignored. Relevance and attractiveness make for increasingly frequent visits. The investment made by companies in their subsidiaries in virtual space will not pay out immediately. They cannot expect sales to leap solely because they have a virtual office in the shape of a Web site.

Access to the Internet

The potential consumer and user of the Internet today normally dials his way into the Internet via an Internet access provider. In addition to access to the various services such as e-mail, Telnet, Usenet, FTP and Web-Access, these internet providers enable all persons and companies to install a Web site on the provider's computer. The Web site represents the minimum presence on the Internet.

Larger companies have their own Internet server on the network. They are present on the network via a dedicated computer and maybe have a great deal of information on this machine. However, in addition to a computer, there is also a need for a firm communication link to the network. The computer is allocated an IP code. As well as direct addressing via the domain, there is, at the level of the physical computer, a special form of address. Today's IP code is to be replaced by a new one during the next few years which will enable up to 200 million addresses to be processed in the future.

Depending on data throughput, a simple telephone line may be just as feasible a vehicle as a high speed line. The computer can also be configured as a node point for the entire enterprise. The decision on whether to incorporate others will hinge on the particular activity, the number of users, anticipated access to the information and the cost. In many cases, access via a commercial Internet provider is advisable initially.

In practically every country, Internet providers are burgeoning like mushrooms. All private network operators such as CompuServe, AOL (America Online), Prodigy or MicrosoftNet offer access to the Internet. Wherever the Internet is mentioned in the following, it goes without saying that these commercial network suppliers are included.

Other functions on the Internet in addition to the Web

The WWW stands in the spotlight of public attention. However, the Internet is more than the WWW. The other functions are supported in different ways, depending on the browsers and access software used. Certain functions lend background support to the WWW. In the near future, these other functions will be integrated into the browsers and therefore become easily accessible for the users.

Electronic mail

Internal and external communication is a very important reason for companies to use the Internet. Smaller companies in particular and those operating from different sites can set up a communications structure on the Internet using electronic mail which is highly efficient due to being rapid and cost-effective.[55] With e-mail, the sender can respond directly and personally to one or more addressees, in the same way as he can using letter post: a message can reach a contact within seconds or, at the worst, which is very seldom the case, within a maximum of 10 hours. Worldwide fax communication at local rates is a very attractive way of using the Internet. The addressing of mail on the Internet takes place via the DNS (domain name system). This system overlays the physical computer IP address to give increased clarity. The DNS addresses are translated into the IP address by special computers. DNS application in the USA is chiefly on the basis of subject-related name giving, whilst in Europe the geographical area plays a major role.

With e-mail, the user has a gap-free record of the correspondence conducted. Electronic mail also reduces the barriers between people at different levels within a hierarchy. For this reason e-mail is regarded as a significant communication medium in flat level organisations. Other data files such as text, picture, sound, video can be appended to e-mails at no expense and sent or they can be sent several times without any trouble.

In marketing, e-mail with additional functions such as automatic answering functions and electronic address lists, is becoming a very important instrument. If a new product is introduced on to the market, the relevant announcement can also be sent to all interested customers via electronic mail. In addition, the electronic address for information about this new product appears in all media. If an enquiry is received, a standardised but individually formulated reply is generated by means of a software routine. One message will answer the majority of questions posed. Moreover, the prospective buyer receives the addresses where the product is being demonstrated or from which the product can be ordered. For highly information-intensive market services, an electronic questionnaire may be sent to interested customers. They fill in the form with the necessary details and the form is then used for final drawing up of the quotation.

If a customer wishes a company to provide him with information about a specialised area in the future too, then his address will be placed on a suitable distribution list. Book publishers, for example, use this method to send highly personalised advertisements for new publications – at an unbeatable price.

Within the public relations sector, press announcements can be made very quickly and, most importantly, with good timing. A company with a global operation would have had major problems reaching the press simultaneously with the media available to date. It would have found itself constantly having to work with advance notifications and waiting periods. Now we have e-mail addresses for press contacts, this is no longer a problem. Announcements to the world's press can be made simultaneously and at a precisely controlled point in time from a single office.

Two important aspects of e-mail are access to addresses and the use of the addresses. There are available on the Internet certain visual options for finding addresses. However, these are still highly unsatisfactory. The simplest way is for companies to give their customers the opportunity to get in touch with them via e-mail. In this way they obtain the sender's details including his address. Traditional communication options are used to obtain the addresses initially. An important aspect of the customer database is the fact that customers can be contacted electronically.

The e-mail addresses cannot, unlike letter post addresses, be used for mail shots. Established usage on the Internet shuns mail-shots utterly. One publishing company, by way of a test, sent advertising for a book to 2000 addressees via e-mail. The reaction was overwhelming. Within a matter of hours the publishing house had received masses of replies. The irate Internet communicators threatened to list the name of the publisher and the book in information bulletins, together with a call to boycott. Other attempts to apply mass marketing on the Internet have ended in veritable avalanches of letters which hopelessly overloaded the sender's computer and rendered it inaccessible.

In this respect, the Internet is not only a form of technology, not only an aid, but also a concept representing a particular culture, a culture that refuses to allow aggressive and penetrative marketing any longer. The supply of information is controlled by the market. The dialogue is very simple but it is, in principle, triggered by the prospective buyer and determined by the customer.

The Eldorado of Telnet: stalking the competition

Terminal emulation for computers on the Internet is made possible by the Telnet service. With Telnet it is possible to use a great number of computers on the worldwide network. One exception is the IBM mainframes which can be dialled using tn3270 instead of Telnet. As far as marketing is concerned, Telnet does not play a direct role, apart from the possibility of searching for information on competitors' computers. Telnet is a paradise of diverse information which betrays more about markets and competitors.

It is estimated that a minimum of 6000 gigabytes of cost-free software and other data files, for instance, graphics and audio data, are publicly accessible on the network. It is as easy to find photographs of famous actors as it is to find satellite photographs from NASA. Since the data files are highly comprehensive, this information is mostly made available on the Internet in compressed form. After the data files have been downloaded on to the user's local machine, these are unpacked and processed in non-compressed form for their application. Data file transfer on the Internet is made possible by FTP (file transfer protocol). If companies make extensive data files, complete with photographic material, maybe even video material, accessible to their customers, assistance should be given to the customer to help him successfully unpack the data files, even if he has no knowledge of the details. This particularly applies to company reports, product presentations and extensive information which is filed in compressed form and accessible by means of polling.[56]

Usenet – the living world of the special interest groups

Defining the criteria 'market segments' and 'target groups' in traditional marketing is a fine art. The criteria may be purely external characteristics: age, education, income and other data which can be determined statistically. The internal picture of interests and inclinations within the target group psychograph is being opened out by external traits.

There are on the Internet thousands of special interest groups which organise themselves into Newsgroups.[57] For marketing specialists this is a dream. Nevertheless, this fact can cause sleepless nights as the external characteristics of the individual persons are missing. In addition, the unwritten laws of the Internet forbid the wonted direct-to-the-masses approach of the real world.[58] Why should this be so?

As a global virtual community, the Internet naturally also offers the opportunity of a world-wide interchange of opinions. To this end there are currently almost 5000 Newsgroups in existence. Each Newsgroup is dedicated to a single defined subject. This Internet function of communicating with the special interest groups is termed 'Usenet'.

Initially the Usenet existed independently of the Internet, as the Usenet had been developed on the basis of the UNIX to UNIX Copy Protocol (UUCP). As is well known, the Internet communicates on the basis of TCP/IP for data transfer. The interchange of information between the two systems is made possible by means of a special protocol. The Newsgroups in the Usenet have become, for many Internet users, a natural and highly-rated part of their on-line activities. The majority of users are not aware that it is not an original Internet service.

The individual Newsgroups on the Usenet are divided up hierarchically under subject headings. The top level of this initial stage comprises seven headings, in addition to which, over the course of time, a few 'alternative' subject areas have become established.

In view of the the enormous diversity of what is available, it is not possible to characterise the Usenet in terms of its content. Nevertheless, it is true to say that, within the Usegroups, any subject you may care to think up is being addressed in some way. Since the Usenet is constantly changing, it is subject to continuous change; every day new Newsgroups are being set up whilst other special interest groups are no longer available due to a lack of initiative or interest. You enrol as a participant in a group and receive all the information that comes into the Newsgroup.

The majority of Newsgroups can be viewed internationally. This means that any announcement made by such a group will be read throughout the world. Frequently another member of the group will subsequently send a comment on the first message on a certain subject to the Newsgroup. In this way a proper conversation will develop, which is also termed a 'thread'. These conversations can be picked out of data file archives using keywords and also read at a later time.

The Usegroups are very important in cyber marketing in that they enable trends, up-and-coming interests and also opinion makers to be identified.

Netiquette: correct form in virtual space

This notion has given rise to certain 'rules of behaviour' on the Usenet.[59] These rules are often termed the 'Usenet netiquette' or 'netiquette' for short and they have become established in all the other sectors of the network. Since the discussions take place globally, the Usenet in a way also represents a challenge in the sense of international understanding. The sender of a message or a comment cannot be identified positively. Communication therefore harbours a certain degree of anonymity.

Naturally manners and practices vary greatly between the different groups and for this reason different Usenet rules of conduct have become established over a period of time. This is the reason for the recommendation that new members initially spend one or two weeks reading contributions before posting their own messages.

One general rule is not to overload Newsgroups which have hitherto been very well 'visited' with unnecessary messages, for instance, by means of 'test messages' which are used to try out the functions of the Usenet. In the majority of Newsgroups there exist so-called 'FAQs' (frequently asked questions) in which frequently asked questions on a particular subject are listed together with the answers. For questions on a particular subject there is mostly an e-mail address given with the FAQs.

A further peculiarity of on-line communication is the fact that passages of text written in capitals are construed as SHOUTING. This is just as unpleasant as it would be in a 'proper' conversation and should therefore only be used where the context is particularly appropriate. Some groups react very angrily to contributions which give the impression of being even to the smallest extent commercial. Winning interest and customers in the Usegroups therefore calls for a very special flair.

The search instruments

The size of the Internet and the fact that the borders of this virtual universe are constantly being pushed outwards, calls for instruments of orientation. How can we otherwise locate the infinite amount of information, data files and programmes available?

The importance of the search systems for efficient cyber marketing should not be under-estimated. A user searching for something on the network will sooner or later make use of the search instruments available in virtual space in order to shorten the search time.[60]

Archie

One of these search systems is Archie. Behind this name is concealed a powerful tool for searching for data files available on FTP servers. The function is carried out by means of keywords.

In this system, information on the data files offered on FTP servers is constantly being filed away in a central database, which is up-dated in this way every 30 days or so. In other words, during this period the search system runs through all the FTP servers managed, gathering information on the data files available in each.

This information can be made use of via a link to an Archie server. There are three possible ways of effecting this link: Telnet, an Archie client or e-mail.

In addition to Archie, a second database exists in this system called 'Whatis'. If Archie looks through the names of the data files of the entries filed in its database in accordance with the search-concept indicated, the abbreviated information stored with the data file names is used in a Whatis search. However, the list for the Whatis search does not give any addresses for the appropriate FTP servers but only an overview of the data file names along with the relevant description.

Often it is not easy to guess which sequence of characters is used in the name of a particular data file and it is therefore in many cases worth detouring via the Whatis database. Once we know what data file it is we are looking for, we can initiate an Archie search using the file's name as a keyword; the result will be a list of FTP servers on which the information for which we are searching is stored.

In cyber marketing, a duty exists to make the path to the relevant information as easy as possible for interested cyber marketeers. For this reason it is very important that they should know how users find their way around in the world of the Internet. It is only in this way that the relevant systematics can be used to lead those interested into their own information sectors. The following principle applies: the more communication can be effected via the desired data file, the more rapid and precise the result of the search will also be.

Gopher

Gopher is another system which makes it possible to navigate sites and services on the Internet. Travelling through the Internet with Gopher does not call for any knowledge at all about the information which is being sought. In the case of an FTP meeting, it is necessary to know which server the data sought is on and in which directory it is located. In a Telnet link, the log-in ID will even be required to get to the data. Gopher does not require any of this information to reach the desired target.

There are almost 1000 Gopher servers to make navigation possible on the network. They manage Internet resources over the entire world and can be accessed using a simple user guide. The link structure to the individual computers operates in the background, unseen by the user. However, there is a short waiting period with this process. Gopher is so popular that the Internet resources managed by Gopher servers are also termed 'Gopher space'. Access to Gopher space is either by accessing an appropriate client programme or via Telnet. In addition, Gopher offers the possibility of storing interested stations on the way through virtual space with the aid of so-called 'bookmarks'. This means that one can return to these sites at any time.

These characteristics make Gopher servers the ideal anchoring point for marketing activities. Skilled negotiation of Gopher space can produce a great deal of interest, especially bearing in mind that Gopher servers are currently not yet overloaded with commercial information. As Gopher space grew, it became increasingly more difficult to find certain information quickly, because the number of new servers was growing at an impressive speed. As a result, information being sought often lay buried 15 hierarchical levels deep in an area which it was more or less impossible to find. Staff at the University of Nevada in Reno, however, came up with a brilliant idea to solve this problem. They developed 'VERONICA', a tool which helps to find something defined within Gopher. The development of software tools which help the user to navigate in his odyssey in cyber space is poised to increase in leaps and bounds in the future. We should never forget that publishing information on the Internet is not difficult, but finding it on the other hand is!

Search services as a communication strategy

The difficulty of finding one's way about the Web has created new opportunities in terms of the transmission of information. Yahoo is a search service whereby suppliers pay a fee to have their presence on the Web and the services which they offer registered. Visitors approaching Yahoo with an enquiry will have the search results for the subscribing suppliers downloaded as a matter of priority on to their screens.

Communication strategy in cyber marketing will centre less on the question 'How do I contact my target groups?' than on 'How will my potential customers find me?' This turn-about question as regards the conduct of communication illustrates how important it is to acquire presence in the popular and highly-frequented search instruments by means of registration: presence with high-priority advertising within the search instruments means existence in cyber space.

Commercial Network Suppliers – On-line Services

Various commercial on-line services offer companies the possibility of setting up an on-line presence. In the USA, CompuServe, America Online (AOL), Prodigy and Delphi are the most widespread. In Europe, CompuServe has succeeded in establishing a presence. T-Online or Europe Online from Bertelsmann, as well as various local continental suppliers, are set to make their mark on this growth market. Larger companies such as AT&T and MCI have recently started setting up their own on-line services.

The commercial on-line services offer their users a well-ordered electronic world with improved navigation facilities and specialist information services which are, as a rule, easy to find. At the same time, the content of very many contributions has been checked out by secondary supervisory personnel prior to being made accessible to the general public on the network. The larger on-line services offer various functions on their networks.

On-line services such as CompuServe have copied Usenet's function. Theirs are called 'forums'. Each individual forum has a special keyword allocated to it, which may be a particular field, a company or have geographical or subject-related connotations.

Forums where people organise themselves into a meeting to have a chat and where information can be lodged in data libraries are of great interest as far as marketing is concerned. The user groups or forums offer a natural vehicle for the formation of diverse target groups. One of the most important functions in cyber marketing is to find Newsgroups which correspond to a certain target group profile. One further option is to form such groups and manage them in the background by exercising moderation. Nevertheless, companies too can set up entire forums using these commercial on-line suppliers. In these forums, business activities are not frowned upon although the suppliers do stipulate boundaries which must not be overstepped.

Using a commercial on-line service may have major advantages, for instance, little known firms stand a very much better chance of raising their profile within the framework of a commercial service than on the Internet. The use of polished sound and graphics messages is currently more successful via an on-line service. These firms are constantly working to improve comfort. This also applies to customer guidance. Even novices feel that they are better able to find their way about in an on-line service than in the chaos of the Internet. Another area to which this applies is that of technical support which is offered via electronic media. Customers who are not software freaks or computer gurus are better off with a commercial supplier. The commercial service can, by means of its promotional opportunities, bring hundreds of thousands of possible customers to the electronic door. The commercial suppliers use different rating methods for on-line services and charge them to the customer's credit card.

CompuServe subscribers can post electronic mail into the Internet at large or, for example, to a Prodigy user. CompuServe was the first of the larger suppliers to make direct access to the Internet possible by way of its dial-in nodes. Today an on-line service without integrated access to the unconstrained world of the Internet has become unthinkable.

A disadvantage of using a commercial supplier is that control of communication is handed over to a third party. In addition, all suppliers charge a fee for using them.

CommerceNet

In the USA, the CommerceNet consortium is one of the most important sectors when it comes to transacting business. CommerceNet was designed as an Internet-based infrastructure for the purpose of doing business electronically (e-commerce). The American government made the formation of this non-profitmaking organisation possible under the TRP initiative (Technology Reinvestment Project). TRP was part of President Clinton's 1994 economy revitalisation programme. CommerceNet offers services aimed at making electronic business possible, e.g. services such as specialist directories and reference information, certification of manufacturers and credit information, notary services on the network as well as financial services and the arrangement of transport capacity. CommerceNet makes access to the Internet particularly easy and holds software tools for companies to enable them to easily make their presence on the Internet a reality, as well as software programmes for security mechanisms, authenticity tests and coding which can be supported from within the application. CommerceNet's services are aimed primarily at the medium-sized and smaller companies within the USA which are in a position to set up a global presence using this medium.

CompuServe information services

CompuServe is one of the leading lights when it comes to on-line business.[61] With the acquisition of Spry, the company which developed Web browsers, CompuServe became the first on-line service with an open door from its own network into the Internet at large. CompuServe is poised to intensify its efforts in respect of the integration of functions, both as regards its own network as well as the opportunity of journeying on the Internet. This company already has more than 3000 different products and services available. CompuServe began its on-line activities in 1979; in 1989, it became active in Europe and is now operating globally with an increasing number of nodes and countries.

Barry Berkov of CompuServe is anticipating a markedly structured segmentation of on-line services aimed at servicing the various interests of users in years to come. With improved functions in the speech communication sector, the on-line service can increasingly become a cheaper alternative to the telephone. The advantage of private, commercial on-line suppliers such as CompuServe lies in the comparably high level of security in transacting business electronically. The functions for actioning payments for information services or sales via CompuServe are sure and simple.

This fact is reflected in the range of business activities on the networks of commercial on-line suppliers. Examples include the flower shop 1-800-Flowers or JC Penny in CompuServe. People throughout the USA can select a bouquet or a flower arrangement from this virtual flower shop and send it to a target address. The products of J.C. Penny, a large warehouse chain with a mail order arm, are accessible via CompuServe.

America Online

America Online (AOL) is one of the larger on-line services. It started in Europe at the end of 1995 as a joint venture with Bertelsmann. America Online is very strongly geared to electronic commerce and offers a good platform from which to contact end customers. AOL has demonstrated extremely high growth rates in the USA over the past two years and is extremely aggressive when it comes to acquiring new users.[62] Jack Davies, President of AOL International, feels that AOL distinguishes itself by offering the new generation of 'infopreneurs' a good platform for their businesses.[63] AOL's strengths lie in the fact that they offer basic services which make it easy for the user to orientate and find his way about. Questionnaires reinforce this view: many consumers prefer the structure of an on-line supplier to surfing on the open Internet. AOL tries to keep content – including commercial content – exclusive and non-recurring.

Microsoft network

The most recent, but at the same time the strongest player for influence and a dominant position among private networks, on-line services and access to the Internet, is Microsoft, Bill Gates' enterprise. With its new operating system, Windows 95, Microsoft created direct access to Microsoft Network (MSN), but this has not succeeded in establishing a dominant position in the market. Bill Gates regards the Internet and, in particular, the development of WWW as the most important happening since the development of the PC.[64] Microsoft had lost the race for predominance in the browser sector even before it began: Gates' giant company had slept through the start and only woke up when Netscape were dominating the market.

As Microsoft see it, the digital revolution can be split into three generations. First of all, the mainframe generation, today often called the 'legacy system', marketed by companies such as IBM. Secondly, the personal computer generation, which was made famous on the market by APPLE with its Macintosh machine. The third stage is public digital communication by means of the Internet, triggered by the development of WWW. The first phase of the information super-highway is being initialised by the PCs which make private and business communication possible through the Internet. Digital television will be incorporated into the communications structure as a secondary item. Other terminal equipment developments will follow those two terminal machines that we know today – PC and TV. Microsoft aims to remain true to its company philosophy and to dominate the end user market with its software programmes in terms of access equipment to the information highway, as well as to generate even more end-user business in selected areas with content related to the network.[65] On the other hand, Microsoft's horizon is no longer free of clouds or question marks as to whether Bill Gates will really succeed in equipping a large part of the approximately 280 million PCs sold up to 1996 with the key software for cyber space.

AT&T and DEC

John Petrillo, President of AT&T Business Communication, stated at a conference during Telecom 95 in Geneva that AT&T had been very surprised at the success of the WWW. The WWW will bring about a massive change in the structure of the on-line industry. The approximately US$250 billion turnover on the Internet between mid-1994 and 1995 is a strong indicator for the future of this market to which AT&T has devoted itself. Strategically speaking, the telecommunications companies are in an unusually good position to dominate the network over a long period. They are in possession of the access ramps, the telephone keys and, with their rates policy, they determine a considerable part of the costs which arise for the users.

Very similar statements were made by Henri Gouraud, who is responsible for Digital Equipment (DEC)'s Internet business in Europe. Although DEC had actively participated in the development of the Internet since 1982 and were following the development intensively, the company had been absolutely amazed at the resounding success of WWW. These statements underline very clearly that, in the competitive environment of the information era, time no longer ranks as a barrier to entry.

The classic computer giants such as IBM, DEC, Hewlett-Packard or Compaq are finding it difficult to get along with the new developments. With the launching of a network computer (NC) by the database and software company Oracle in the middle of 1996, the boundaries of the hereditary fields of activity within the TIME industry are becoming blurred.

Current Challenges and the Future of the Internet

There exists, in conjunction with the Internet, a whole series of challenges which will need to be addressed in the future.[66] In addition to legal questions, security considerations are very much to the fore. Technological development is being driven on with absolutely no regulation or influence on the part of any state. The communications industries will be setting up band widths with good transmission capacity. Purely using the Internet throws up fewer problems than questions about how to deal with it.

One thing is certain: the cyber world will never be any more perfect than our real world – it was after all shaped by very different people – but the cyber world parades the ugly, diverse and loathsome aspects of human existence very much more globally before our eyes.

The laws and justice which apply to our world also apply to the cyber world. However, due to the lack of geography in cyber space, quite a few interpretational problems are bound to crop up. There are certain allusions in laws and decrees which are geographically based and cannot be easily transferred to the virtual world. Legal standards which are binding network-wide will no doubt be drawn up. The political will to do this is also evident from the statements made by the leading states at the G7 Summit at the beginning of 1995. However, the political and international process of trying to agree firm rules and regulations will not be particularly easy. The various positions are highly diverse. Authorities in the USA support a moderately liberal viewpoint. The European states, especially the apparatus of the European Union, is anxious to ensure that the content and the development of the global information infrastructure are strongly regulated.

Points of contention exist as regards permissible coding methods, state intervention in the preparation of politically undesirable propaganda or the accessibility of information which infringes ethical or moral principles under the catchword 'pornography'. These questions will no doubt be occupying both the public and political factions in the future. Another sure thing is that commercial influences will have an important role to play in this opinion-forging process.

Technological development

A longer-term view can be taken of the technologies which are ripe for marketing within the hardware sector than is the case in the software sector, where new developments are taking place along a broad front.[67] Many functions which open up new possibilities for the user will be realised based on developments in the realm of software.

The TCP/IP protocol will be replaced during the next few years by a new standard which will considerably simplify the transmission of multimedia. The addresses available on the Internet will be extensively extended by means of a new address system. This is absolutely essential if the growing number of users are going to stand a chance of being incorporated in the network. The language for hyperlink applications, like the programming of Web pages, will be replaced by a new generation, for example, 'Java' from SUN Microsystems.

A fundamental and long-term predication as regards the technical development of the Internet is almost impossible. This applies in particular to one very great weakness of the Internet – real-time interactivity. If we talk about the Internet as an interactive system, this statement, from a strictly technical point of view, is incorrect. As the link between a client and a server on the network only exists as long as a transmission is taking place, Internet is not really an interactive real-time system. In a system of this kind the communication link exists regardless of whether a transmission is taking place at the moment or not. A telephone conversation is a real-time link, but the Internet is not. For certain applications, such as direct video communication or trading in electronic markets, real-time communication is, nevertheless, essential.

Security

Jim Clark, one of the founders of the company Silicon Graphics and currently Chairman of Netscape Communications, says that the Internet is no less secure than the telephone. The combination of security procedures at the level of both hardware and software affords a good degree of protection. The employment of codes in particular makes for highly secure communication. Many of the security problems we hear people complaining about are primarily a matter of handling and managing the relevant systems. Looking back on the development of the Internet, it is clear that security within the network has not been a priority and that, when decisions were taken in regard to communication barriers and user identification, the aim was to achieve good universal communication capability. The discussion about security will certainly never die down completely. It will, however, lessen once people in general understand that absolute security can never be guaranteed in a human system. The important thing is to enlist the help of suitable specialists in the spheres of network security, coding and access authorisation.

Cybercash and banking in the virtual world

By the very nature of the business, banking services in particular are predestined for the Internet. Nevertheless a number of institutes in Europe are hesitating for security reasons. The Bayerische Hypotheken- und Wechselbank was the first German bank on the WWW. It specialises in providing information on capital assets. The DIRI (Dresden International Research Institute), a Dresden Bank company, was one of the first to offer current information and publications on different sectors of the capital market. The DIRI server pursues the 'most closed policy' here. This means that most of the data is only available to visitors with an appropriate access permit. Part of what is offered is also accessible to anonymous individuals without any specific user recognition. Anyone who wishes to have access to all the information can obtain the conditions of use by e-mail.

This kind of application clarifies the background to the discussion about 'micropayment'. If it were possible to charge a minimum amount for each Web page read and transmitted, then the cost of information, documentation and enquiry services could be very efficiently reckoned up. In the long term the results of all the research and analysis conducted by all the banks should be available on the network. This is very obvious as the majority of investors or those who bear responsibility for investment policy already possess screens on which they monitor happenings in the markets.

Securities dealers in the USA were active on-line at a very early stage. Brokers such as Quick & Reilly, E*Trade Securities and Max Ule's Tickerscreen can be reached via America Online or CompuServe. Net Investor, National Discount, Lombard Institutional, Charles Schwab or Aufhäuser are on the WWW. Others, for example, Fidelity Brokerage, can only be contacted direct. The charges made by these dealers cannot be undercut by conventional practice and the trend towards the discount broker via the network will strengthen in the future. Salomon Brothers use their Web page to propagate services such as research asset management, securities dealings and information on company structures and career options. J.P. Morgan is in no way inferior to its competitors.[68] Stock companies, too, have discovered the Internet as a very efficient way of communicating current rates for their investment stock. Investment banking overall can, using the network, become very much simpler and more rationalised. This is achieved by affording individual investors direct access to their actual day-to-day portfolio. Likewise, it should be possible for transaction business to be input directly into the system by the investor. In the same way this can be forwarded to the electronic markets system via the internal systems.

Bank Austria was the first bank in Austria to make accounts accessible via the Internet. In Germany, the direct banking section of the Commerzbank has adjusted to the new kind of banking.[69] Worldwide it was possible at a very early stage to peruse Home Pages, with the services offered by the Bank of America, Barclays, Chase Manhattan Bank and Citibank.

The first real virtual bank became active on the Internet in October 1994. First Virtual Holdings Inc. (FV) is the umbrella company for the performance of finance and marketing services, particularly in the sector of buying and selling information for everyone with access to the Internet. FV was the first bank to introduce a specific technology for a system of payment on the Internet. Within only nine months of the commencement of its activities on the Internet, First Virtual had customers in 64 countries, had 500 sellers (such as Apple Computers and Reuter) endorsing this method of payment and was recording 200,000 new accesses every day. First Virtual developed a very simple, user-friendly and highly cost-effective transaction system to guarantee the link between the supplier and the buyer. Buyers do not need any special software for this and may remain anonymous. Purchasers can register with First Virtual for only US$2. Other suppliers are quoting registration costs of US$10. The sucess of First Virtual is based on a profound knowledge of problem-solving in the coding and data communications sector.

The Netbank is a further pioneer of virtual banking in cyber space. Netbank makes transactions between customers and dealers possible by means of Netcash. This system is similar to the transaction of cheques in the real world. The monetary currency of the Dutch company Digicash is called 'E Cash'. This third-party payment system works with special software which is required as a supplement to the browser. It models cash from the known real world in the form of digital coins. Of course, it is quite possible that these will be lost, for instance, if the hard disk where the coin is located crashes. A further form of cash transaction is cybercash; this models an electronic payment transaction which is transferred in key form to a cybercash server account.

Efforts to introduce a standardised currency or, at the very least, the opportunity of secure payments and financial transactions, are set to gain momentum in the immediate future. Given a successful breakthrough, major profits beckon all those offering a virtual payment system in cyber space. One thing can be predicted almost with certainty: the impulse for a future standard will hardly come from an established and renowned banking institute. These are, in terms of their thinking and actions, too deeply immured in their conventional structures, the truth of which was already being demonstrated decades ago at the start of plastic money's rise to triumph.

The Principality of Liechtenstein is, in the shape of the Liechtenstein Landesbank, prominently represented on the Web and this to some extent reinforces its reputation as a safe haven for investment. The principality has, however, acquired more of a reputation through offering the opportunity to play bingo on the Internet. So-called InterLotto can be played for an outlay of just 5 Sfr.

Strategic and Tactical Significance of the Network as far as Marketing Is Concerned

The long-term strategic importance of the Internet lies in the fact that the network is the prototype of the future information highway, the foundation stone of the information society. Its short-term significance is based on the question of whether money can also be earned by means of the Internet.

Some companies are of the opinion that their presence alone on the Internet and the image acquisition connected with it makes it all worthwhile. Other companies ask, justifiably, whether the money invested in this technology and in the resources will ever be recouped and, indeed, whether any sort of presence is in fact necessary?

The strategic viewpoint

From a strategic viewpoint, the Internet and its further development will doubtless gain in importance. Whereas, 15 years ago, it was the development of the personal computer that was important, it is now the development and expansion of the Internet. No enterprise can get away from this fact. In the long term, every management team will have to come to grips with this new instrument of communication. In the case of enterprises with a global operation it will happen sooner; as regards companies which operate regionally, it will happen later.

Many companies will, initially, be looking to restrict themselves to starting up a small pilot project within this sector. This has a number of advantages. It is possible to monitor the progress of development oneself. If a decision is made to extend activities within this medium, there is always know-how within the company to fall back on. In addition, it may well be feasible for experience and progress in terms of productivity to be gathered internally initially, for example, by means of the extended use of electronic mail between individual subsidiaries. This initial step makes possible not only a change of culture but also a team-orientated approach to working, although these teams do not have to be physically together all the time. This change is not only necessary within advertising companies, but also in a number of other companies, banks and insurance companies.

From a strategic viewpoint, the only question that arises from it is one of timing entry correctly and of procedure, which is something which management will need to detemine. If entry is required by the customer then it may well already be too late, for, in this case, competitors will already have the advantage.

When dealing with technology, it is possible to consciously follow three very different paths. Leaders in the sphere of technology are very quick to make use of new technology once this has become available, or they may even have been involved in developing it. The declared aim is to fully utilise the potential offered by early involvement. Moderates are interested in proceeding cautiously and not having to pay for development mistakes. They adopt new technologies at a stage which offers a guarantee of being able to link up without having to incur major additional expenditure. The stragglers are the ones who only employ technology when, as far as the general situation is concerned, there is no other choice left for them.

Tactics – and their significance in terms of advertising, promotion and sales

The Internet is already a low-cost communication medium. Communication is world-wide and is capable of reaching a significant target audience. Within a very short time, the number of different target groups on the Internet is set to undergo a massive increase, even taking into account readiness to use this new technology increasingly in purchasing. There is no other medium which displays similar growth rates to the Internet. This applies both to pure Internet users and also to commercial suppliers of on-line services. The number of users will, similarly, undergo a massive increase in the future, thanks to the increased use of Windows 95.

Aspects of advertising

The advertising industry is poised to experience powerful changes along with the spread of network usage. Advertisers were, until recently, the equal of the instruments of communication. There were a number of very large agencies spread across the world, all specialising in various subjects. There were copy-writers who were fully conversant with the spoken word. The art directors are definite visionaries. Even today, the scene as far as advertisers is concerned continues to honour individualism. Accordingly, it was individuals who set the tone in the relevant offices, even when attempts were being made to set up an international organisation. This was necessary in order to launch international campaigns. On the Internet, global communication is becoming possible from a single computer. This may be installed on an out-of-the way mountain or on a remote island. World-wide communication takes place via a satellite or radio link. If success is to be achieved, it is essential to understand the network and its features and to anticipate developments. In addition, multimedia cannot be mastered by a single individual. Modern-day talents within the different agencies and specialist facilities will be faced tomorrow with organising themselves into a team if they wish to register resounding successes. In the advertising sector, the individual is being replaced by the team. This means that, within a team of this kind, the creative individual will demonstrate to a much more marked extent the features of a computer artist, because he will need to be familiar with the limits and possibilities offered by the relevant system with which he is working. It is no longer enough to simply capture a creative idea in words or pictures.

In practically all local markets, it is generally the norm that, initially, offers are made by Web consultants and Web advertising agencies. Pioneers who wish to make what they have to offer accessible to a local market are very often book dealers, music companies, fashion companies or travel agencies.

From a tactical point of view, the Internet represents, even at this stage, an extension of what is on offer in the way of communication media for companies and market services. This new medium has its own rules which are very different from those which govern the traditional media. Nothing gets on the nerves of Web users more than boredom. Their ability to deal with the electronic media is determined by their Nintendo mentality. Interaction must be full of tension as well as informative. Users also have high expectations as regards technology. The advertising sector, especially the creative branch, was for a long time untouched by modern information technology. As far as dealing with it is concerned, the new medium must be handled with the same seriousness as every other advertising medium. To this end the necessary professionalism needs to be built up. In order to enable it to be successfully set up, the strengths – interactivity and emotionality – of this medium need to be acted out. It is also essential to adopt a professional approach. What is needed is a new way of thinking, as this medium is not solely a possible additional alternative to the existing one. The medium of cyber marketing will trigger massive changes in communication practice which, in turn, will undergo a marked change because of it. What today's Internet has to offer will, in the long term, become the dominant way forward in communication.

Internet in comparison to other media

If we analyse the media, the differences towards the public media become obvious.[70] Via the Internet it is impossible to carry an aggressive campaign on to the market. In the traditional media, offers are brought on to the market by means of newspaper and television advertising. The target group is confronted with the offer whether it wants it or not. On the Internet there is no such guarantee. The Web site may be extremely attractive but suffers from lack of use. Advertising success, of which there is at least some tangible evidence with the traditional media, cannot be quantified. Although it is very easy, when dealing with the traditional media, to evaluate market penetration, this is not the case on the Internet. Whilst the Internet may know how many 'hits' there are on a Web site, that is, the number of accesses counted, this is purely relative as there is no information available on how often or with what frequency the same user has accessed the site. It is even less simple a matter to make any kind of definitive statement as regards the profile of the consumer. What is lacking is detailed information on age, income and sex – all that it is possible to establish is the geographical point at which the subscriber dialled into the Internet.

A rough estimate can be made regarding the current demography of Internet users. In 1995, 50% of users in Europe were between 16 and 25 years of age. In the USA, 60% were betweeen 16 and 45 years old with fairly uniform distribution. The difference arises due to the unequal spread of network acceptance in the two continents. In the USA the adoption rate is much greater than in Europe due to the higher level of Internet acceptance. It is true to say that, based on this factor, certain conclusions may be drawn in respect of the overall acceptance of information technology on the relevant continents. The average income of a typical Internet user in 1995 was US$69,000 and almost 10% in the USA (6% in Europe) already use the Internet for regular shopping. The value of the purchases made is 60% less than US$10, 22% betweeen US$10 and 100 and 18% above US$100. This means that a majority of purchasers are going for favourable share ware. However, the factor that is highly crucial to the profile is education: 6% have had professional training, 57% attended a high school or technical college, 20% have a university degree and 7% are qualified to PhD level.

As far as the number of accesses and their duration are concerned, contacts can be assessed purely in terms of figures. It is also possible to maintain statistics on what information is of most interest, e.g. how long visitors actually spent at the site.

The often quoted maxim 'Think globally but deal locally' is no longer applicable in the information era. Proof of this is displayed by the Internet. 'Local potency with global presence' is the message propagated by the Internet. Locally controlled communication is no longer possible as the Internet represents a global form of communicating. Potency because even the medium of the Internet does not guarantee automatic success just because the opportunities for communication can be perceived globally. Potency may lie in original products, in ideas or services which can be communicated globally. The more original the local skills and the more easily transferable they are, the greater the likelihood of success in surviving world-wide.

A further criterion is interactivity. Here the traditional media all fail – apart from the seller in discussions with his customer. All the traditional media are basically founded on one-way communication. Reply cards and freephone numbers are attempts to satisfy a basic human need – communication. This profile shows clearly why the Internet is not just one more spoke in the advertising wheel, aimed at overwhelming the customer with messages, but is instead a new medium with other qualities.

Success in this medium will only become established when full use is made of strengths to compensate for corresponding weaknesses.

The web page – visiting card to the network world

On the Internet, as is the case everywhere, time and money are in short supply. The volume-dependent costs or the time-related charges for connecting those interested to the Internet are making this a matter of urgency. If WWW pages are properly laid out, companies will be able to save their customers time and money. The structure of the offer which is to be communicated via Web pages must be planned prior to implementation. Every WWW document should contain in its footnotes a hyperlink to the index of contents. This will make it easier for the user to navigate. A uniform appearance means that corporate identity is more strongly emphasised and this helps the user to get his bearings.

Longer texts must be structured so as to permit a clear overview. Graphic elements can be used both to improve clarity as well as to catch the eye and as access points. The internationality of the Internet calls for English on the front of the home page with the option of making it possible for different users to access their own native language. The subsequent index of contents should offer a clear overview of information. At the same time, a uniform menu structure will not only make it easier to find one's way about but will, besides, save on transmission costs as the graphic data files which are used over and over again will only need to be transmitted once. The pictures are no longer built up via the slow network but from the rapid local memory of the user. Text hardly takes up any space in data volumes, by contrast to graphics, sound data files or even video films.

If graphics are used, they should be small as this will reduce data transactions. Overall a larger number of smaller Web pages are better than an enormous document which takes a great deal of time to transmit from the server on to the local machine of the user. Text colours represent a very good and cost-free creative element. Various colours, combined with a background picture on which the text is superimposed, make for a very attractive arrangement of Web pages. If graphics are superimposed over the background so that they are transparent, then both text and graphics will still be recognisable against the background. For the observer transparent graphics act like a foil laid against the screen. As regards colour representation, 8 bit patterns with 128 or as few as 16 colours are generally adequate. The usual pattern, however, contains 256 colours, although pictures constructed in this way are very slow and awkward in transmission. As regards the build-up of graphics, too, there are various techniques available; on the one hand, there is the option of portraying the graphic as a full picture from top to bottom in its full resolution or of starting by quickly making a rough outline sketch of the picture and then gradually refining it with colour. The second method is very much more pleasant from the user's point of view.

The best training prior to setting up a Web site, your own 'Home Page', is to move around on the Web for a few hours, visiting competitors and looking for good examples of Web pages. The lesson learned through direct observation will build up experience and bring in a number of ideas on how the company's advertising should be fashioned and what it is better to leave out.

The decision to log-on

However and whenever a company decides to log-on to the Internet, there is one immediate step that every marketing boss should take and that is to register his company as a DNS address. In 1995, the USA witnessed the outbreak of a fierce fight about names allocation. This was not only within the company sector but also as regards brand names. As a rule the owner of a brand name also gets the relevant DNS address. In the USA, legal battles had already been fought over allocation of DNS addresses. Thus we find IBM under the address IBM.COM and the PC division under the address PC.IBM.COM. As the number of possible DNS addresses is not a random matter, those responsible within the marketing sector should reserve the DNS address for their company through an Internet provider. The hamburger chain McDonalds found that the address McDonald.COM had already been registered by a private individual when they came to register their company name. In litigation at court McDonalds nevertheless obtained the address. McDonalds were lucky. Had the name of the previous owner in fact been McDonald, the world-wide company would not have stood a chance of obtaining this particular DNS address. In August 1995, Kraft Foods registered 133 product names in the USA. Proctor & Gamble registered 52 brands as DNS addresses in the same period. Some weeks later, Kraft was no longer registering brands but instead product categories such as 'Cereals' and a DNS address 'Drinks'. Proctor & Gamble had even secured the DNS addresses for itself with the names of parts of the body, such as 'Arm' or 'Eye' and ailments such as 'Headache' and 'Diarrhoea', which is a logical consideration when we think how users search for information on the network. Companies are better off registering their good name and their brands as DNS addresses before it is too late.

Master plan for the electronic track

The first step in cyber marketing clarifies what is needed to make direct contact with every customer with the question: 'How do I reach the customer at his terminal from my screen?' The terminal equipment can be a PC, a fax machine or an interactive TV. Which items of terminal equipment are our customers using today and what communication trends will they develop for the future? These facts and ideas can be ascertained from customers. At the same time it may be assumed that, sooner or later, PC owners are definitely going to link up to the data highway. If we are already aware of what their preferences are in terms of current and future communication media, then the question that presents itself is, in what sequence the relevant steps will be made to set up the communication infrastructure. One fact is definite: 'control' of all communication will be via a database. This database will need to contain information from already existing information technology systems as well as the data to be made possible by the new communication systems, for instance, the electronic mail address and the PC operating system which the customer uses. The operating system is necessary so that we know in which format data files are to be relayed. The design and implementation of the basic item, the database, will take up a considerable amount of time. In the majority of cases connecting the instruments of communication takes place in a very much shorter time than it takes to set up a customer database which has to depend on data warehousing services. Before a customer database can be implemented, there must be a clear and practicable marketing concept to establish the basis for it.

A preliminary period of at least one year is usual before the customer database and the integrated communication instruments are fully functional. However, implementation does not have to take place sequentially, but can also be undertaken in parallel, although this is something which calls for extremely good project management.

The obvious conclusion to be drawn from this situation is that there must be an actual marketing vision by way of a target for the marketing programme. This forms the basis for the realisation of the necessary infrastructures.

Different Ways of Accessing Cyber Marketing

Various ways of accessing cyber marketing result from the combined use of different Internet functions and the option available to the user of either working on the Internet in general or on certain on-line supplier networks. The degree to which the lifeblood of the information era is used is, in addition, a critical factor when it comes to the various different modes of access. The level to which it is desired to use an access variant begins with the pure acquisition of information via competitors and through the developing market. The utilisation level is achieved in full when all income comes exclusively from activities conducted via the network and the world outside only needs to be considered as a vehicle for fulfilling the physical supply of material products.

Getting to know variants

In the forefront of the level of utilisation is the pure acquisition of information. The acquisition of information is a very important activity, but one which does not always generate direct sales. In this variant it is of paramount importance to know which competitors have already decided to log-on and the level at which utilisation is to take place.[71]

Intranet variant

Nevertheless, communication may take place globally within a group of affiliated companies. The medium of electronic mail is a good one for simplifying and compressing into as short a space of time as possible the exchange of information from and to the associated distributors, dealers, wholesalers, agents, franchisees or sales points. In this way, the time taken for a company to react on the market will be considerably reduced. This in-house use of the communication network is also termed 'Intranet'.

One example of the use of the Intranet in marketing, which can be decisive in terms of competition for vehicle insurance companies, is: 'We aren't just reasonable, we're the fastest. We deal with your claims for damages within 24 hours or we waive a year's premium for you'. How can an insurance company which exists to sort out reports of damage to motor vehicles cut its reaction time to this extent? The damage to the vehicle is photographed on the spot using a digital camera. This equipment is available commercially for less than £500. Different models incorporate the facility to check the photograph immediately on an LCD and establish whether or not it is usable. Close-ups taken at up to 15 cm can be reproduced using special macro-devices to give crystal-clear photographs in brilliant colours. The camera weights 200 g and is completely silent. The pictures are directly transferred to the PC and passed on to the central office via the Internet. There the necessary authorisations are undertaken in response to the applications made by the damage assessment officers and the relevant papers directly despatched to the parties involved. Less than 24 hours go by between the visit from the damage assessment officer and the administrative arrangements and the point when the paperwork is consigned to post or sent off on fax.

By means of internal communication, the company, if this is not already the case, can be introduced to the realities of the information era and prepared for cyber reality.

Being present variant

A presence on the Web means that products and services offered by the population of the Web are brought closer. Customers can select the particular product that is tailored to their requirements and obtain information on where the product can be ordered from. We would specially recommend Hewlett-Packard as an example of a Web page on the Internet.

From electronic distribution to marketing dialogue variant

This variant incorporates the initial steps towards a business transaction. The customer may make his selection from among various standard products and communicate the order. This is as a rule confirmed by means of e-mail. Depending on the particular country and the level of software development, payment may be made by fax communication using a credit card or directly via the private network in the case of commercial on-line suppliers.

As of this stage at the latest it will be necessary to use a database to identify prospective buyers individually and to take active care of customers.

Mass individualisation variant

At the next level of utilisation, the customer configures his own product via the network, which may, for instance, be the specifications when ordering a new vehicle, as the range no longer consists of a limited number of standard products. The customer may in addition choose how the service is to be performed. This means in this example, how and where delivery is to be made. Neither the handling of the contractual aspects nor payment takes place completely via the electronic medium.

Electrical commerce variant

The most complete level of utilisation is the selection, ordering, payment and delivery of the products exclusively via the network. This level is only ever achieved today by software companies and other enterprises whose business is based on pure information, such as information bureaux, lawyers, investment specialists and stockbrokers.

Access Conditions

Technology

Having made the decision to join, it is sensible from a technological point of view to choose computer systems which are open. That means that companies should not depend on one single manufacturer alone. The decision to join should be taken within the framework of the planning for the information system infrastructure. Since, as far as technology is concerned, a great number of changes have yet to be anticipated, no unequivocal fixed decision can be made which, within a period of years, will not need to be revised.

The attachment of existing information systems to the network, in order to enable direct polling in response to applications, is not a simple undertaking, although it is certainly possible. Within this sector, it is well worthwhile calling in the appropriate specialists.

Positioning

The more directly market performance is linked to information technology, the sooner link-up is advisable. As regards companies which work primarily with information or offer services, the network provides an ideal medium for developing contacts with customers. It also provides a vehicle for information bureaux or specialised information services and, in particular, the economic services and performance analyses produced by banks and credit services. Enterprises which work directly with software will be well advised to make friends with this new medium with all possible speed, for it enables communication with customers to take place openly and very rapidly.

Suppliers on the network

The suppliers who will establish themselves on the network are those who have, at a very early stage, gained experience in the perversities and advantages of the network. One difficulty encountered by the visitor to the Internet lies in being able to find his way in this very large and confusing world. Companies who resolutely and single-mindedly concentrate on using cross-references to enrol with the various navigation servers will achieve a very good frequency. However, for this a knowledge of rapidly changing technology and development is as indispensable as the ability to bring real content on to the network. Pure advertising statements are not regarded as adequate content. This means that the company's internal resources need to be mobilised in order to parade existing knowledge and ability within the relevant sector of a broader commercial environment visibly in the market place without making key know-how generally accessible. Sensitivity as regards the information and knowledge required for this which, by contrast to generally known content, is crucial as far as competition is concerned, cannot be awakened throughout the entire organisation within a very brief period of time. Cultivating the rules and conditions for business success within an organisation calls for a massive mental change at every level of the hierarchy and in all sectors of activity.

Conclusion: The Route to Cyber Marketing via the Internet

The Internet and, in particular, the World Wide Web, ranks as the prototype for the implementation of virtual realities and cyber worlds within the global information society. Originally academic and commercially neutral, the Internet is currently transforming itself into the global on-line market which up to now has not been centrally controlled or subject to any form of continuous legal regulation. On the other hand, the global networks operated by commercial on-line service suppliers offer a well-structured and relatively secure operating environment for the first steps towards cyber marketing. Companies will, in the future, find themselves compelled to accept the reality of the on-line markets, something which calls, not for their response to the question about the use of the Internet for marketing purposes in principle, but merely to that regarding which access variant and time a firm should choose.

III – Practice, The How

7 MARKETING PROGRAMMES

How does the ability to see into the cyber age and the opportunities for marketing – that least defined of activities which is at the same time the most crucial one in terms of sales – affect the practical perception of profit margins and the difference between black and red figures? The question being asked is how those responsible should implement cyber marketing. The marketing programme spans the arc from the vision of a far horizon to the current state of the organisation. The marketing programme is the marketing performance of a team in terms of the organisation of a project incorporated within a methodical procedure which is established throughout the company. There are common links with projects to implement technology. The aim of the marketing programme is different to those of the implementation projects for cyber technology which we shall be discussing later, although the basic organisational principles are typical of both activities.

The statements as regards the framework of the marketing programme are very much abbreviated and are not comprehensive in the sense of familiar marketing theory; instead, this is to a great extent assumed to be already well known.[72] In the relevant observations on the stages of the programme, reference is made primarily to experience gained from practice and to the requirements of cyber marketing. Practice shows that those responsible for marketing need to set aside a number of working days to consciously prepare for all the theoretical and practical aspects of the marketing programme activity. In a procedure of this kind, mostly conducted in the form of a workshop, the theoretic principles are freshened up and new knowledge and experiences are related directly to the current activity and operationalised as a marketing programme.

Basic Principles of Marketing Programmes

From the entire spectrum of a company's marketing activities which are recorded in programmes it is possible to compile a portfolio. This portfolio makes an overall view of marketing activities easier for the company management if the marketing programme is standardised and the language used has been introduced on a uniform basis throughout the entire organisation. The programmes provide information on advances in terms of time, costs and yields.

The work carried out in the form of marketing programmes must be enshrined within the organisation in clear management principles. The principles governing marketing programmes as well as other projects associated with information technology can be derived from the service sector, for it is here that costs and success are directly dependent on time and the quality of the people entrusted with the tasks. The basic tenets are therefore as follows:

One: it is not the number of people but the quality of their brains that is decisive as far as performance is concerned.

Two: identifying the correct target is crucial for success.

Principle 1 – no programme, no marketing activity

No activity within an organisation can take place without a programme. The programme displays a clearly standardised framework and offers a guarantee that the
aim, the purpose, costs, yield, time and basic data are all fixed. For every programme there is a fully responsible person, the programme manager. Hence the
allocation of activities in relation to responsibility is clearly and ultimately regulated. Every programme should be implemented within the shortest possible space of
time. The shorter the time taken to implement a programme, the lower the costs
and the greater the comparable market advantage. The advantages of time-based
competition on the market can only be guaranteed by the application of this principle.[73] The marketing programme is decided by top level management and periodically checked to see that progress is being maintained as planned.

The programme manager's responsibility embraces the achievement of set targets. In any case, it is up to him to collect and coordinate. This applies in respect of
information as well as in terms of activating other management levels to respond to
particular incidents. This duty allows the programme manager only a very little
room for manoeuvre when it comes to foisting the blame for any unscheduled incidents on to lack of progress or external circumstances. He is of course responsible
for budgeting and for keeping within all the costs chargeable to the programme.
Likewise he bears full responsibility for time scheduling and keeping to deadlines.
The sphere of activity for the person with responsibility for the programme is clearly defined in the contract and the relevant procedures laid down in the marketing
programme. He has every authority necessary to implement the programme and
fulfil the contract.[74] Such authority includes, in particular, the selection of the team
members when planning and implementing the marketing programme.

The following comments may be made briefly on these very short guidelines.
Under normal circumstances, the person responsible for the programme should be
directly answerable to the decision committee. Marketing programmes are, in the
majority of cases, so vital to companies that this direct relationship is wholly justifiable. Very frequently – in software projects too – a particular position emerges for
the responsible programme manager within the organisation which, by bringing in
an external coach, can be emphasised and at the same time improved. However, in
practice, the model of an internal mentor has also shown itself to be a good solution. Mentors are, in most cases, long-term managers who may have retired from
the day-to-day round but continue to take an interest in important projects as
active members of the Board of Directors or of the Supervisory Board. Thus the
mentor is the confidant of the programme manager. He is, thanks to his high level
of involvement and good network of connections within the company and, in many
cases, also among his customers, capable of exerting a strongly integrative effect.

Basically, this approach, like the employment of an external coach, is exclusively dependent on the interpersonal relationships of those concerned.

The programme manager has, within the framework of the company guidelines that are generally applicable, a free choice of means and procedures to steer the marketing programme to a successful conclusion. The basic idea, certainly in larger companies, is to strengthen individual initiative and to encourage the person responsible to employ guerilla methods within the framework of the existing, general instructions.

It is essential that the management of the company allow the person responsible to make his own mistakes: only he who has the possibility of making mistakes and of correcting them will ultimately be able to bear responsibility. The management climate must, therefore, allow errors and mistakes and rectify them in an open manner. It is only a climate of openness when dealing with failures that will enable an organisation to learn. The will to learn is a key ability when it comes to success in cyber marketing. Cyber marketing makes use of the newly emerging opportunities right at the very source of technology. Any progressive movement, including the emergence of the cyber age, will not appear stable at the moment when it emerges, but, rather, chaotic by comparison to that which already exists. This factor – change through chaos – is the basis for the fact that a number of decisions, when it comes to implementing programmes in cyber marketing, will of necessity not be at the peak of perfection or may even be wrong. This underlines the importance of tolerating faults, linked with a high awareness of learning as a basic condition for the success of an organisation which has made up its mind, as a pioneer, to realise the earnings potential offered by cyber marketing.

Principle 2 – togetherness with the customers

The yardstick for any transaction is the customer. The basis for success is a market performance which the customer accepts and is prepared to pay for. The basis for every marketing programme is a conscientious analysis of customer and market needs. Empirically defined values show that almost 100% of innovations derive from impulses from existing customers, 76% of the most important new features and 58% of smaller improvements were prompted from the market side and not from within the company.[75] The obvious conclusion to draw from this is: customers should be included as early as the planning stage and before implementing the marketing programme. In the case of highly innovative activities, such as is unarguably the case within the cyber marketing sector, suitable customers or customer groups should be called in to help prepare marketing programmes. The sooner customers are included in planning, the less the risks which may be anticipated due to erroneous decisions will be.[76]

Different types of customer are approached in the course of a product's lifecycle. Initially, at the stage when the product is first introduced, it is the innovators. After them come the early adopters at the commencement of the growth phase. By contrast to the remaining types of customer, these first two are frequently enthusiastic about innovative technologies and new methods. Statistically, the innovators make up around 2% to 4% of the customer base and the early adopters something between 10% and 15%. Individuals who are always up to date with technology and very well informed about what is going on in development areas are ideal when it comes to cooperating in marketing programmes. These individuals very often transfer their personal inclination to their business activities. A company that is truly and exclusively innovative will be proud of the fact and will also give this side of its character prominence in its company profile and its corporate image.

The person responsible for the programme also takes care of customer relations and market research (by which we mean the procurement of information) and for any communication involving the collection of a debt from the debtor's residence. Any communication with the customer should be documented in such a way as to enable the relationship to be reconstructed by the company agents who would normally assume responsibility in such circumstances.

Within the framework of a programme activity in cyber marketing, success can be measured very quickly by the reaction of this small group. If the innovative customers do not 'buy' cyber marketing, then its chances of success will also be minimal as far as the remaining market is concerned. This underlines the importance of planning both offer and activities with the customer and of exploring the suitability of the concepts and plans with them. Once customers have identified opportunities for personal advantages they will certainly react very positively.

Principle 3 – taking the right steps quickly

To achieve 80% of effect with 20% of expenditure is the central rule when implementing a marketing programme. This calls for effect, result and action to be clearly projected within the marketing programme. Unplanned activities spell confusion and not, as is often postulated, improvisation. The plan forms the basis for improvisation, for this is always an activity which is intended to achieve a target, but also incorporates an awareness of deviation from an original plan. The starting point for the plan is the assessment of the company's own strengths and opportunities compared to its weaknesses and the threat posed by competitors. In cyber marketing, the aim is a further extension of existing share of customer and market position using the new marketing instruments with the aim of increasing profits. This means that the basis is the already existing competitive advantage.

The suppliers of advice and services in the cyber marketing sector are building up an entirely new market performance spectrum in conjunction with cyber marketing. As far as the majority of companies are concerned, cyber marketing is, in its emergence phase, an instrument for optimising what exists with a view to making profit or for replacing it in order to reduce costs. This also applies to any company activities which develop organically. Organically, that is, as opposed to growth based on acquisition and partnerships where the competitive position is purchased as an extra item. Successful marketing programmes call for existing market performance with clear benefits for the customer. Without a basic range of products, services or software it is impossible to build up any competitive advantages which will enable a company to achieve the required level of market strength that is necessary to ensure that its balance sheet stays in the black.

Having formulated the concept and procedures for the marketing programme, the steps towards implementing it are also listed. If the concept and the procedures are wrong, then failure will be pre-programmed at the point of implementation. For this reason, it is essential to know whether the level of market performance achieved by means of the instruments of cyber marketing will be more successful in terms of solving the customer's problems than the competition, or whether the level of performance overall is seen as being more favourable for the customer and, hence, more lucrative. Furthermore, the question is whether the the company's own market performance – which may incorporate products, services, software or a mixture of all three – is being adapted to meet requirements more quickly than that of the competition.

The programme manager who follows the basic internalised precept of the 20/80 rule will quickly carry out the correct steps. This rule represents an unrelenting principle for judging the person responsible in terms of his efficiency. He himself must advocate and live this pragmatic approach.

Principle 4 – setting the example of a budget mentality

As regards independent entrepreneurs and their employees in small firms, the budget mentality is the norm. Cost awareness manifests itself in such a way and is safeguarded by the boss to such an extent that this point is actually an anathema.

In medium-sized and larger companies, employees have to be constantly reminded to exercise the same care in handling the company's resources as they do when handling resources in their own private households. At the same time, this statement should not only be seen in relation to direct costs such as salaries, external contracts and expenses, but, to an even greater extent in terms of the hidden costs which arise due to the implementation of a marketing programme. An awareness on the part of the management of how to sensitise the person responsible for the programme, predominantly to the on-going costs which will be incurred, is very important, for example in data-bank marketing as regards on-going maintenance aand support or, in the case of on-line marketing on the Internet, the costs for transactions and maintenance of the Web sites on the WWW. A high level of quality awareness in the development and implementation phase is absolutely essential. If this is not available, the management should formulate a guideline for developments within the IT sector and, especially, software. As regards outsourcing, this guideline is in any case a pre-condition for quality assurance.

A lasting competitive edge can only be assured by cost leadership. The person responsible for the programme must take into account the principles of cost leadership in every aspect of the programme, such as planning, preparation and implementation. This also applies to strategies which involve the pursuit of differentiation.

Principle 5 – know-how status

The decision on whether to buy or to make in the industrial era was always related to supplies of the necessary product components. The discussion as regards the outsourcing of projects and implementation within the IT sector is raging vehemently today. In the information era, the definition of a company's strategic know-how is the catalyst on which the decisions on whether to build up the resource internally or to obtain it from outside depend.[77] Strategic know-how should always be available on the company's own premises. If strategic know-how is obtained from outside, then it is important to ensure that a transfer to one's own employees takes place, through whom the know-how will become established within the company. This means that the transfer of the know-how is contractually regulated and made a condition in agreements with those who are to perform the service. Very often advisors make a very good living by only allowing diluted know-how to flow into an enterprise with a view to prolonging the duration of their consultancy for as long as possible. Strategic know-how should be built up within the company as quickly as possible. Its acquisition and distribution should be regulated by means of guidelines and management recommendations in such a way that a cluster risk is avoided by not concentrating the knowledge on one employee. The know-how must be documented and be capable of being called up in comprehensible form from internal locations.

If need be, rules may be set up to prevent certain suppliers from making any know-how obtained jointly in projects available to a direct or potential competitor over a specified period of time.

In order to implement these points effectively and unequivocally, it is essential to define, in the form of guidelines, which know-how is strategic in nature and which not. This is a task that falls to the top level of management. The programme manager's achievements will be measured by the extent to which he has observed these guidelines, with which he must be familiar.

The question as regards strategic know-how is closely linked to the core skills within a company. The discussion about strategic know-how may be symbolised using a wheel. The hub is strategic; we cannot do without it, the same goes for a minimum number of spokes and the tyre wheel. The hub is the knowledge about how all the elements and relationships are kept together. The minimum number of spokes are skills, such as processes and technologies, as well as organisational procedures and guidelines. The tyre encompassing the wheel symbolises the customer base and effectiveness in the market place. This market effectiveness can be completely gummed up by an advertising agency or a media consultant. The tyre may not be the supporting element in the wheel construction, but it is the contact surface.

If a service is obtained outside, the supplier should be in a position to perform this service faster, more cheaply and better. However, in some cases it is desirable to set up the service internally, as, for instance, in cases where it is not possible to guarantee or monitor the speed of delivery or the quality of the external service. If the net value added is above-average, potential in terms of profit will also go outside and this should not be allowed to happen. What if the person from outside who is to perform the service should come into contact with the company's own customer without its having been possible to come to a contractual arrangement on how the external supplier should deal with customer relations? In such circumstances it is advantageous to deal with the task internally. The marketing context needs to be characterised by a very high degree of sensitivity when it comes to dealing with customers through external suppliers.

These five principles should act as an aid to orientation for every person with responsibility for a programme and every line manager.

The Marketing Programme

There is a standardised blueprint available on which a marketing programme can be based.[78] This standard simplifies dealing with the marketing process and, primarily, makes a common language possible within the company. This does not happen overnight, rather, in the majority of cases it is the result of working meetings. A company should take the time to work out these basic principles in formal workshops at middle and top management level. The various marketing activities based on the programmes can be stored in the form of a portfolio which will make them relatively easy to refer to.

In the following we have, having given an overview of a typical marketing programme, gone on to briefly outline the basic ideas which lie behind the individual points. As for those readers who are interested in going further into the material and details, may I refer them to the relevant bibliography. However, a seminar providing an overview of essential marketing terminology would be very useful by way of an introduction to ways of thinking when it comes to working on marketing programmes. Today, the basic science of marketing is fragmented and exists among employees at different levels. In the final analysis, what is relevant is how the knowledge is to be transformed into practice within an overall context and how results are going to be achieved for the company.

The programme framework

The stimulus for a marketing programme is the target and an appropriate mandate from the management. The contract must be sufficiently precisely formulated to serve as a suitable guideline.

In addition to the contract, the framework contains, by way of the first point in a top-to-bottom approach, the strategic points of view, then the resources to be achieved for the targets. Here it is already evident within the model framework of this book that the problems of personnel and their skills, that is, their abilities, will be accorded a central role. Finances, materials and much more rank as the property of all and are easier to acquire or to use. The central point lies, however, in the human involvement. The information era lives off people who understand how to handle the latest technology and who are able to create value by using information.

Naturally, the information in itself is available within the company, but it takes the right employees to make correct use of it. If new programmes are set up in the Internet marketing sector, then the combination of marketing and modern technology at its peak is not easy to find in a single person; hence the person responsible for the programme should also be able to share in the decision on the use of the appropriate resources.

Marketing, finally, does not only directly serve the customer, but it also indirectly serves the company through good results. Only a company which demonstrates a strong earning capability will be able to maintain itself long-term in the market place and will therefore be of interest to customers. It is now, at a time when a change of paradigm is taking place, that a company's stability may represent an essential factor for a purchaser when making his decision. Through networking – not only in the philosophical sense but primarily in the technical sector – stability plays a major role, as communication of this kind may be connected, for example, via EDI with an initial investment in finance, time and personnel. Benefit should continue to be drawn from this investment for as long as possible and it should only be replaced by a more attractive substitute. Everything concerning the sales revenue plan should be agreed with the company controllership. On the one hand, there is the need to create a programme-related opportunity for financial management whilst, on the other, the principles of book-keeping need to be transferred to the programme management. The line of demarcation between costs and investments, guidelines on whether and, if so, how, an ROI should be calculated, whether a cash projection should be undertaken, should be defined by the controllership. A marketing programme, together with other company programmes, will be measured against formulated targets. These must be known and communicated. The guidelines will be set out within the framework of a defined strategic orientation.

Readers who are not employed in a large company may find these statements disturbing. Nevertheless, it has been established in various investigations that many entrepreneurs who are capable of building up business with potential, are not very strong on the financial management side. Cynics take the line that, if they did understand something about it, then they would not contemplate the risks in the first place. The financial aim of a start-up company is relatively simply formulated: 'How can I implement the plan without outside finance or with the resources which I have available?' As a result of this constraint, young entrepreneurs are frequently more resourceful and more creative as regards project realisation. Never to fall into the liquidity trap is, to a certain extent, the acid test as far as commercial activity is concerned. The first three points also represent a suitable framework for discussions with the finance providers and for convincing them of investment opportunities.

The fourth point encompasses the traditional marketing activities. These activities take up the greater part of the time. They cover all aspects of the marketing mix together with the relevant aspects of cyber marketing in each case.

The fifth point gets to grips with the execution of the marketing programme. The view that the first four points contain the organisation of the structure and the fifth the running organisation is correct. The nature of a project is that it is of limited duration pending the implementation of standard activities. The person responsible for the programme will, depending on how fast-moving the relevant industry is, draft out a new programme or, using the programme that he has already developed and drafted out, put it into active operation for a time.

The final point incorporates programme control. This is more rigid in the initial phase and is included in the standardised report together with the performance. The programme termination criteria also constitute a point.

The marketing programme framework features a clear division into life phases. This division would appear to be highly appropriate because practically everyone involved has an understanding of it based on his own personal experience.

Some strategic aspects of cyber marketing

A strategy consists of a fundamental pattern of existing and intended targets, action-guiding principles, the use of resources and interaction between an organisation and the market, competitors and other environmental factors.[79] The information aspect is thus doubly taken into account in the strategy employed. Firstly, in the action-guiding principles. These are the essence of knowledge, know-how and experience within an organisation. The second aspect lies in the organisation's interaction with the market, the competition and other factors. This interaction is to a significant extent pure communication, i.e. mutual information.

The interaction with the environment, the market and other factors was formulated first by way of a strategy as such. The definition came from the great-grandfather of strategy – Sunzi. He lived around the year 500 BC and was appointed by King Wu to be the top general in his army. The soldier and philosopher had attracted the attention of his army commander with his paper 'The Art of War'. This was the first treatise on strategy to appear in written form.

Sunzi began his treatise with the following paragraph: 'The art of war is of crucial importance for the state. It is a matter of life and death, a road which will lead to safety or destruction. This is why it may, under no circumstances, be neglected'.

In his thirteenth and final chapter Sunzi holds forth on the most valuable skill of a commander: Obtaining and using information about the enemy.[80]

> *Opposing armies may face each other for years and struggle for the victory which will one day be won. Since this is so, it is the peak of inhumanity to remain ignorant about the enemy's constitution solely for the reason that you are reluctant to spend a hundred ounces of silver by way of payment or reward. Anyone who acts in this way is not capable of leading men, he can be of no valuable help to his lord, nor can he win the victory. What enables the wise ruler and the good general to strike and to win and achieve things which lie outside the capabilities of ordinary men is advance knowledge. This advance knowledge cannot be elicited from spirits, nor can it be gained from experience nor from drawing conclusions.*

> *Knowledge about the enemy's plans can be gleaned from other men.*
> *Knowledge about the spirit world is obtained from the oracle; information*
> *within the natural sciences can be gained from empirical values; the laws of*
> *the universe can be substantiated by means of mathematical deductions. But*
> *the plans of the enemy are determined by spies and only by spies.*

With the right information an enemy can be beaten without a single soldier having to go to war. The thought pattern on which this kind of strategic approach is based, was primarily established by the representatives of American business schools and company consultancies, for instance, the discoveries relating to the curve of experience of an organisation made by the founder of the Boston Consulting Group – Bruce Henderson,[81] the widespread systematic approach of combining market share with product life cycle in the easily remembered manner of the Boston Matrix. Michael E. Porter from Harvard defined the analysis framework for determining strategic competitive positions as well as the fundamental strategic options.[82]

Economic life is not determined by a single competitor but by a multitude of unknown people. The art of surviving in an uncertain world therefore also depends on action-guiding principles. The earliest principles were written down in a very profound form around two thousand years after Sunzi.

In 1584, Miyamoto Musashi was born in Japan, in the village of Miyamoto in the province of Mimasaka, to the west of Kyoto. He was the most famous swordfighter in Japan and begins his book entitled *A Book of Five Rings* with the sentence: 'I have spent many years training in the ways of strategy . . . and I now wish, for the first time, to expound on this in writing'.

Miyamoto Musashi gives clear instructions on how to learn his strategic ways:[83]

1. Do not think dishonourably.
2. Practice is the way.
3. Become familiar with every art.
4. Know the methods used in every trade.
5. Distinguish between winning and losing in worldly matters.
6. Develop an intuitive judgement and understanding of everything.
7. Penetrate those things which cannot be seen.
8. Pay attention to detail.
9. Do not do anything which has no point to it.

This tradition of action-guiding principles was formulated in Europe and the USA by means of Mewes' Bottle-neck Concentration Strategy. Practically ignored by the universities, this was applied with great success by very many enterprises such as Belimo AG, a company which, in only twenty years of existence, grew into a global market leader in a niche market within the air conditioning and ventilation technology sector. Whilst one school is more inclined to emphasise targets, the other is more orientated towards ways of getting there.

Marketing strategy must define not only the targets, the resources required and the application of such resources but also the action-guiding pattern for creating competitive advantages. Synergies must be identified, planned and established within the existing organisation.[84] Strategies are defined at various levels such as overall enterprise, business unit or marketing. It is very important to know from the outset where the organisation stands in the overall network of relationships.

A marketing group within an overall company which operates on a local or global basis has a completely different way of looking at things than those responsible for marketing in a national subsidiary or a wholesale distributorship. It is important to be aware of the 'power to influence'. Whereas marketing within an overall enterprise may have a very direct effect on a particular aspect of market performance, as, indeed, should be the case, this 'performance power' as far as the person responsible for marketing within a distribution organisation is concerned, is considerably restricted. He may concentrate on fine-tuning logistics and communication and decide which product he will carry in his subsidiaries. In the information era, the question of 'performance power' will come to the fore very much more than has hitherto been the case. As distances no longer form barriers to markets and contact between the producer and the consumer can be made direct and without the need for any intermediate links, physical distribution networks are becoming relativised in terms of their role in marketing and communication.

Rick Rose of San Pablo Avenue, El Cerrito in California, advertises on the Web pages and his advertising is seen by several dozen million people. Peter Swart in his doctor's practice in Oudtshoorn in South Africa may be interested in it, or Nadia Nabinur at the University of Almati or Talayjane Aonsriprapai in her home in Hong Kong. But the likelihood of his concluding a deal with these three people varies greatly. Rick Rose is the Honda representative of the Hendrick Automotive Group. With some justification, he advertises on the Internet. His business near the University of Berkeley on the Bay of San Francisco lies in the intellectual centre of gravity of the information era. The area around San Francisco has an extremely high population of contemporaries of the new perspectives. In what, though, does Rick Rose's individual performance power lie? Honda produces the actual product. Hendrick Automotive Group is the distributor. What has Rick Rose got to offer? Technical details and specialist matters can be dealt with confidently by the most competent of producers. Peter Swart, Nadia Nabinur and Talayjane Aonsriprapai are agreed on that and would initially seek out a Honda Web site and put their questions there. However, Honda, when responding to questions about list prices and deliveries, would probably have to refer to their individual national agencies in South Africa, Kazakhstan and China. How does Honda solve this problem? Are enquiries sent on and dealt with on a decentralised basis or are questions answered via the central office because it is only there that they have implemented a database marketing programme? Is the matter dealt with centrally? How do they communicate with Nadia Nabinur – she speaks Russian, Kazahstani and German?

The national agency or a distributorship such as Hendrick Automotive Group can help to overcome these barriers. Performance potential is limited to communication and product distribution. One further possibility is customer bonding incentives such as replacing the car free of charge.

Rick Rose has the opportunity to give the individual customer good service on the maintenance side and as a rule makes use of personal contact. He gets to know his customer's preferences and may, under certain circumstances, influence him when it comes to selling him another new car.

Where do we find individual performance potential? Based on the fact that the Honda product comprises not only a motor car, but also involvement in the sales process and, above all, includes service components above and beyond service life, different components of the overall market performance are produced by different organisations. This means that Honda, as the producer, has maximum performance potential and, along with this, maximum power to boot. Honda may employ agents or build up its own organisation. Honda's voice also makes itself heard when it comes to choosing sales and service points. Honda is responsible for the core service and has the opportunity of determining the remaining aspects of it.

The opportunities for determining aspects of the service vary according to the particular sector. Microsoft is not familiar with the problem in this guise. Microsoft can supply its products direct via the network. Microsoft does not require a distributor in Kazakhstan to be able to supply Nadia Nabinur with an Excel table calculations programme. However, Microsoft also finds it very difficult to protect itself against the eventuality that its software will find its way from Hong Kong into the Chinese interior and there be copied and re-distributed without Microsoft receiving any licensing fees from it.

Knowing one's own area and becoming aware of the extent to which it is possible to influence performance is a very important pre-condition when it comes to implementing a marketing programme. The correct evaluation of the defining magnitudes within a company's marketing operation is very central. The prevailing conditions which are created by the adjacent station occupy a central position as far as the preparation of the programme is concerned. Even before any analysis has taken place, these pre-conditions should be addressed and formulated. Either a critical examination of these facts will strengthen these assumptions or other opportunities may present themselves. As a result of the massive changes due to the transformation from the industrial to the information era, these pre-conditions are altering very much more rapidly and thus exerting more influence than the changes which are taking place in specific markets.

In times of major change, the model of bringing action-guiding principles to the fore is a more promising ploy than pure target strategising. One fundamental principle employed by successful chess-players is to leave oneself as wide a range of options as possible. The constant creation of new options is, as an action-guiding principle, robust and successful. The steps taken will be the right ones, if they create positions of success within the context of the market and vis-à-vis the competition. However, those responsible for marketing must also be aware of the risks. By contrast to bankers, entrepreneurs are inclined to put chances very firmly in the foreground. They hardly ever ask about the risks and are often hardly or not at all aware of them.

Analysis

Today we find the traditional methodical framework, along with the driving forces within a sector such as suppliers, purchasers, substitution, being increasingly invaded by the media and other interest groups. As one example of a special interest group we would like to mention environmental protection organisations.

The precision analysis of communication skills and possibilities is a new but necessary activity within the analysis phase. The pure fact of knowing the competition and potential new players in a competitive arena is no longer sufficient. It is essential to have a detailed analysis of how competitors communicate within the market and the cyber world. Metro Holding, with group companies such as Kaufhof, Cash & Carry Markets, Asko Deutsche Kaufhaus, Vobis and the media markets throughout the German-speaking world, dominates trade. The creation of its own on-line service Metronet took place in the realisation that the access ramp to the communication paths such as Internet or interactive cable television is of strategic importance. Metro recognised very early on that the power of the TIME industry could only be confined within limits by applying its own infrastructure. The strategic significance of the subsidiary networks of trading groups will extend to the communication media in the information era. The struggle for 'shelf space' is poised to turn into the battle for the 'slice of the screen' and 'cyber space', that is, from today's conflict on the shelves we are set to join battle in the future first of all for the VDU and then for a place in cyber space.

Equally relevant is the current phase of the branch's life cycle. Factors relevant to branch surroundings include trends in supply and demand, technological and demographic factors, economic activity and political, social and cultural factors and those which relate to the legal regulatory system. In addition, market structure and, in particular, market saturation also represent significant factors. It is possible to assess potential by means of the degree of saturation and the size of the market.

In conjunction with cyber marketing or marketing in the information era in general, a high level of attention should be paid to substitution. Whereas signals relating to changes emanate from suppliers and purchasers, which of course have to be received and interpreted, substitution is a market factor which is considerably more difficult to grasp. Cases of substitution may cost companies their lives. When, to speak in the spirit of Sunzi, weapons change, then the art of war needs to be adapted. The weapons are and always were a reflection of technological progress. Their replacement by new technologies is, therefore, good for major surprises. Chances which open up as a result of innovation can be used positively; it is, however, fatal if they fail to be recognised. In contrast to the industrial era, today information on new technologies is very easily accessible. Anyone who knows how to evaluate innovations quickly and commercially will gain competitive advantages. Rapid innovation skills still need to be developed and instrumentalised in very many companies.[85] Substitutions are contingent on three factors:

1 Price/service relationship of substitutes in comparison to existing market performance.
2. Costs involved in modifying or replacing the production systems.
3. Pressure to substitute.[86]

One important substitution will stretch throughout the economy and that is the communication medium. The Internet and the opportunities associated with it are accessible to all sectors. The initial positions are, essentially, the same for all industries, even if the computer industry does enjoy certain advantages due to its having had the longest experience of dealing with software and information systems. Nevertheless, a replacement technology, for instance, in the data management or multimedia sector, will find this branch once more constrained to adopt new measures.

Those who doubt the power of substitution may care to recall the change in the typesetting and printing industry. Within a decade an entire profession – the typesetter – had disappeared. Even fifteen years ago they and the print unions represented a powerful association within the print media in practically every country in the world. Today there is nothing more to see of them in London's Fleet Street, for decades the stronghold of this branch. Many people working in this field were completely overwhelmed by the innovation of computer layout techniques. Typesetters had been proud craftsmen with good knowledge of language. Many of them did not want to have anything to do with electronics. For them, computers and PCs were toys for children or for madmen. How could a computer ever affect their precious professional status, nurtured over centuries? The phrasing of the argument is well known – as are the changes that took place and the present-day situation.

Substitution processes are very brutal procedures as far as companies are concerned. Massive substitutions are generally based on highly innovative technology which it is very difficult for the relevant branch managers to assess. Particularly dangerous are views like the one put forward by Charles H. Duell: 'Everything that can be discovered has already been discovered'. The Commissioner of the US Patents Office made this statement in 1899 and was obviously not able to persuade himself to the contrary, for, in the fifty years since the Second World War, as many discoveries and innovations have come about as in the entire previous history of mankind.

New products and markets, as well as the renewal of existing market performance features, can only be identified if the fundamental possibility of substitution is recognised. Company management, entire sectors, frequently wallow in such a high degree of security that they fail to notice the changes – or fail to accept them as real – although these may well be happening in full view on the other side of the street. An example of this is the quartz clock which, in the lower segments, has completely ousted the clockwork wristwatch. Although the Institut der ETH in Zurich has built prototypes of quartz clocks and submitted them to the Swiss Association of Clockmakers, no interest has been shown. The clockwork clock would survive, was the conviction. Decades after the victory parade for the new technology, launched on to the market by Japanese and American companies and lapped up by the consumer, the Swiss clock industry has succeeded in extricating itself from the crisis for which it was itself responsible. But even the American Western Union stated in an internal memo in 1876: 'This "telephone" has too many shortcomings to be seriously considered as a means of communication. The device is inherently of no value to us'. We do not only need to look in the last century for examples of missed opportunities in terms of the acceptance of developments. The computer pioneer, founder and president of Digital Equipment Corporation (DEC), Ken Olsen, stated in 1977 with regard to the application and marketing of personal computers: 'There is no reason for any individuals to have a computer in their home'.[87]

Other industries, for example the steel industry, had to undergo a process of shrinkage after steel production capacities had been built up to an absurd level. The possibility of a number of steel parts being replaced by plastic had simply not been recognised.

Analysis of a sector sheds some light on how communication is conducted. This type of communication is set to undergo a massive change in the course of the next few years. Communication with the customer will take place using a new technology. The perspectives are already defined: the Internet and computer, telecommunication with videophone, interactive television with communication options by way of accessories. All three basic variants are digital. All three variants support multimedia and are interactive and capable of dialogue.

The strengths/weaknesses analyses and the possibilities and threats (SWOT – Strengths, Weaknesses, Opportunities, Threats) must be undertaken quite specifically with regard to the electronic markets. As contact with consumers is to be made by means of electronic communication media, the number of telephone lines, television sets and PCs in a given market is crucial. In an assessment of the markets which can be reached via the Internet, an analysis shows the dominance of the English-speaking countries. The USA, the UK, Canada and Australia have a total population of around 470 million with an average 20.2 PCs per 100 inhabitants. This market is the most interesting, not only because it is the largest from the point of view of population, but because it displays the highest density of PCs. The market with the second highest density of PCs is Denmark, although with a population of only 5.1 million. Other very large markets well served by a telecommunications infrastructure are Japan, the German-speaking world and French-speaking Europe. Korea is in fifth place ahead of Italy, Spain and Holland with 11.2 PCs per 100 inhabitants. By contrast, in China there are only 0.2 PCs per 100 inhabitants in a country with a population of 1,190 million. On the other hand, China's density of television sets beats, at 23 per 100 inhabitants, that of Greece by 1 set, i.e. a good quarter by comparison to the 79 sets per 100 inhabitants in the USA. The possible speed of the spread of the Internet within a country is not only determined by the number of PCs, but also by how quickly the computer can be connected to the communications network. In China, the average waiting time for installing a telephone connection is three and a half months, whereas, in Greece, for instance, it is almost ten months.[88]

Targets (quantitative, value, time)

Marketing activities have a target; they are pragmatic in the information sense. The intention or the mission to conduct a marketing programme gives information about the purpose. The targets outline what is to be achieved by this purpose. The strategy should show how the targets are to be achieved and describe the operational or tactical statements of how the steps are to be achieved. Finally, the way in which progress is to be measured should be clearly established.

The targets must be specifically and measurably defined both in terms of quality and quantity. The programme's target should be characteristic and clearly understandable. The objectives must be capable of being measured with the instruments available within the company. The target should be set so that it is attainable under the given conditions. The objectives should be relevant for the company and clear statements should be made as regards data and times. If unclear or unmeasurable objectives are formulated at the beginning, the outcome will only be disagreement over the extent to which a programme has been successful. Based on these objectives, the relevant forecasts and financial estimates are then set down in a detailed paper.

Any increase in share of customer must be measurable and the same applies to market share. The statements made by the objectives as regards quality must also be clearly formulated. What is the aim of the marketing programme? Is it to open up a market, to penetrate a market or to extend a product life cycle? Depending on the particular intention, various points of focus will be encountered. Market share as a principal objective is justified in a new market, whilst an increase in share of customer will be the logical consequence of a saturated market. Is the market performance new or existing? Is the market new or already in existence? Depending on the combination, four different aims emerge: market penetration, extension of the market, product expansion or diversification.[89] Market penetration is achieved by gaining market share and/or increasing share of customer.

Competitors/positioning

Competition can be compared to a triangle. The three corners stand for one's own company, one's competitors and, thirdly, the customers. This triangle undergoes dual analysis – on the one hand, in the real environment and, on the other, in virtual space. The intensity of competition depends on various factors which a programme has to identify. The fundamental factor is the life cycle of the sector, its entry and exit barriers as well as the structure of the field surrounding the sector. Further factors are the number of competitors, cost structures, capacities and product differentiation. Essentially, competition in mature, saturated or shrinking markets is characterised by customer loyalty. The programme must be correctly positioned within the competitive situation and cope with the possible reactions of competitors if it is to be successful in the future.

Sufficient depth of focus should feature in the analysis of competitors. There are innumerable instances of major group companies who are eclipsed in terms of their pathetic market performance by medium-sized or even very small firms. The analysis must uncover the extent to which resources are being applied within a particular segment. In the past, the amount of capital a market participant had behind him was highly significant. This is set to undergo increasing change. It is not capital or the power to create production capacity that is crucial to success in the information era, but rather intelligence, speed and concentration on customer potential. If a multi has first to be able to find the appropriate staff resources and secure them for itself, a great part of the available time window, which enables market potential to be opened up and used, will already have been used up.

The market perceives the different suppliers with the services which they offer and their prices. The sole distinguishing feature between the different suppliers is the difference in their presentation and in what they have to offer. The simplest differentiation lies in the price. This is true for every sector. Many potential buyers like to keep their lives as simple as possible. A very strong sales argument is needed to get away from price alone. It is the programme manager's job to build up this argument for sales or for marketing communication and to make it available. This argument must tackle the specific needs of the target groups.

Target group/market segment

Generally, the term 'market segment' designates a group of purchasers who have the same needs and display the same purchasing patterns. Those customers within a market segment who may be approached with very high expectations of success are 'target customers' within a 'target group'. Great care should be taking when compiling information relating to individual target customers. Clear and helpful answers to a variety of questions must be found and given. How do I identify a potential customer? Which potential customers are especially valuable? How does a valuable potential customer develop into a prospective buyer? Which performance characteristics must be fulfilled to make a prospective buyer a launch customer? How are the different types of customer, such as 'casual customers' and 'multiple customers' defined? How can the share of customer of a launch customer or a casual customer be increased? What steps to bond customers are necessary and meaningful to make real regular customers out of potential ones? What is the definition of the term 'regular customer'? Are all the customers who generate 70 – 90% of annual sales also regular customers? What features characterise this group, which makes up around 10 – 30% of all the company's customers? Are there different and defined stages in customer bonding programmes? How are regular customers served?

The old rule about segmenting the market and conquering the segments by establishing dominance in terms of market performance, applies to growing markets which are opening up. Segmentation can no longer be undertaken from a purely geographical viewpoint, such as, for example, the nine sociographically built up artificial nations in America, with Ecotopia in the Californian West, Dixie in the Southern States, Mexamericana, New England, Quebec, the Bread Basket in the centre, the Empty Quarter in the Mid-West and the Foundry in the East with the dying industrial cities and the islands with Miami as the capital.[90] Segmentation by interests and current reaction is becoming much more important. The different user groups on the Internet offer a taste of a fine-tuning of interests yet to come.[91] The electronic protocols of direct interaction with surfers on Web sites are the 'snapshots' of the current reaction of customers and potential buyers. It is important to differentiate between interest groups that are of a generic nature and those of a current nature. General interests, such as Chinese cuisine, travelling in the Andes, Eskimo culture, are interests which are of long duration. The individual members may, under certain circumstances and viewed over a lengthy period of time, migrate away from these groups and turn to other interests. Research into individual aspects of special interest groups and the development profile of the trends in terms of interests of individual consumers will, however, assume major importance for future communications work.

Marketing mix

The strategic aspect of the marketing mix is the original marketing mix of market performance for the relevant target groups and the planned change of marketing mix over and above the market life cycle. How best to bring together price, trading channels, market communication and market performance over the phases of introduction, growth, maturity and phase-out within a product's life-cycle? Which instruments are used in communication and how can customer bonding be achieved? How is share of customer systematically increased?

The term 'market performance' has been chosen on purpose. Market performance may, in essence, consist of three different components: a pure product – e.g. durable consumer goods, staple goods or an item of equipment. Market performance can also be purely a service: transport, lending on credit, supplying energy, body care or training. The third type is software, the transferrable and replicable application science, mostly in condensed form. Software is a typical product of the information era. Market performance may be made up of all three components, with one component representing the core on which the others depend. The three components' share in market performance will change over the life phases cycle. Often, but not categorically, the product is termed a 'system'.[92]

Completely new forms of market performance, for instance, the production of three-dimensional prototypes using stereo lithography, call for intensive training to open up the market for the core service. The service aspect is necessary to open up the market. Three-dimensional prototypes are being used increasingly in medicine. This involves the exact reproduction of any part of the body in plastic. This is based on data determined using computed tomography. The technique is used in very difficult operations on the skull and enables the operating team to run through the necessary stages of the operation on a realistic artefact before carrying out the operation on the patient.

Once the manufacturer's market performance has been introduced and disseminated, expenditure on training will fall. Under certain circumstances, however, the supply of software can extend market performance within the life cycle.

Resources

What has the aspect of resources got to do with a marketing programme? The resources to set up the core service are to a major extent determined by production. However, the increasing personalisation of customer relations and the increasing significance of the most diverse services and software in terms of market performance call for clear ideas on the development of resources within the product life cycle. As market performance is characterised by the increasing service share, the question of personnel resources is very central. Like materials and information these are important, but in cyber marketing the right people, together with their skills and knowledge, are poised to assume a central position. This may be to perform a service or, something which is even more accentuated, in the creation of software.

Personnel

Too much stress cannot be laid on the importance of choosing the right person for a particular job. Those with responsibility at company level and, in particular, personnel directors have, during the industrial era, developed a very peculiar attitude towards human resources based on the production line mentality. In many companies, personnel directors are merely administrators and contact points for external recruitment agencies. Directors with responsibility for personnel are often not properly qualified to judge activities in their own company. For this reason they are unable to correctly assess the skills and abilities of their employees and of new applicants. Employees are often declared to be the human capital of a company. However, it is only very seldom that principles for evaluating this capital are available and still less actual measures which serve to increase its value.

The successful implementation of marketing programmes calls for an individual who knows his way about the company and is familiar with its market performance, besides knowing the market and being conversant with technology. As regards personality, he should be of a disposition which enables him to lead a team, keep it together and moderate it. However, this person is only one part of the team; the other members are equally important. As one single person is hardly going to be able to meet all the requirements, the necessary skills and knowledge will need to be guaranteed by several people within the team.

If a team is being brought together for a particular task, it is normal practice to keep a look-out for suitable people in the immediate vicinity, for instance at the company's headquarters. Those responsible for the project will put their heads together and come up with some possible names. The result in practically every company is quite amazing: it seems that there is only a very small number of really top-flight people to be found in individual companies.

The company will need to take appropriate measures to counteract this human shortsightedness. So what do investors have in common with personnel directors? Both have to be able to give information at any time on the current composition of their portfolio. Both need to be constantly keeping a look-out on the market for assets which will bring about an increase in the value of their investment target, the portfolio, not necessarily in the short term, but in the long term, corresponding to the vision. It is possible, using the existing portfolio, to compile teams, something which would simply not come about using traditional methods. A portfolio is not drawn up solely for a subsidiary or a single group company, but for the entire enterprise. Using an Intranet it is possible to rapidly access and obtain a clear overview of employee skills profiles internally. Team members scattered all over the world can, thanks to modern-day communication methods such as Intranet, work together and systematically foster their abilities.[93] Scientific research and academic activity have already demonstrated this in the first 20 years of the Internet's existence.

The fact that the relevant data protection regulations need to be observed when setting up a portfolio of this kind containing information on individual personal skills within a company goes without saying.

Skills portfolio – credit/debit

The person responsible for the programme will set up the required profiles for his team members in accordance with the company's scheme. The people with responsibility for human resources will play a very important role in this phase of the actual compilation of a team to implement a marketing programme and this should be borne in mind when structuring the team.

Internal services

Highly conscious decisions will need to be taken about which activities and services are to be performed by internal stations and which are be obtained externally. The person responsible for the programme should, when making these decisions, allow himself to be guided by the company guidelines on strategic know-how.

External services

If there is sufficient time and excessive financial expenditure is not called for, an outside quotation should also be obtained for services rendered internally. This will provide a healthy opportunity to relativise internal cost estimates as well as the costs taken into account within the organisation[94].

Finances

At the end of the day, once the intended market performance has been defined, the external analysis concluded and the resources determined, the marketing programme itself must pay as far as the company is concerned. The financial aspects of a marketing programme incorporate the following steps: sales estimating, cost and investment planning and, deriving from this, a sales revenue plan.

This step in the planning of a marketing programme will be influenced to a major extent by accounting and company controllership directives. Many companies have clear rules at their disposal here. The person responsible for the programme either has a person placed at his side who is familiar with these aspects or he works in accordance with guideline directives. It is very useful to introduce those responsible for company planning to marketing matters. This extension of knowledge is, in most cases, highly expedient, as financial planners have, almost without exception, had a career in accounting and often lack proximity to and feeling for market feasibility. This is particularly necessary when costs and investments in conjunction with a marketing programme are to be capitalised.

The financial plan is based solely on estimates. The assumptions on which the figures are based in relation to turnover, costs and investments, should be fully and properly documented and recorded in the form of a condensed and intelligible summary. The current trend is simple: sales expectations are being pitched too high whilst costs and investments are too low. A good way of examining the financial plan for a marketing programme is to call the statement in question with assumptions of double the expenditure and half of the stated income.

Sales estimates

Many company activities, including marketing programmes, are justified, in accordance with the intentions of company politics, by means of flawed, careless, incorrect or manipulated sales expectations. A very serious discussion should be held about turnover and sales volume. A proper distinction is very frequently not made between the concepts of 'market potential', 'market demand' or 'market volume' and 'sales volume' or 'possible company turnover'. Possible turnover is dependent on the realisable market share, price and number of performance units. For this reason the marketing mix must be loosely determined at the strategic approach stage, the details being finalised at a later point in the planning.

Expected sales should be determined using both current methods. Market potential is determined using the 'build-up' and 'top-down' methods. The possible potential of a defined market is defined in terms of units and time. The inclusion of a time span in relation to markets and customer bonding is very much a fundamental consideration.

As far as pure products are concerned, the period of time in which saturation of the market can be assumed is the entire life cycle of a market. This is broken up into the individual phases of the life-cycle. Then the potential is split into the individual phases, after which the company's own market share in these phases is evaluated in accordance with the market strategy. Market share per phase is the basis for determining the different share of services. This system outlined illustrates that estimating sales is not a simple matter and should not be undertaken lightly.

The 'build-up' method originates from the individual customer. The question here is: 'What is the value of a customer above and beyond the life cycle that is to be expected?'

Costs

The cost aspects are, as a rule, the least problematic when it comes to forecasting. Very important and often neglected in practice are the recurring costs. With the accumulation of fixed day-to-day costs, the profit threshold and opt-out costs rise. These two aspects are central considerations in high-risk ventures.

Investments

Software developments are investments in the infrastructure of a company. Not all accountants and book-keepers see this as a fact. Traditional accounting is often ready to carry the warehousing facilities and the company car park as assets but not the instruments with which the preconditions for the supply of the service are created, such as databases and special software which cannot be allocated to a single product alone. Making full use of all opportunities to capitalise on development costs can be a decisive factor as far as undertakings are concerned, especially in the case of companies which are subject to the provisions of company law and hence to regulations governing the rendering of accounts and audit, where these opportunities will be fundamental. If the accountants continue to mentally cling to material values and only appreciate software, which is not physical, in terms of a cost, then it is only by recourse to official and recognised accounting rules that the situation can be illuminated.

According to IAS 9 (International Accounting Standards) which deals with book-keeping for research and development applications, a consistent policy is desirable for dealing with capitalisation and write-offs. Development costs can be capitalised only when clearly defined criteria are met. These must be demonstrated unequivocally and allocated to the development project. Allocation takes place at the point when the technical feasibility of the development is proved. Furthermore, the precondition for capitalisation is the intention to use the product resulting from the development and the certainty that there is a payback option available. Finally, evidence has to be provided that sufficient resources are available to see the development through to the end and to make use of it above and beyond the period forecast.

The level of capitalisation is limited by the fact that all costs (development, production, sales and administrative costs) have to be covered by the income that can reasonably be expected in the future.

The amortisation of costs can either be undertaken in conjunction with sales or linear over a fixed period. It is important that the method is identified and maintained. Should the preconditions underlying capitalisation cease to apply, then the non-amortised capitalisation should be charged off immediately to costs. This check should take place at the end of every accounting period.

Bearing in mind the importance of this aspect, in the USA guidelines are also issued by the FASB (Federal Accounting Standards Board) and GAAP (Generally Accepted Accounting Principles). The details are regulated in No. 86 of the Financial Accounting Standards.

Decisions on fundamental principles

The level which is responsible for making decisions may, based on information received from the station with responsibility for performance, assign to the programme manager, together with information relating to strategy, resources and finances and a budget to enable the programme to proceed, the decision on whether the programme should be completed in all its details. In this sense all work carried out hitherto will have the character of a preliminary project, which will be used to help with refining the marketing programme.

Marketing, planning and preparation

The different influencing factors of society, business and technology should be taken into account at the planning phase and be incorporated in the preparations. The changes in society are coming about due to the interaction of consumers and purchasers world-wide and rising demand for customised market performance with high quality, low prices and rapid availability. The clear social frontiers are becoming increasingly blurred due to multi-culturalism and diversity and this is reinforcing the fragmentation of the mass markets into actual micro-markets or single-customer niches. This is leading to a decline in the efficiency of mass communication media, such as television, which, because of increased advertising pressure, are also losing the power to approach customers with messages at all. Some figures from Germany, for example, underlie this: in the ten years from 1986 to 1996, the average viewing time per day increased by 21%, from 149 to 181 minutes. In the same space of time, the number of advertising spots transmitted increased from 162,000 to 1,250,000 per day, an increase of 671%. In view of these figures, it is not surprising that, today, 42% of TV viewers feel that the advertising spots are intrusive and try to protect themselves from advertising by switching from one channel to the other, something which is leading to a massive decline in viewer's ability to recall advertisements.[95] The business factors include global competition in particular, branch deregulation and regulation of industries, as, for example, by the European Union. A very decisive influence is exerted, furthermore, by conditions prevailing nationally which arise from interstate or multilaterally regulated agreements and are giving rise to a re-consolidation of competitive factors.

Product/service

Market performance, whether this means products, software or services or a combination of all three, is becoming increasingly customised, personalised and information-determined. Information relating to market performance should be recorded and this activity should be stepped up in the course of the ensuing life cycle. In virtual space, a supplier's ability to allow the attributes of market performance to be defined by the customer has an extraordinary effect in determining the level of success that can be achieved in the market. The ability of companies to create virtual products; i.e. products prior to physical production, within virtual reality, and offer them as finished products so that customers can test the functions and advantages in cyber space, will present those responsible for marketing in the information era with a completely new set of demands.[96] The nature of marketing capability must undergo a fundamental change and be completely customer-centred in terms of all its efforts.

In all industries and especially in the business-to-business area, there will be an increase in the pressure to develop products simultaneously with the customer. Traditionally, products have been designed and passed on to marketing for distribution. Product development was almost completely dependent on the intellectual and physical capacity of the producer to generate new product ideas and to translate them into market performance. These enterprises are mostly very technology and product orientated. Customers only appear when someone is required to pay for the finished products. One example of this is the American automobile industry prior to 1985. Marketing had to make good the deficits which arose due to the manufacturers concentrating far more on what their production facilities were handing out than on what the customers actually wanted. This smouldering problem only became apparent when the Japanese competition appeared on the scene, along with their vehicles which lived up to customer expectations.

Customer segments and reference customers

Customer segmenting is the process of extracting from the market potential purchasers in measurable and approachable groups who have a high probability of conforming to the customer profile which has been matched to a company's market performance. Whereas mass marketing had not encountered segmenting, in the post-consumer epoch of the industrial era, this was based chiefly on demography, socio-economic profiles or psychographic models and was to this extent location-related. Even today factor analyses and cluster simulations are being used to extrapolate future expectations based on patterns from the past. The basic data for this comes from a handful of companies which specialise in market analyses. This fact explains the slight differences in the analyses despite using the same kind of methods, which does not throw doubt on the results as such, although it probably affects their usefulness in developing a convincing competition strategy based on them.

In cyber marketing, the actual reaction of the customers is crucial to segmenting. The history of individual customer reaction is managed by the companies themselves directly on a proprietary basis using databases in such a way that it can be evaluated. This information has a completely different quality to the market studies and consumer analyses carried out in the past, where customers were not actually statistical determining magnitudes but merely statistics. Using their own data as a basis, companies are able to determine the essential values: the customer's potential in terms of expenditure, share of customer and degree of customer bonding. From this the profitability of the individual customer can be determined, as well as the potential for the future and, with it, the value of a single customer or of actual customer groups.

If segmentation in marketing was traditionally construed as an art, then understanding and dealing with customer segments in cyber marketing will be a matter of using data warehousing techniques and the skilful handling of marketing databases, methods of extracting data and building up information, as well as the means of depicting what are, in part, highly complex statements, in the most user-friendly manner possible.[97]

Making the closest possible contact with selected customers as early as possible is highly crucial to the preparation and creation of market performance. Added to this is the need to develop customer bonding programmes so that they come very close to what customers expect or will accept. For these purposes, reference customers at an early stage are extremely vital to success. Reference customers with prominent names are, for many prospective buyers, one more reason to decide on a particular supplier.

Companies should consider whether the relationship with their suppliers is better than with their own customers. Where relatively close bonding with suppliers actually exists, the basic attitude of the company management should be reviewed. The customer relationship will ultimately decide the success of the company more directly than the suppliers in a contract relationship. Customer relations should be formulated on the basis of cooperation and not under the premiss of antagonism.[98]

Advertising, promotion and communication

Laymen very often equate marketing with advertising. However, the experts know that this is not so. Cyber marketing, on the other hand, transforms advertising to a massive extent. Traditionally, advertising consisted of placing a small number of advertising messages in an optimum position within the mass media. Due to advertising pressure, however, the actual message became increasingly of secondary importance, because to register at all became increasingly the maxim. The effect could be determined by means of objective measurement criteria, such as range, audience, costs, or, in the case of radio and television broadcasting, by the time of day. The price for using it is not determined by the effect of the relevant advertising but by the position of the individual medium by comparison to the market.

In cyber marketing the traditional media do not simply fall away, but are supplemented by on-line options. The traditional advertising media need to be used this way in order to draw the attention of potential buyers to the opportunities of direct interaction in cyber space. Cyber marketing using databases targets the single individual and tries to co-ordinate advertising to take account of the relevant profile in terms of interests and response. Advertising in respect of a particular brand is no longer a matter of being as open and general as possible so as to reach a maximum number of market participants, but, instead, it is individualised and stresses the personal note within the context of the brand. This can only be achieved by full mastery of databases and electronic communication media. Even today there is technology available on the WWW for digital bank deposits and pop-ups. This makes it less possible for the competition to imitate the advertising because the advertising techniques used are no longer broadly visible and even individual examples only become representative once the relevant customer profile is known. Overall the object of the advertising becomes increasingly aesthetic and is to a lesser extent characterised by grandiose creative notions and the inevitable transformation into one-sided messages than by the ability to carry on actual communication as well as being in a position to deal with feedback customer statements. In cyber space, the advertising sector loses its halo of elitist creativity; it will have to be prepared at any time to submit its former claim to exclusive dexterity in communication in each individual instance of contact to measurable proof.

In addition to promoting sales, promotional activity in cyber space will be to a major extent aimed at obtaining detailed customer information, based on which a promotional programme tailor-made for a specific user can be created quickly and dynamically. Compared to 'Princess Advertising', promotion traditionally has the ranking and assumes the personality of the 'Frog', hopping about in the every day swamp of sales pressures, chasing glamourous advertising successes and trying to reach budget targets by rather unspectacular measures. Promotions have something erratic about them and are not routed through the channels of actual customer response.

In cyber marketing however, promotion becomes an intimate conversation with the customer and in essence changes fundamentally – the frog for   his part, has become a handsome prince and, in terms of his future function in cyber space, is more than the equal of 'Princess Advertising'. In a really personally managed promotion, the data on the relevant customers forms the basis and dealing with this data is a highly sophisticated process. Individual market potential and respective share of customer can be very precisely balanced against the costs for the relevant promotion. Viewed in this way, the incoming flow of costs incurred in customer bonding simply mirrors future earnings potential. Something that is becoming a crucial factor in terms of promotion is timing; it is not the particular point in time when a specially good offer can be made that counts, but the moment when customers are interested in making a purchase. Hitherto these aspects have been left to one side in low-tech promotion. Overall, in cyber marketing, advertising and promotion make the transition from the one-sided transfer of information to communication: instead of confrontation, we have interaction.

COMMUNICATIVE INTERACTION CAN BE DISTINGUISHED BY THE FOLLOWING POINTS:

- *Communication from the time when contact is first made, through the first sale right through to the point where a relationship is established will become increasingly more personal and strive towards an indissoluble bond.*
- *Communication prior to the respective sales is a special service to the customer.*
- *Interactivity is an incentive to gather data about the customer so as to understand him better.*
- *Even when the time of communication is determined by the customer, the respective content of the communication should be managed by marketing using digital and interactive technologies.*
- *The co-ordination of corporate reality in cyber space with the company's actual appearance is central to the overall customer relationship.*
- *The fundamental approach within the customer relationship must be universally present and perceptible in all media and also in personal contacts made by company representatives.*

Pricing

The item 'Prices' in the marketing mix is just the tip of the iceberg in the overall sales/purchase agreement. In markets dominated by sellers, customers must accept prices. Today they no longer do this and will be increasingly less prepared to simply accept prices, given the complete transparency of prices in cyber space. Whereas suppliers today adopt a very simple approach to pricing, because a large number of different conditions, such as delivery and payment deadlines and volume-based scales of prices, are too expensive to administer, the situation in cyber marketing is completely otherwise. Yes, prices are primarily determined or chosen by the customers. But suppliers have, within certain parameters, the opportunity of varying their policy so that the individual price which the customer feels he is justified in demanding is also based on individual terms and conditions.

The refinement of terms and conditions and commitment to a correspondingly cleverly devised price structure is further promoted by the possibility of micro prices. In the modern business world, certain prices lie below the administrative costs of carrying out the transaction. This means, in reality, that it would be cheaper not to supply the products at all or even to give them away. Because of certain customer expectations this is not done, for, ultimately, a customer may go over to a competitor completely if he is forced to make the unprofitable purchases from the competition. Companies who have made adjustments to their range on the basis of product profitability are familiar with this dilemma.

Due to the reduction in transaction costs, micro prices can already be applied to low costs on-line today and, in the future, in cyber space. There is currently a problem on the Internet in that, for instance, electronic publications of print media, such as the *Wall Street Journal* or *Playboy* have to make their contents accessible free of charge because network users are not prepared to pay an electronic subscription. It is equally unreasonable, bearing in mind the current cost of credit card transactions, to charge for calling up individual pages. The possibility of charging micro prices puts a totally different complexion on matters.

Support strategies in micro pricing are basically aimed at increasing frequency and incorporating the time axis in price determination. It actually adds a completely new dimension to price determination. It originates from combining the time axis with the traditional quality, performance and quantity axes.

In the area covered by the suppliers of information, for example, the combination of frequency and immediacy gives rise to a completely new price structure. The value of information declines with time; this is particularly so in the sphere of stockmarket and finance data. With the decline of immediacy, the price charged in good cyber marketing will also fall, going through five different pricing grades from real time immediacy through up-to-the-minute relevance to day- and week-related values and, finally, on to statistical values.

The price structure in cyber marketing is characterised by high variability in relation to terms and conditions, the high level of application of micro prices and the use of new pricing parameters, such as time.

People

Certain ways of looking at the marketing mix incorporate people in addition to product, price, promotion and placing. Instead of the classic four P's we talk about five P's. This is a justifiable viewpoint as, at the end of the day, people are always involved in any activity. Nevertheless, this point is a particularly legitimate one in a marketing context with a number of different distribution channels including the direct sales form.

Cyber marketing, in the final analysis, is a form of direct selling on a non-personal, digital basis. Success in cyber marketing cannot, as a rule, be ensured by individual persons, because the craft of marketing needs to be teamed with mastery of information technology and telecommunication. The team is the actual organisational unit, which means that team work must be accorded appropriate recognition within the culture of an enterprise.

The typical team in today's on-line marketing comprises, in addition to the team leader, in most cases a marketing professional, the Web Master, the Content Master, the Customer Relations Manager, the Business Fulfilment Manager, the Marketing Managers for the respective market services and the creative individual responsible for multimedia communication. This team has a large number of other specialists working for it. In cyber marketing, these functions will continue to exist and a Context Specialist will be added to the team.

Customer bonding

Whereas, in the past, marketing was responsible for 'communication' with the market but not for the quality of such communication, this undergoes a fundamental change in cyber marketing. Responsibility for customer bonding lies with marketing. It has every possibility at its disposal of not only increasing but also measuring both its circle of customers and customer bonding.

Marketing in cyber space without a customer bonding philosophy is naïve, rather like enrolling in a chess tournament without having familiarised oneself with the basic rules of chess.

Customer bonding is worthwhile – for both sides. Thanks to the continuous dialogue with the supplier, customers are better informed about new products and special offers and this leads to increased requirement, purchasing frequency and sales. In the case of customers of the IKEA Family Club, the average amount purchased is 15% higher than for the other customers.[99] Many other company marketing departments have had similar experiences with customer bonding programmes. The open customer club is, in cyber marketing too, an important basic element which contributes to customer bonding. A customer club is termed 'closed' where the link with the members is forged by means of a commitment other than pure customer registration, for instance, in the form of a membership subscription. In the case of airlines, it is normally a minimum number of miles flown or flying frequency that puts up the barriers by ensuring that only people who need to travel a great deal are included. By restricting access to the clubs, potential in terms of customer expenditure can be segmented, thus facilitating handling. The other link in improving customer bonding in cyber space is based on the high degree of person-alisation in dialogue and interaction with the customer based, for the one part, on his externalised profile of interests and, for the other, on his actual response.

Logistics

Linking the marketing systems, the systems which give access to cyber space – cur-rently the Web servers – to the existing productive systems is important and ne-cessary for raising cost efficiency. Commercial activities and communication in cyber space must be connected to the delivery systems in the real world in order to ensure a continuously smooth-running process. We should be looking for the best possible way of incorporating the 'instant' mentality in cyber space into the struc-ture of logistics. With the traditional response of mass marketing being to make a 'sale' and not to bother particularly about any further relationship with the cus-tomer, certain marketing people had a tendency to assign less importance to the post-sales phase. The customer relationship in cyber marketing is a 'til death do us part' relationship and the first business transaction has a honeymoon significance within this community of interests. Logistics, customer service is an everyday structure and is a crucial factor in determining whether the relationship breaks down or not.

Contracting/legal aspects

Current legislation as far as very many aspects of marketing are concerned is, in itself, very clear. The legal interpretation – on the Internet today and in cyber space in general – is, however, bedevilled by the fact that, as an activity, it has no fixed location. Laws, decrees and guidelines ultimately rely on geography as an ordering principle; they always apply to a definite terrain over which a society or political power claims jurisdiction. If the location cannot be unequivocally identified, seri-ous problems will arise. Geography, and, along with it, the states, reflect the respective views of their politicians and their societies. This fact is extremely inter-esting in terms of the philosophy of law, but does not help with current problems.[100] And it is not as if there is an improvement in sight. First of all, opportunities on the network are developing more quickly than the legal experts' understanding of how to interpret the technical innovations within the context of the existing legal sys-tems of around 120 countries linked to the Internet, and, secondly, these interpre-tations inevitably founder on the lack of physical location, something for which no provision has hitherto been made in law.

The rule of thumb can only be to operate as well as possible within the frame-work of the existing conditions, always being aware that changes can happen. For certain areas, such as intellectual ownership, the area of copyright and brand name protection, co-operation with leading legal experts from the relevant country is being imposed. The broad sector of data protection is currently well covered by lawyers and publications.[101]

Internal launch

The inception of a marketing programme should also be announced internally within the company. The organisation's employees must be able, broadly speaking, to give information about activities in the market and in cyber space. A company's employees are important communicators within their respective environments.

In addition, employees can also be useful in field tests. Why on earth should a customer bonding programme be accepted by the market when even a company's own employees cannot be convinced by it? Good communication begins at home.

Training

The philosophy of cyber marketing is a rejection of traditional marketing thought. Cyber marketing makes use of a large number of progressive technologies and is in a process of powerful development. Other company departments, such as Production and R&D, but also Controllership and the Personnel Department, have hardly been aware of even the bare principles of the old-style marketing. To introduce and implement the programmes based on this new approach, it is essential that all departments co-operate with one another. Training in the basics is, therefore, very important for all sectors within the company and not only for marketing specialists.

Sales planning

Before sales planning can take place in cyber space, experience has to be built up. It is geared to short-term opportunities. As the time span from idea to presentation on the market has been massively reduced, thus sales too can be stimulated by promotion to give a number of short-term actions. Sales planning is primarily based on existing experience but this experience is broken down into more precise time periods.

Support

Many of our contemporaries are technophobes – they have an aversion to technology – either from a personal nature or, increasingly, for ideological reasons; which does not matter. The minimum level of support offered should be a telephone number with a person at the other end. This minimum facility opens up the borders to stretch to a virtual classroom for a customer training course or a course for salesmen within the company's field.

Nationalisation

Closeness in terms of communication is achieved primarily through language. Closeness to customers is therefore expressed in one's choice of language; this even applies within the English language. In 1996, English-speakers were represented on the world-wide on-line market of the Internet by around 480 million people with more than 100 million PCs between them. However, as far as the language is concerned, very great differences exist both between the USA and the UK, but also between these two and Australia. Fine-tuning in customer communication must take account of this fact. Complete linguistic nationalisation is necessary for the other already well-developed markets. Linguistically speaking, the second largest market is Japan with 124 million inhabitants and a PC density of 12 for every hundred inhabitants. The German-speaking market, with 94 million inhabitants and a population of 15 million PCs in Germany, Austria and Switzerland, is in third place. In fourth position comes France with a population of around 68 million people and 10 million PCs. Korea occupies fifth position.[102]

Execution of the programme

It is only at this stage that we have proof that our assumptions and the steps taken to implement the programme were correct. Management attention is very important in the early phase of execution. Significant adjustments may still be appropriate.

Organisation

The integration of the programme team into the existing line organisation and the adoption of activities by the respective stations which are already institutionalised is an important transition process. The programme team's knowledge must be transferred to the follow-up organisation, if the programme members are not themselves integrated into the process organisation. As a rule, integration is recommended only once the programme team has been able to demonstrate success with the marketing programme.

Programme checking

Checks take place periodically based on the original target guidelines. A marketing audit is recommended after the introduction phase to disclose any possible improvements. Ultimately, the decisive factors as far as the success of the programme are concerned are sales volume and net margin, together with share of customer. However, regular assessments by customer relations panels are indispensable as regards introducing corrective measures and improvements.[103]

Risks/critical success factors

A significant aspect of programme objectives at director level is risk. In the final analysis, the risk must shed light on the chances of realising the declared objective. In addition to the risks inherent in the product, such as intensity of competition, speed of market change and the risks associated with implementing the project. This latter is the main risk as far as those responsible and other participants are concerned.

Conclusion: Marketing Programmes Aimed at the Achievement of Customer Bonding and an Increase in Share of Customer

Marketing programmes stand for the systematic marketing philosophy within a company which is operationalised in a standardised manner. Core points in cyber marketing are long-term customer bonding and the logical pursuit of increased share of customer in a customer relationship characterised by interaction. Communication in cyber space is a personal process based on customer characteristics registered on line, such as information given by the customer himself, interests expressed and actual response in cyber space. The planning and implementation of marketing programmes is team work under the charismatic leadership of an individual with responsibility for marketing. The technical systems are means to marketing's end, which is the achievement of company targets.

8 IMPLEMENTATION PROJECTS

Control of Software Development Projects

Software and habits are character-related. What one has, one disregards. What one does not have, one desires. Awareness of change arises through pressure exerted by the environment. Change, in turn, is uncertainty. Those responsible for change experience uncertainty as a risk and those affected by it as fear. Obvious to all concerned is that the beginning is arduous and the venture certainly means a great deal of additional work, but the driving force lies in the prospect of change leading to success.

Opinions on how new software should be created are as diverse as they are infinite. Many instructions and suggestions are systematically and theoretically underpinned, others have grown out of practical experience. Practical success seems to feel more comfortable with the character of a gambler than that of a dogmatist.

This only applies to one of the two different basic types of development activities; these are development tasks which are, on the one hand, aimed at improving an existing product and at the creation of a completely new product on the other. The first activity is part of the daily round within the company. It is permanent or periodically recurring and established organisations should cope with it. It serves to address further development or product expectations in the broader sense. In the case of software, this is regulated by an appropriate policy of release and version planning.

The creation of new products is, in the final analysis, a tangible achievement. It is non-recurring, of limited duration and does not progress automatically along an established course. These are the characteristic features of projects.[104] If the new product scores in a competitive situation because of its novelty value, then we can talk about 'innovation'.

A demand for innovative software development projects will, as far as the majority of managers are concerned, sound warning bells whilst the spectre of risk rises in the background – deadlines undermining completion dates, additional costs breaking like waves over budgeted items and quality levels stranded far from the original tide-mark: a situation akin to a storm on the high seas. But weather conditions can be overcome – seamen know that – everyone in the team knows the objective, his task and is fully conversant with the elements of his craft. This applies equally to the pilot, the helmsman and the captain – the management crew.

The risk associated with a product depends to a considerable extent on the development team. Specialist capability in the fields of methodology and tools for software development as well as a high level of experience in the sector where the application is to be used must be present within the group. But smooth communication will enable the team to bring its own abilities and the specialist knowledge of the users together in a single product.

As far as software development management is concerned, it is possible to reduce the risk as far as the following aspects are concerned:

- Quality.
- Responsibilities.
- Planning, organising, monitoring and controlling the development process.
- Calculation and observation of deadlines and costs.

By observing relatively simple rules it is possible to obviate the risks associated with implementation and reduce them during the course of the project work.[105]

No development without users

Co-operation with users goes beyond merely formulating their requirements and is active in all the phases of a development. If the development work is not aimed at an application for individual and therefore non-recurrent usage, but instead targets the multiple marketing of the development as a product, then it is important to ensure, by means of suitable collaboration, that requirements which may be all too individual do not infiltrate the general basic version. Co-operating with more than one user group will ensure this. In addition to the IT specialists, the users should be involved in the development project at each phase of its development. As in a Web process, the knowledge of two fields – that of the user and that of the person developing the application – are brought together to form a whole. If the product is to be marketed then prior market studies are essential.[106]

Prior to commencement of the project, a commitment to exploration must prevail over the rough functionality of the system. The expression 'commitment to exploration' underlines the fact that, on commencing the development of application software, the functions and qualities contained in the final application cannot be defined to their ultimate extent. This calls for a general objective and functionality of an application to be agreed in the knowledge that the specification will be jointly worked out in the first part of the project.

Agreed sequence of phases

The fact that, at the beginning of a development project, only a commitment to exploration exists, is a vital point in assessing the risk. In the case of development projects, it should as far as possible be reduced and/or managed. It is in this procedural aspect that traditional phase models often fail. They are based on breaking the development work down into individual steps in order to promote a supreme solution.[107]

The phase model must be so operationalised in co-operation with users that both developers and operators can work in conjunction with the model and, as the project progresses, an increase in the certainty of realisation must be identifiable. This means that the consequences of individual actions and responsibilities must be clearly perceptible with tangible results to assist in dividing up the phases. Instrumental aspects include planning, control and communication. In alignment with the individual phase targets, the allocation of tasks, project responsibilities and guidelines for resolving conflict situations should be contractually agreed prior to commencement of the project.[108]

Binding project agreement

The rules of the project are reflected in the structure and content of the contractual agreements relating to a project between the parties. 'Parties' means the development team, promoters and participants as well as users/operators and any control bodies such as, for example, audit companies. The contractual implementation of the project guidelines must be such that any infringement will be construed as a contravention of the mutually acknowledged objectives.

Quality based on requirement-targeted software development

Behind every specific activity (which is what any new software development should be) there is a requirement. The formulation of requirements arises from the need to solve a problem. Problems may be perceived highly generically; excessive costs by comparison to competitors or failure to process information quickly enough. Often an attempt is made to remove an existing application with its limitations and target 'embroidery' in order to simplify activities or increase working capacity. Sophisticated users today are very quick to recognise needs. They expect answers to existing problems. These are the sources of innovation. They are, without exception, to be found where the needs of operator, customers, employers or other users have been formulated.[109]

Project Dimensions

The dimensions of a project are provided by the level to which functions, time and costs are fulfilled. The functions are wholly defined and fulfilled in the course of the project. According to the detailed specification, a risk of under-fulfilment exists. As a rule both the completion date and the costs are subject to fixed agreement prior to commencement. This constitutes a fulfilment risk.

Functions

An initial commitment to exploration is formulated in the initial phases and the functions are definitively determined. On commencement of the project, the functions of the software to be produced should be roughly sketched out, i.e. formulated so as to permit workable decisions at management level. The progress of the individual steps to fulfil the functions will be evident from the portrayal of the phases.

Deadlines

Deadlines should be realistic but ambitious. On the other hand, in certain projects, such as connecting to the EBS (Swiss electronic stock exchange) deadlines will be specified. Here a feasibility study should be carried out. By contrast to production processes, it is not possible, when developing software, to shorten the length of the project by providing more staff. As the number of development employees increases, so the costs of co-ordination within the development team rise. The limit is around a dozen staff – and this assumes tasks that are easily modularised. Innumerable examples exist to back up the theory that a project should not extend over a period of more than 20 months. The maximum project size for a single team thus amounts to 20 person-years and/or 240 person-months. Very large projects must be modularised into appropriate part-projects.

Costs

The costs of a development project are, to a considerable extent, influenced by two factors; the types of cost are dealt with in detail below. The most significant factor in terms of cost is staff costs which are expressed in person-months in direct proportion to the size of the project. Added to this are the costs of development licences or other licences to third parties. If the deadlines are adhered to, this can as a rule also apply to the costs.

Project structure

Participants

Clear group structures are important for the organisation of the project. The project leaders must demonstrate a high level of ability to communicate as well as of leadership. However, when it comes to leading the development team in particular, it is not so much the formal skills of the project leader that are important as his personality. It is in the nature of developers not to see themselves in a hierarchical way and not to have any sympathy for excessive bureaucracy.[110]

One dozen people is the maximum for a project team. Various studies have shown that, with different size groups, the amount spent on co-ordination increases in excessive proportion to the gain. The quality of the project team is not dependent on the number of participants, but solely on their specialist and interpersonal qualities. The development team must be able to communicate with the operators within their individual specialist areas.

Of all the operators participating in the project, it is of primary importance to take into account those who pass on knowledge. People on the operating side who have good abstracting abilities are very useful within the context of a project. Both on the operating and the development side it is essential to include management. In addition to information meetings geared to the individual phases, management must, in principle, be easily accessible for communication purposes at any time.

The project coach or, for instance, the individual piloting the development project, has a significant role to play in this important aspect. He is not part of the team, but, in this situation, he is a member of the team. The pilot is responsible for observing the project code as the development progresses, in all its aspects and phases.

Project code

The code is binding for and known to everyone involved. Discussions which do not serve to clarify mutual understanding, but which are concerned with decision variations should be based on the following principles.

Thinking through to the end

'The end' in this context means usage by operators and the maintenance of the application by the relevant specialists. The various considerations and questions must be related to the prime factor, which is the use of the application. Only decisions made on this basis will result in the desired benefits.

80-20 Approach

When it comes to determining the benefit to be achieved, the awareness that, with 20% of expense around 80% of the benefit will be achieved, must be pragmatically implemented. The remaining 20% of the benefit must obviously be acquired with 80% expenditure. Increasing benefit by means of major expenditure can always be a further development activity during the use of an application. Failure to consider this disparity logically will have a significant effect on deadlines and costs.

Talking – immediately and openly

Those concerned, in particular the development team, should identify with decisions and the procedure implemented. Identification is only possible where partici-

pants are fully informed. This fact is often argued and dismissed in the face of more
informed opinion. An attempt may be made, using a number of wily tricks and
material incentives, to achieve identification nonetheless. In the last instance,
incentive management will be brought to bear instead of project management. The
wisdom of teams is proverbial and only exists when full expression is given to communication and information. Any resistance on the part of those involved must be
discussed immediately and openly. Resistance as regards the matter itself needs to
be dealt with by recourse to the project rules, whilst personal objections should be
settled directly by the project leader.

Growing with the project

The project can be more than simply a job for those concerned. Employees everywhere have jobs. The individual is motivated to apply himself with greater vigour
when he is given the opportunity to achieve a benefit for himself personally, i.e. to
grow with the job. This may also be termed 'vision management'. Thus interpreted,
the project acquires an additional plane. This 'meta'-level is a starting point for
reflection and permits a level of objectivity which it will not otherwise be possible
to achieve here.[111]

The map is not the landscape

Instruction manuals about how to conduct successful project management are
picked out with models showing how to proceed. In practice, many of these models fail because they are insufficiently operationalised. The procedural model must
be comprehensible to everyone concerned and be handled in a logical manner by
the person responsible. Phase models with just a few clearly defined activities are
easy to understand.

In practice, however, the creation of links with previous phases is usual. But
reiterations of this kind are mostly related to individual aspects and seldom to the
totality of the project.[112] Feasible alternatives very quickly present themselves as far
as decision-making is concerned. Instead of reiterating variants, it is more worthwhile to conduct a analysis of risks and contingency planning.

The map is not the landscape. Nor is the project procedure the project itself.
The procedural framework makes it possible to determine the situation at any
time and acts to a major extent as an orientation aid for improvisations. The only
thing to bear in mind is that improvisation without an underlying plan spells
chaos.

The target first

Phase 1 is the objective of the future application which is to be realised by the project. The objectives should be devised jointly with the operators. Increasingly, tasks
consist of removing an application which has been in use for many years. The

application to be worked out must, as a minimum, cover the existing functions and provide additional features.

For such situations Reverse Engineering is often suggested as a developmental procedure by way of an alternative to a new development. Essentially, the functions should be abstracted from the existing application and implemented in a new technology. This alternative is the least desirable of the two. The current popularity of business process re-engineering explains why. In pure software engineering, no new functions will be brought into the application from the business's current daily routine.

In this phase it is important that the employees involved in the project, the development staff and the users should agree on a mutual language and/or be familiar with the language of the other sector. The developers of the application in particular need to be able to find their feet very quickly in the language of the operators. As far as the public who are to use the software are concerned, the handbooks, as well as the different screens and the evaluations, must be produced in the language used by the operators. Phase 1 concludes with a detailed specification. In essence it answers the question: what must the application be capable of? The functions of the application should be clearly listed in the document presented.

The particular trap in this phase is the tendency of the operators to want to describe the application in detail at an early stage. Stimuli are very frequently present, primarily at the beginning. These should not be shut out but taken into account and retained for the following phase. A feel for communication on the part of the person responsible for the project is an essential factor in ensuring that the initial cooperation does not founder on detail. The phase sequences can be used as a clarification aid with a view to structuring the activity and to maintaining its continued smooth flow.

It is by means of dialogue and mutual effort that the expectations of the operators are brought up to the correct level. As far as the developers are concerned, it is possible to identify strict project boundaries. What is not important in terms of functions within the application should, without exception, be very clearly formulated. Here it is worthwhile taking on board any other desired points and bearing these in mind for a further development or a follow-up release based on what has gone before. For practical application, the 20-80 rule should be applied as a basis in this phase.

This target formulation can, overall, be between 5 and 15% of the overall project. The level of ability of the project leader is fundamental as far as the exact proportion is concerned.

Purposeful analysis

Phase 2, Processes/Functions, is triggered once an audit of the actual situation has taken place. Identification of the phase represents the two steps of analysis and design in software engineering.[113] When assessing the current position, the already existing IT media should be identified in addition to the 'real' situation. Depending on complexity, this activity may be of the magnitude of a Business Reengineering exercise. The principles which different authors have highlighted should be borne in mind here.[114] Particular attention should be paid to the following IT aspects in the target situation to be formulated:

- Data model and data holding as the foundation of the application.
- The location of operators is not significant.
- Decentralisation of decisions, concentration of control centrally.
- Discussion of organisational consequences with management.
- Avoidance of media breaks.

The data model is the basis of a modern application. Functional objects can be inserted and/or substituted relatively simply, particularly where the procedure is object-orientated. The data holding cannot be changed very quickly and easily and this may be due, for instance, to legal constraints. Finally, every organisation should maintain a certain minimum level of 'history'. This involves the continuation of past values in as congruous a manner as possible. Let us take a book-keeping situation as a simple example. New requirements within the context of business activity conflict with this. In the data model, these two factors with their conflicting effects are united, namely, the continuation of the information which was relevant in the past and the integration of new data.

Modern means of communication bridge the physical location of those involved in the commercial processes. Even if all are united in a single location today, this may still alter in the future. When designing the system, this should be taken into account from the very beginning. In this way the modularisation of the application into individual processes will be achieved.

By holding the relevant data in the system and reviewing it, with the addition of rules and framework conditions, to provide information, it is possible to decentralise decisions. Decisions should be taken at the point where effectiveness is achieved. The decisions can be centrally tracked and monitored by means of a 'meta' level (frequently also MIS: management information system).

Newly created or very rigid processes and their imaging within an application will, in their very nature, lead to changes in organisational form and thus affect areas of management responsibility. Where an alternative base is used, the possible consequences should be pointed out to the management at an early stage and agreement obtained for the variant selected, as otherwise internal company problems could arise at the implementation stage. This is one of the fundamental reasons why the coach and, if possible, the project leader too, need to have regular and unrestricted access to the management level of the commissioning body.

Media breaks are in many organisations today the main impediment to the efficient handling of data and the flow of information. Very often data is re-typed from manual applications into another application. The most frequent form of media break is in the figures sector. Absolute mountains of figures are printed out and then typed in again using a table calculating application. Media breaks should be avoided and minimised wherever possible.

Blueprint for operators

Ascertaining what the task of the operator is and how the job is to be done is one of the main tasks of the analysis sector. This consists of the detailed recording of operations and the data structures necessary for them. Co-operation between the development team and the operators is highly intensive in this phase. In the subsequent working discussions, it is important to bring out what in the application is necessary and what is merely desirable.

In order to achieve a broad-usage application, reviews with third party users are necessary. These may be experts from other companies but also third parties, such as audit firms and specialised consultants. Specialists in a number of commercial activities and sectors can be found at technical colleges and universities whose knowledge can be made good use of in the new design.

Phase 2 concludes with a logical data model and protocols for specifying application objects.

Experience will show that these documents are, as a rule, not easily understood by operators as a good entity model hardly contains any hidden superfluities and has a high level of abstraction.

Up to now not a single line of programme code has been produced. The acceptance of these phase results will describe an application almost completely in terms of its inner workings. But the operator cannot do a thing with it.

Operators obtain an understanding of the application through the system definitions in Phase 3. In this phase, all screen masks and analyses are clearly defined by means of prototyping both on paper and screen. In the same way, on conclusion of this phase, the communication interfaces with other applications should be completed.

The use of prototyping has proved very useful in this phase. It gives the user a good feeling as far as the final state of the application is concerned. Operators can find their way about more easily from the application's 'packaging' than was the case with the documentation from the previous phase. Working with the user guide, the operators examine, on the basis of the Phase 1 functions, whether the Phase 3 targets have been achieved or not, and the system is accepted accordingly.

After the first three phases, the system will be sufficiently precisely defined. The operator can see exactly what he is getting by way of an application.

Implementation by means of user tests

Phase 4 is initiated by the use of coding. Realisation incorporates the effective work required for setting up the software, tests and acceptance. The important factor in this phase is the fact that the specifications are 'frozen in' and no allowance is made for modifications in the specifications. It is quite feasible that, during the course of realisation, the need will arise to make adaptations to the specifications already agreed with the operators, but this tends to be the exception rather than the rule.[115] The test concepts are important as far as the quality of the application is concerned. As regards quality, the level of fulfilment of the application should be tested out using actual scenarios.

Quality

Quality can be described as the level to which the demands placed on a product by a customer are met (ISO 9001). If a software product meets the customer's requirements, we talk about high software quality; otherwise it is low. The level to which quality requirements are met can be identified by reference to a number of criteria. The most important one is the functional level of fulfilment of the application. Failure to fulfil the projected functions is therefore the greatest risk that can befall a development project. Within a risk management context, the main criteria are defined in the different phases. Proceeding along these lines, the risk of lower quality cannot be excluded, but it can be minimised by means of control. It is, in particular, very important to see where the cause of suspected low quality lies. One frequent source of error, namely unclear specification, can be avoided by applying the model of procedure. Low quality comes about either due to low quality requirements or by failure to meet quality guidelines. The former is caused by the operator and the latter is due to mistakes in development.[116]

It is only ease of maintenance that cannot be established until after acceptance has taken place. However, it is during the course of the project that data is established and target data controls are embarked upon.

Communication

As regards communication, many individuals and those in authority are of the opinion that one either communicates or does not communicate. This is utterly wrong. People constantly communicate and nobody is incapable of communication. In a software development project, the creative elements of which are immaterial, since thoughts, ideas, concepts and knowledge are processed, communication ability within the development team is a prerequisite for success.

Team members mostly communicate verbally but in any situation they may communicate non-verbally. Information is communicated within the team either openly or bilaterally concealed on the part of those involved. We talk about 'hidden' communication when the transfer of information and relationships take place mainly outside the overall team or partially outside the working social area and are addressed to selected individuals. Both non-verbal, open communicators as well as individuals who respond verbally but in a covert fashion can be identified within the team and, by applying appropriate leadership skills, be brought to open verbal communication. The covertly non-verbal type is difficult to integrate into a team and hence into a project.

Formalised communication should be kept to a minimum, since otherwise more written comments and reports will be produced than progress made towards declared aims. Larger organisations tend to adhere too rigidly to the report form.[117]

As a rule, reports are supposed to serve as a vehicle for justification when mistakes are made. Mistakes are bound to happen, but justifying them costs even more in terms of time, energy and money.

Project coaching

It is often advisable to engage an independent project coach. The reasons for this are obvious. The project leader is normally caught up in the general hierarchy of the company. In this sense he is subject to the normal political constraints of the existing structure. As far as the operator side is concerned, the other employees engaged in the project are also likely to be compartmentalised. A link should also be established in terms of this organisation which is not affected by hierarchical constraints. An external project coach will cope with all this. His main task is to ensure communication between the agents of the organisation, such as developers and operators, at every level. Essentially, his task will be to direct the systematics of the procedure and ensure that the principles established at the outset are adhered to. At the same time, his specialist skills in the application sector or his expert abilities as regards software development projects are critical if he is to be accepted by either team.

Project controllership

A rough estimate of costs should be established at a very early stage for both the overall project and the individual phases. The rough cost breakdown should incorporate the following types of costs:

- Personnel costs.
- Materials costs.
- Costs for third party services.
- Expenses.
- Project investments for items of equipment, licences for development environments, etc.

A minimum breakdown would include personnel costs, expenses and third-party services. Whilst the personnel costs bear a direct relationship to the number of employees involved and are thus in proportion to the size of the project, expenses and third-party services should be assessed in relation to the project.[118]

The company's accounts department will feel that it has to draw up a cost unit statement in which the project costs can be itemised in a classifiable manner. It has proved worthwhile to deal with the individual project phases separately, even within an accounting context, as some overlapping between the phases is practically impossible to avoid. This solution is based on the neat and logical documentation of hourly expenditure with corresponding statements of working hours.

A company will be well advised to conduct its accounting in respect of operations within the same framework as the relevant cost estimate for the individual phases. On conclusion of the project, the management will be able to obtain valuable fundamental principles by carefully analysing the original ballpark costs, detailed planning and the expenditure that has effectively resulted. These principles will make a significant contribution towards reducing risk in subsequent projects.

Project controllership should be systematically documented since these documents form the basis for the capitalisation of the development costs in financial statements and will therefore also be scrutinised by the audit department.

Conclusion: The Conquest of Cyber Space through System Development

Good project management will ensure system development in accordance with marketing requirements within a short time and with minimum risk. Transforming the objectives of cyber marketing into software systems calls for the combination of engineering systematics with marketing creativity, something which can only be achieved by team work. Abortive developments can be avoided by means of clear phase structuring, strict delineation of responsibilities and periodic progress controls as regards the project dimensions of function, cost and time. Investments in the infrastructure of connection to the cyber world can be capitalised in the balance sheet and written off over their anticipated useful life.

9 ESSENTIALS OF CYBER MARKETING FOR MANAGERS

Intellectual leadership, management of the migration from the values of the industrial era to the paradigms of the cyber age, the competition for market positions in virtual space and the logical increase in share of customer as a result of high levels of customer bonding may be postulated as the hinge points on which competition in the information-based and knowledge-determined future of the cyber age will be based.[119] At the same time, organisations need to become smaller, better and more knowledge-based so as to be able to develop full competence in the core skills. It is only in this way that companies will be able to survive in the future. How is it possible to make a statement of this kind with such conviction? The top manager in an organisation, whether it is local or multi-national, has a responsibility that no-one can take away from him. This is concern for the future of the company which has been entrusted to him or which he has built up himself. How then can a perspective on the future be established?

Seen from a historical point of view, we currently find ourselves in a phase of upheaval in the transition from the industrial society to the information era. The future is, therefore, set to be played out within the framework conditions pertaining to the information society. A pre-condition for the success of a company is its specific skill in handling information. The importance of this can be divided into two areas of creative ability: one is that the level of skill within the organisation should correspond to the most up-to-date level of know-how within one's own sector and the latest knowledge of the relevant communication technologies whilst, on the other hand, the information society is characterised by the opportunities for exchanging information, i.e. of communicating.

If the in-company aspect can be seen very substantially as a forward projection of the computer technology of the past, combined with the Web technology in the Intranet, then the ability to communicate on the part of society and the markets based on direct networking quite simply represents a completely new situation as far as the environmental conditions applicable to companies are concerned. These technologies not only affect day-to-day commercial practice but also have a major effect on society, the kind of effect which was attached in the past to such developments as the invention and introduction of railways and motor cars or the discovery and use of electrical energy, all of which have fundamentally shaped the face of the twentieth century.

The conclusion is obvious: the factors which promote success undergo change both within the environment and within companies. The more emphatically a decision with a short-term effect points in the correct direction within the context of the future, the less will be the need for corrections. This is the reason for management interest in estimating long-term developments, even as regards decisions which have immediate relevance.

Key Success Factors for the Information Era

What are the key factors for successfully coping with the future in the information era?

In the first place, companies must be geared up to the new framework which, after the end of the transformation phase, will develop out of the existing situation and to the commercial rules of the game which will apply to the information epochs.

In the second place, these call for an increase in information-handling skills and in communication within organisations – as well as in the use of new technologies – and for the establishment of commercial process structures based on knowledge.

Thirdly, the strategic opportunities offered by the assumption of competitive positions during the current emergence of the new virtual markets in cyber space should be utilised quickly and in a purposeful manner.

Fourthly, marketing needs to cope successfully with the promotion and smooth integration of the cyber market into existing marketing effort and company processes, taking into account the new rules of the game. The mastery of conventional telematics, in particular, data warehousing, decision support systems (DSS), applications for the electronic maintenance of customer bonding, communication with various digital media such as the Internet, interactive television, computer-aided speech and fax communication and the ability to quickly and purposefully harness the services of the Internet and its future mutations, multimedia technology and Web products and services, are becoming crucial factors in addition to the fundamental marketing philosophy of customer bonding.

The New Framework Conditions

Four industries that are today independent have the potential as well as the intention to determine the framework conditions and the future of the information era. Telecommunication is the oldest and, to date, the least liberalised industry. It has the best network structure at its disposal, even if transmission options are still, in a number of networks, based on analogue sound and data transmission, for instance, in fax communication. The youngest of the four industries ranks, as its name suggests, as a driving force – the computer industry, which has been offering information technology and computer science for four decades. The media industry has a trump card – the cable networks – which Net providers have built up for themselves and which, in the highly developed regions of the world, guarantee access to the more prosperous consumer sectors. The entertainments industry has now chalked up exactly one hundred years since the invention of films. It plays a significant role as a producer of content such as films, music and other audio-visual products. Within a decade the four industries will converge to form the TIME industry. TIME stands for Telecommunication, Information, Media and Entertainment. What effect will this new industry have on the market, the purchaser, the customer, the supplier or the seller? Within the information society the TIME industry (see figure 1) will dominate a continuous and multi-layered communications infrastructure which will be indispensable as far as both commercial and social life are concerned.[120] In the same way as roads and railways today provide a satisfactory transport system for people and material goods, cable, radio and satellite communication is becoming a highly efficient and potent global infrastructure for the interchange of information and knowledge. The information highway will not only be based on high-tech cable systems under the control of telecommunication companies, but instead we may expect that other network operators will create a real competitive situation and, primarily, create major transmission capacity. Every company, every household may well have at its disposal more than physical access to the world-wide communications infrastructure; we may be looking at the successor of today's telephone connection and the replacement of the cable television link. These new framework conditions for companies in all sectors world-wide are being shaped predominantly by the TIME industry: this has been developing since 1992, first of all within the USA and now on a global basis, through mergers, acquisitions or – as demonstrated by AT&T – by means of splits and as a result of the deregulation of the state monopolies within the telecommunications sector in Europe. The climax of these strategic restructurings and re-alignments of the industry which is fundamental to the information era still lies before us. Multimedia as a technology does not only open up new dimensions for PC freaks, it also changes the perspective on the future for those TIME industry companies that have hitherto been separated due to media breaks. In the future they will all come together as activities within the context of the TIME value chain, producing and communicating content as well as transmitting, something which, within a few years, may well bring about massive competition and over-capacity in terms of communication possibilities in the networks of the global information infrastructure.

Viewed from this angle, the Internet is the prototype of a digital infrastructure which will be made available by the TIME industry in the information era and is set to become the essential foundation for global economic activity. Together with Intranets, information-based activities within organisations as well as outside companies will be made significantly simpler, quicker and cost-effective. The world-wide network of information highways will establish a new market where mastery of the virtual value chain will represent a decisive factor in terms of competition.

Communication and transaction as an information activity

But what relationship does 'information' have to the economic process, to commercial activity, to the management task within an organisation, and what is its significance? Information and how to handle it is of central importance both to the economic system and to human life. The enormous importance of these factors is reflected in the following categorisation of information-based activities. This covers all activities associated with information such as:

- Procurement of information.
- Dissemination of information.
- Communication.
- Transaction.

Information-based activity is aimed at reducing information deficits, i.e. the fact that decisions always have to be taken even where there is a certain lack of relevant information. The possibility of having more information at one's disposal brings increased opportunity, as a decision once taken or a business transaction once effected means another opportunity relinquished. However, this relinquishing only becomes a conscious option if the alternatives are known and available. Hence protectionist markets and cartels, by their very nature, also invariably represent a scaling down of alternatives; the less information is available with regard to alternatives, the more likely this is to happen. Opportunity denotes the alternative choices available. The TIME infrastructure reduces the transaction costs. For the costs of a commercial transaction – even if it is only the purchase of a bar of soap in a supermarket – are costs which arise in conjunction with information-based activities to reduce information deficits, costs which arise in terms of the communication necessary to agree the transaction and costs involved in the exchange of information to coordinate the handling of the transaction.

Information-based activity

It is important to differentiate between communication and the handling of information. Electronic information-based activities, namely, the procurement of information, the dissemination of information and communication, are already becoming increasingly digitally-based, multimedial, global, very rapid and capable of being implemented without difficulty as well as at low cost and this will, in future, be wholly the case once the necessary technology is available and accessible and users are sufficiently familiar with it. From this point of view the Internet, at the very least, represents the stimulus for the basic concept, if not actually the prototype of the future infrastructure which is developing for information-based operations and communication (see figure 2).

A transaction may be interpreted as standardised communication in commercial dealings. Buying and selling represents a form of transaction which takes place throughout the world and in all sectors, innumerable times each day, whether it is in the supermarket or the taxi, on the stock-exchange or at the theatre box-office – the specific conditions governing the transaction are pre-determined in each case. Standards for transactions on the Internet are beginning to develop and will, in the future, play a major role in the rapid and positive functioning of cyber markets. The possibility of low-cost transactions on the Intranet will completely restructure the world of work – i.e. the relationship between employer and employee – and have a sustained effect on future company organisation.

Figure 2   The evolution of marketing

- Robinson Crusoe — Local handicraft
- Mass marketing — Mass production
- Marketing by differentiation — Segmentation
- Marketing on relationship — Customer retention
  - Direct marketing — Relationship
  - On-line marketing — Interaction by contents
  - Cyber marketing — Interaction by contents and context

Copyright TeleTrust SA Neuheim, 1998

It is essential to distinguish whether the information-based activity or communication is happening within the company itself – i.e. internally – or whether it is taking place in association with the environment. Outside the confines of companies people make use of the publicly accessible network; within organisations the Intranet was created for this purpose. The Internet, like the Intranet, is based on standards which permit inter-operability and communication in networks and provide various different services for actual communication or information-based activities. The Intranet recognises, in addition to the basic services offered on the Internet – which do not all have an equally important role to play – additional services such as video-phones and the possibility of video conferences. Although the Intranet is set up based on the central idea and technology of the Internet, its actual use cannot and should not be adopted on a 1:1 basis. The Internet as an instrument in many specialist areas of a company addresses questions of organisation, company culture or company management only marginally, whilst the Intranet's approach is, by contrast, fundamental.[121] Companies will be well advised, when it comes to making use of the new opportunities offered by the Internet and the Intranet, to effect the practical introduction of the two options sequentially and in two conscious steps. Any sequence can be used and should correspond to the company's basic cultural approach to dealing with change and its attitude to innovation.

Information deficit

Managers are decision-makers and responsible for parts or entire sections of an enterprise. The job of the management can be divided into two essential activities: firstly, decision-making and, secondly, communication. Information forms the necessary basis for making a decision. This means that managers, as active or passive recipients of information, are empowered to take decisions which will define actions and activities on the part of third parties that are as relevant as possible and which will promote the aims of the exercise in the best possible manner.

As far as practical decision-making is concerned, there is a very significant problem which may arise. A prerequisite for the decision is information which may, in a real situation, be at best incomplete or, at worst, not available at all. In practically all these situations – and this also applies to commercial activity in general – decisions have to be made where there is a choice between one or the other item. In other words, decisions are a conscious relinquishing of alternatives to the selected item. The basis of this is, however, as we have already shown, suitable information about the options offered. Anyone with an information deficit, i.e. anyone who is inadequately informed or not informed at all about alternatives, and is not able to disclose these creatively for himself, has no options in terms of choice and cannot/does not have to decide. Information deficits can be conscious or unconscious.

The causes of information deficits in decision situations can be viewed in a number of dimensions:

Quantitative
- Information is not known.
- Information is inaccessible.

Qualitative
- Woolly definition of information requirement, maybe due to complexity of decision situation Information of correct quality not available (too low/too high).

Time-related
- Decision situation changing so quickly and hindering processing of information. Procurement time for information is too long.
- Half-life of information causes its quality to decline too quickly.

Costs
- Procurement of information is too expensive.

Management are concerned to reduce their information deficits by means of specific information-based activity. Successful top managers pursue this aim in a structured way.[122] First of all, the necessary information is obtained for purposes of analysis. In this step, the Internet and the sources of information outside an organisation which are accessible through it can provide very valuable services. Following analysis and decision, this should be disseminated, for example, as an objective. The Internet offers two services for this – electronic mail is the more important of the two. Even at the information-based activity stage, an experienced manager – especially when he finds himself in a new field of operation – will be making good use of this time to build up a network of what are, for him, relevant information sources and important people when it comes to implementing decisions.[123]

Managers make deliberate use of communication to reduce uncertainty and misunderstandings. Very often the propaganda work and executive functions involved in the implementation of decisions are regarded as clarification of the objective.[124] However, it is essential to establish a social network for electronic communication too and it is only in this way that managers can be effective at all.

The procurement and dissemination of information plays a central role in decision making and communication is the dominant factor when it comes to implementing decisions and realising objectives. The Intranet is very much better suited to these activities. This reinforces the forecast that, by 1998, expenditure made by companies in the Intranet sector will amount to an estimated 8 million US$ overall, around four times as much as the Internet.[125]

What is the significance of the Internet as far as the management function is concerned? The multiplicity of external information is becoming clearly and much more easily accessible, procurement times are being reduced dramatically and relevance is being better sustained. It is proving possible to reduce the quality-related deficits and, through communication, to target an improved quality of information. The most significant factors are therefore time and, more importantly, cost. Information can be obtained so inexpensively via the Internet that financial clout no longer plays any significant part in accessing information (see figure 3).

Figure 3 The shift of paradigms in marketing

Aspects	Conventional marketing	Cyber marketing Cyber space	Shift to
Market focus	Geographical	Cyber space	Virtual structures
Segmentation	Demographic	Behaviour	Databases
Positioning	Local	Global	General Brands
Advertising	Push	Pull	Interactive
Promotion	Mass	Customised	Individualisation
Power on pricing	Seller	Buyer	Negotiations
Communication	Content only	Content and Context	Corporate Reality
Distribution	Intermediaries	Direct channel	Individualisation
Media	Singular	Multimedia	Digitalisation
Management	Marketshare	Share of customer	New metrics

Opportunity

Decisions are sometimes considered in relation to opportunity, that is, the possibility of missing a chance. Economists refer to this approach as 'opportunity costing', pointing out the financial resources necessary for it.[126] Opportunity costings are implicit costs, which means that they are not declared. In practice, it is possible to introduce a further, highly important, implicit cost element into this approach, namely, the costs related to expenditure for the procurement of information relating to alternatives and/or options other than those that already exist. The implicit expenditure is only accepted to any degree with far-reaching and important decisions. This fact applies to all aspects of life, whether private or business; it reflects the subjective, yet consciously categorised importance of the decision of the individual acting or the group of people concerned and the effort to minimise the risk of a wrong decision through identifying as many alternatives as possible.

Even today the Internet is making it possible to consider incredibly low cost opportunities with amazing rapidity. The building blocks are in place for markets, companies and, ultimately, people to enter into a direct competitive relationship with one another. These had existed in parallel prior to this globalisation but were unable to compete because of the cost constraints affecting reciprocal development and communication. The coming together of communal, national and international markets can be traced back over many epochs throughout history, but complete globalisation, thanks to the world-wide simultaneous exchange of information and on-line communication at minimal cost, is a historical first. The further development of communications structures, the precursor of which is the modern-day Internet, will further revolutionise opportunities as regards the handling of information and communication and in this way create completely new framework conditions for economic activity, social systems and politics; it is here that the importance and the potential of the Internet lies, a potential which offers economic attractions in the near future but which is also politically and socially explosive.

Transaction costs

In the industrial era, now in its last days, the manager's perception of fixed and variable costs, as well as the possibility of efficient production functions, formed the basis for good business decisions. A new feature in the information era is that the decision-makers are confronted with very high initial costs and extremely low marginal costs. Crucial to success is knowing how these fixed costs are made up and how they arise, something which calls for the establishment of non-traditional information awareness. This awareness of information recognises the links and dependence on change of the physical and the virtual value chain, as well as the significance and value of information in the economic creation of values, whether these are market performance for customers or enterprise-related figures for the shareholders.

Entry into 'market space' means a completely new cost structure as far as information-based activity is concerned; these costs are very low by comparison to
traditional transaction costs. In conjunction with this highly central cost aspect of
commercial transactions, a further observation has to be made, which is that these
low costs will make possible a sudden increase in the alternatives available, both
for organisations and for the individual. This fact may be illustrated within the
context of the market mechanism, the ideological base for the Western free economy. If a company is seeking a scarce resource, such as a specialist, for a specific task
for a limited period of time, then the costs charged by specialist head-hunting companies for such services will be very high. Making contact with a discussion group
(thousands exist) via the special area will quickly and cheaply bring about initial
contact with suitable candidates. As regards the private consumer sector, let us
imagine that we are hunting for a rare collectors' car. The collector is restricted in
his search to his immediate geographical surroundings and appropriate specialist
publications; at the same time he also has other limiting factors to contend with,
such as the amount of time he can spare for the search and his existing financial
resources. Even with consumer goods the choice is overwhelming. Looking for a
particular music CD on the Internet is generally quicker than going into the next
specialist shop in that it provides, in a fraction of a second, an overview of everything that is available at the most reasonable prices in the world.
Searching for an offer is only one part of the overall transaction. The ensuing
agreement, concluding and handling the contract are other sectional activities
within a transaction which have the potential to save large sums in communication
costs (see figure 4).

Managers in the information era use information awareness to optimise the
handling of information and communication within the organisation. They are
aware of the importance of information in all commercial activities, they understand and extract value in terms of data and information and do not, primarily,
look at the processing costs involved. They endeavour to create market performance with highly original information in order to achieve competitive advantage
and high profit margins on this basis. They know that, where market performance
is exclusively information-based, development and not production will be responsible for the margin. They operate in the knowledge that time is not a barrier to
competition and it is not the number of employees but the quality of their thinking,
their 'brainware' and their ability to use it which determines a company's competi-
tiveness. Market success in cyber space is determined to a considerable extent by
communication which is relevant and interesting.

The systems for informatising information handling and communication themselves form an information value chain.

*The information value chain is a model, as well as the regulating principle
within the system of creating value by extracting information from data. The
elements of data recording/generation, data management, data transmission
and data interpretation can also be found at the level of information which
is described as 'content' by the TIME industry.*

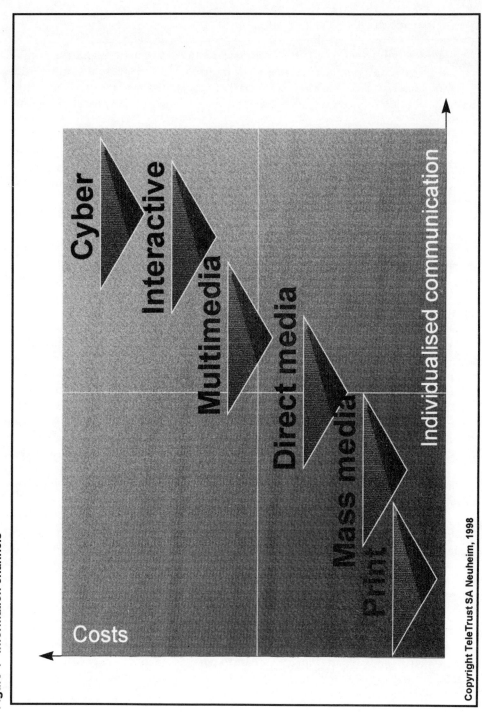

197

Figure 4   Information channels

Costs

Cyber

Interactive

Multimedia

Direct media

Mass media

Print

Individualised communication

Copyright TeleTrust SA Neuheim, 1998

The virtual added value chain

The physical added value chain of intimate reality is contained within a second, virtual sphere consisting of digitalised information; whereas there was at one time only the 'market place' we now have 'market space'.[127] A well thought out linking up of both of these levels will create a great deal of new success potential for companies.

The Internet is the precursor of a new competitive dimension: the virtual world. In addition to physical reality and resources which can be perceived via the senses, a virtual world is emerging, based on data, information and communication, not directly tangible but nevertheless comprehensible. The rules for generating values in real currency within the cyber world are completely different to the value added relationships within the physical world.[128] Even today, on the electronic stock-markets of London, Prague or Zürich, electronic commerce is creating and dealing in enormous sums of money. The dimension of virtual value creation is currently emerging within the context of electronic commerce, on-line market relationships and complete cyber markets. The Internet is, in this respect, an intermediate step permitting online markets and linking up to the TIME infrastructure for cyber business (see figure 5).

A 'trade' commercial transaction which, depending on the party involved, may be construed either as a purchase or a sale, consists of a sequence of information, agreement and handling of the transaction.[129] This applies to the brown cow market in New Zealand just as much as it does to the realisation of a transaction on the electronic options market in London. Whereas, on the brown cow market, only a real transaction is taking place within the physical value chain, the option market is purely virtual, business is conducted entirely via computers and networks. When the Internet is used, both value chains – real and virtual – are engaged in parallel, except where those firms are concerned who sell software via the Internet and where payment as well as delivery takes place via the network. The correct link-up of the real and the virtual steps in the relevant value added chains is crucial for success, whilst the extent to which activities are informatised is crucial as far as costs are concerned. In the pioneering period of Internet usage, the extent of continuous informatisation, i.e. the degree to which functions are performed by systemised rather than personalised information processing, plays a negligible role. With increasing use on the part of competing market participants, the linking up of the systems which figure in the virtual commercial sphere with the information systems which depict and make possible the real productive processes will present a significant competitive advantage.

Today, companies are faced with the decision of whether or not to make an initial investment and thus finally commit themselves to the Internet. Viewed in the medium term, no company can afford not to participate in cyber space and for this reason the matter of which access and usage variants to choose assumes primary importance (see figure 6).

Figure 5 Services in Internet usage

Company	Information		Communication	Transactions	
	Gathering	Distribution			
External	• BBS • FTP • WWW • Agents	• e-Mail • BBS • WWW	• WWW • e-Mail • (IRC) • Videophone	• WWW • EDI	**INTERNET**
Internal	• BBS • WWW	• e-Mail • BBS • WWW	• Videophone • Video- conferening • e-Mail • WWW	• WWW • EDI	**INTRANET**

Copyright TeleTrust SA Neuheim, 1998

Figure 6 Levels of Internet usage

Objective	Information		Communication	Transactions	
	Gathering	Distribution			
Usage level	1. Access	2. Presence	3. Marketing 4. Sales	5. Business	6. Customer service
Users and departments	• Marketing • HR • R & D • Procurement • Marketing • Production • IT	• Marketing • Sales • Customer service • Administration	• Marketing • Sales • Customer service • R & D • IT	• Marketing • Sales • Customer service	• Customer service

Marketing in Cyber Space

When the framework conditions affecting companies overall undergo massive change, then the question that presents itself is what the effects of this are likely to be as far as marketing is concerned or, more precisely, what the new thought-patterns, the new paradigms relevant to trade, are going to be. The paradigms emerge from an awareness of the significance of information which constrains all activities within the enterprise. In the final analysis, without information nothing will happen in a company. The more directly a company converts any advantage it may have over the competition in terms of information into market performance, the greater its possible profit margin will be. However, in the case of market performance which is practically exclusively constrained by information, it is not production but the development work which is critical as far as the possible margin is concerned. By way of explanation: when a company offers new programming languages by way of market performance, the potential profit margin depends to a considerable extent on the innovative value of this 'information'. Software is produced by copying the original at very low cost; therefore it is development and not production that is the critical factor. In the information era, time is not a barrier to competition. Good ideas cannot be protected, but only the instructions for their material formulation in the shape of patents. Good ideas and a clear idea of how to deal with information is not a question of quantity, but rather of the quality of human resources. Dealing with information calls for human beings, not machines who can work with telematic aids. But the quality of the results is not determined by the number of individuals involved but rather by their quality. If a really good product is to be marketed – let us take the programming language again – then it is communication skills which will decide its success on the market and not the financial resources which can be used to fund advertising for the new product.

The new communications infrastructure conveys a virtual rather than a physical reality. The reality we are used to is gradually developing into a new artificial reality which seems hardly to differ any more from everyday reality. Should a user, fully aware that he is not part of the system because a clear sensory dividing line exists between the system and reality, today engage in a dialogue on the system, this dividing line will no longer apply in cyber space. The fact that the user of the system himself becomes, in his own imagination, part of this reality, because he is able, through direct communication between the technical system and his natural senses, to look and move around within the virtual world and thus can open his mind to new dimensions, is termed the 'cyber world'.

However, the present-day infrastructure of the Internet, as well as the broadbased availability of technology, is still some way away from imparting true-to-reality cyber space on-line. Some of the basic technologies are available, in particular, multimedia and the possibility of establishing links between the different media – the so-called hyperlinks. Whereas it is only now that individual elements of the cyber era are becoming available, a specific migration plan is needed to change from present-day technologies to those of the future. It is only in this way that this change can be managed at relatively low cost.

Mass marketing belongs unequivocally to the dying epoch of the industrial era. Personnel and advertising costs are rising to a considerable extent and are crying out for a new orientation. In saturated markets with accelerating predatory price cutting, costs need to be reduced to ensure survival. For this reason more intensive mass advertising with markedly rising costs is not the way to overcome this situation on the marketing front, but marketing needs to respond to the individual target groups in different ways. Target group marketing achieves communication with purchasers by employing greater diversity in the media world. However, within the context of the changing values of society, there are some advertising measures which are already being virtually scorned. For environmental reasons, many consumers are no longer prepared to accept massive direct mail approaches. In addition, studies have shown that, with rising education standards, the degree of acceptance of direct advertising declines. Within the traditional advertising media, a definite information and communication overload has become widespread. Furthermore, consumers wish to be approached in a more personal fashion. However, direct marketing only partially fulfils this requirement because the traditional methods, such as direct mailing, catalogues, private radio and television, fail to make real communication possible.

The fact that it is possible to communicate world-wide via the Internet is opening the consumer's eyes to the significance and the opportunities inherent in being able to acquire information directly for himself. The falling costs of real communication using electronic media such as telephones and telefaxes or, in the future, video telephones as well, and communication via the world-wide network, is making consumers hungry for adventure and dialogue. On the cyber network, the customer will become involved rather than being simply an observer. Marketing via digital networks, in which the prospective buyer or customer acts as a user, is the first stage of new marketing in the information era. The second stage, the actual cyber marketing, will no longer embrace the individual approached in his capacity as a user, but as someone who is involved in a virtual reality. The opportunities to experience the virtually created environment using practically all the senses, in the same way as a real world, make up the cyber era (see figure 7).

CYBER MARKETING IS SUBJECT TO THE FOLLOWING PREMISSES:

- *It is information-based.*
- *It is customer-driven.*
- *It is quick.*
- *It is interactive and highly personalised.*
- *It is contents-driven and context-determined.*
- *It has very low communication and transaction costs.*
- *It operates in a world without distance and has no closing times.*

The webography of cyber space

Webography – the geography of the Web on the Internet – is critical as far as marketing and business activities are concerned. However, the development of the

Figure 7   Phases of a project

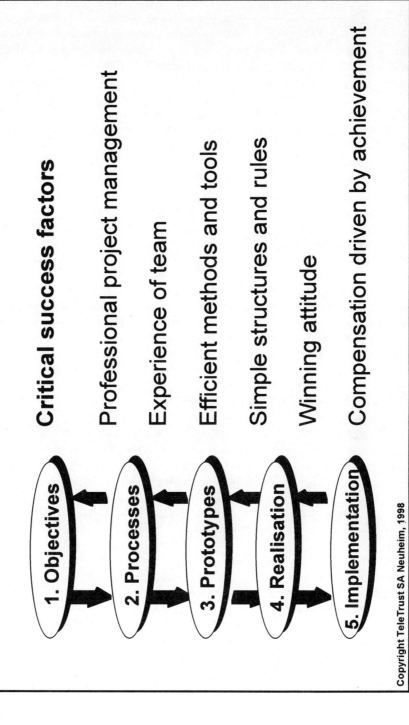

Critical success factors

Professional project management

Experience of team

Efficient methods and tools

Simple structures and rules

Winning attitude

Compensation driven by achievement

1. Objectives

2. Processes

3. Prototypes

4. Realisation

5. Implementation

Copyright TeleTrust SA Neuheim, 1998

Internet differs fundamentally from other information dissemination techniques. Whilst communication technologies such as telephone, telegraph, fax machines or computers initially gained a foothold within a purely commercial environment and then gradually spread into the private usage sector, the opening up of the Web and of cyber space is taking place from the other side, that is, through the private consumer. For some managers who are of a sceptical turn of mind, this is a further reason to doubt the long-term importance of the Internet and therefore to continue to wait, something which is understandable but still unforgivable.

The change of paradigms in marketing is reflected in all aspects of the marketing function. Marketing philosophy is retreating from mass marketing into a relationship with potential buyers and customers. This personalisation of the customer within the marketing activity is a digital process and is information-aided. The market is losing its geographical reference points and becoming place-less, from which it follows that it is important to be able to set up virtual structures. This placelessness is undermining the segmentation which has been practiced in the past and this will be reviewed on the basis of the response recorded in cyber space by means of databases and played with a set of new rules, such as the loss of informational asymmetry. The positioning of firms and brandnames, if this is to be effective, must be global and no longer merely local in terms of its effect, although the expenditure required for this no longer depends on financial ability to utilise the mass media, but is, to a major extent, presented in terms of originality and relevance in communication within cyber space. Advertising is changing over from the penetrative technique of pushing messages to interactive communication which will need to invite target persons to a dialogue if it is to be effective (see figure 8).

Within the marketing mix, customer price control will call for a great deal of innovation together with differentiated conditions and new price models; negotiations may, however, be structured and included in the dialogue. Promotion will gain markedly in importance and challenge the position hitherto occupied by advertising in dealing with information in the market place. The placing of products on the market and distribution channels will undergo far-reaching changes; stages in trading practice which do not entail any obvious advantages for the customer will be eliminated. The conventional laws with their economies of scale, the possibility of achieving a more rapid amortisation of fixed costs per production unit by expanding production volume using the variable costs associated with greater quantities, are disintegrating; due to the high fixed costs of development and the partly marginal costs in production, the experience curve is becoming crucial to success where what is ultimately knowledge-based market performance is concerned (see figure 9).

Market activities are no longer steered by means of objectives and control of market share but rather by means of customer bonding or share of customer.

Customer bonding calls for a knowledge of the customer and this can only be obtained by way of information or customer data, which means that the use of suitable databases will be required.

Figure 8   The benefits of the TIME infrastructure for business management

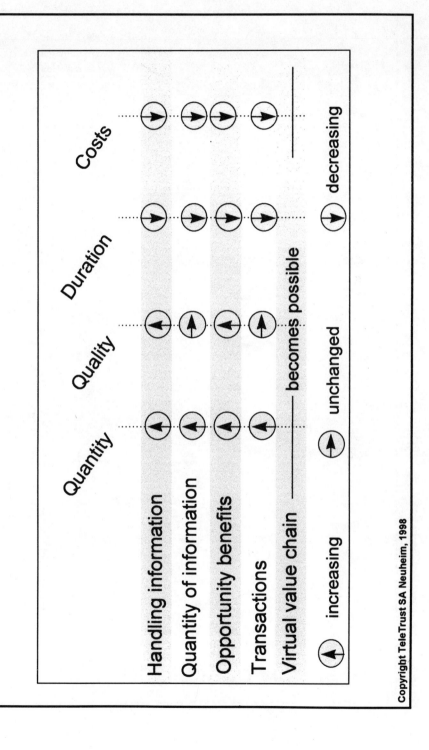

206

Figure 9   The elements of marketing in the cyber age

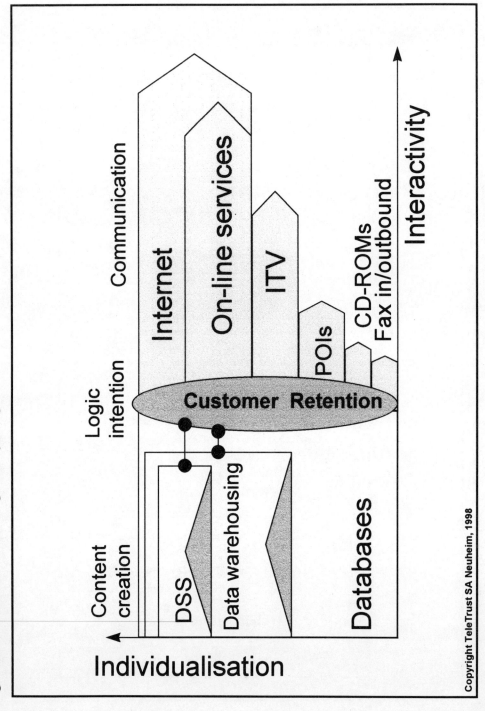

Databases: core of the cyber world

The marketing database is the basis of the actual nerve and information centre. The concept of the database should not be restricted to a marketing programme alone. The database should be geared to long-term company policy. However, its actual implementation certainly lends itself to an approach within the framework of a marketing programme.

THE FOLLOWING STAGES SHOULD BE OBSERVED, SYSTEMATICALLY SEPARATED:

A – *Assessment of current situation and future requirements vis-à-vis the database.*
B – *Evaluation of objectives of the database with costs / benefits / expenditure.*
C – *Performance specification for developers.*
D – *Realisation.*
E – *Introduction.*
F – *Continuous review.*

Steps A and B must be defined within a marketing programme or an overall specification for the undertaking. Requirements as far as the database is concerned should take into account the development of the distribution channels. The company strategy must be incorporated. An important element of B is the actual migration planning of the marketing instruments in various customer segments as well as the manner in which communication with them is conducted. This means clear planning of the migration paths, for example, from letter post to fax communication on to Internet, or from the telephone to interactive shopping on TV. There should also be clarity as regards the sequence in which the instruments are to be employed, for example, when courting a new customer. A few managers will discover that their marketing specialists are, under certain circumstances, not very experienced when it comes to these important aspects of really continuous communication with the customer. For a very long time those responsible for marketing were used to planning individual actions. A continuous communication and the change of the media for the various marketing instruments are new territory for many marketeers, because their individual measures never aim at long-term customer bonding (see figure 10).

The sequence of instruments emanating from the database needs to be defined at a very early stage so that provision can be made for the individual connections to be made from the database to the various types of media. The sequence of instruments, such as fax communication outbound/inbound and subsequent partial migration on to the Internet, should be dealt with both on an isolated basis and in combination; this also applies to the consequences resulting from additive use. Synergetic usage is very important, where the customer constantly has the option of changing from one medium to another.

The developers' performance specification should have at its core those functions which are used first. It is important that the system architecture is kept mod-

208

Figure 10   Communication in cyber space

- No geography
- Irrelevance of time
- High degree of interactivity
- Business transactions by mouse click
- Individual mass customisation
- Customer-driven
- Content and context Are key
- Low information asymmetry

Copyright TeleTrust SA Neuheim, 1998

ular so that new functions can be added to the system. As far as the system architecture is concerned, this should be open.

Managements require assessment of the various approaches within the framework of the marketing programme. This contains all the relevant information
which is necessary for realisation. Contacts in the customer database for business-
to-business transactions should not only be the purchaser and the decision-maker,
but also operators, external consultants, internal influences and the 'gatekeeper'.
There is one very important instance which the marketing people like to forget and
that is those responsible for authorisations and approvals. The decision-makers
may be part of management and able to make a decision on a project or the procurement of an item. However, in really important matters, it is the administrative
or supervisory board which has to approve individual transactions. The decision-
maker therefore also needs to be a good politician in order to be able to get the
business approved by the relevant person.

Managers should check the marketing people's objectives as regards database
marketing. These are: to increase the frequency of product sales and operate cross-
selling, i.e. to introduce and sell other products to the same regular clientele. It is
very important to increase customer loyalty and to strengthen customer relations
to the extent that these customers become immune to offers made by competitors
and appear as cost-free sellers and sales references. The fourth objective is to court
new customers.

Failures come about as a result of the desire to have a comprehensive system up
and running from the very beginning. You would be well advised to set your sights
a little lower and go instead for completing the project on time. Even where there is
personal control and good project management, the applications may founder if
they are based on short-sighted tenets or the desire to achieve success in the short
term and no long-term strategy is pursued. The new beginning is not supposed to
be a leap into a new era but the first step on the road to it. Projects which do not
clearly demonstrate exactly who is responsible and to whom the project leadership
has been assigned never come to fruition. This results in a way of working which
fails to reach an end and the total absence of satisfactory results.

The database is the anchor as far as communication is concerned. This communication can take place in very different ways. Not everyone throughout the world
tools up at the same time to connect to the Internet or to link up directly with cyber
space. The migration of traditional one-way media to the medium of on-line communication is a slow process. This is one reason why, within the context of the
database, provision has been made for fax or interactive television as instruments
of personalised communication. Customers can switch between media and be sure
of the same integral and individual interchange on each and every communication
channel.

Advertisers and those responsible for marketing are faced with a challenge as
regards communication in cyber space. Given a high level of interaction, communication is independent of space and time, yet it is to a major extent individualisable
and customer-determined. The time which elapses between a customer transaction
and the point when a competitor is chosen can be measured in mouse clicks. In pre-

sent-day on-line marketing on the Internet, content is still the determining factor. With the establishment of cyber markets in a few years' time, context will become equally important. The network is transparent and no longer admits asymmetries of information.

Cyber Marketing – But When?

The information era is changing the framework conditions pertaining to economic activity and with this a new kind of company management is emerging. The demand is for a new way of thinking and a way of acting that is in harmony with the prevailing circumstances of the age. The question of whether to get on the bandwagon or not, does not present itself in this form. Anyone who fails to change and adapt to the new philosophy will go under. The question is, when is the best time to get on?[130] If the step is taken too early, one could, under certain circumstances, find oneself paying out unnecessary money for training. The competition will introduce and implement the necessary measures less expensively and more quickly. Getting on too late means relinquishing the advantage of having a lead over one's competitors. Anyone who takes up his position too late will also have to fight for the position in an even more costly battle to oust the competition.

Business – or the market place where business transactions take place – is becoming non-location-related, yet global. The winners, however, are still the doers with a mindset of the unlimited power of creative marketing.[131]

BIBLIOGRAPHY

BARNATT 1995

Barnatt Christopher: *Cyber Business, Mindsets for a Wired Age;* John Wiley & Sons, Chichester, 1995.

BECKER/HABERFELNER/LIEBETRAU 1991

Becker Mario, Haberfellner Reinhard, Liebetrau Georg: *EDV-Wissen für Anwender;* Verlag Industrielle Organisation, Zürich, 1991, 9. Fully revised and extended edition.

BLATTBERG/GLAZER/LITTLE 1994

Blattberg Robert C., Glazer Rashi, Little John D. C., Editors: *The Marketing Information Revolution;* Harvard Business School Press, Boston, MA, 1994.

BÖHM/FUCHS/PACHER 1993

Boehm Rolf, Fuchs Emmerich, Pacher Gerhard: *System-Entwicklung in der Wirtschaftsinformatik;* Verlage der Fachvereine vdf, Zürich, 1993.

BUZZELL/GALE 1987

Buzzell Robert D., Gale Bradley T.: *The PIMS Principles, Linking Strategy to Performance;* The Free Press, New York, 1987.

CANTER/SIEGEL 1994

Canter Laurenz A., Siegel Martha S.: *How to Make a Fortune on the Information Superhighway;* HarperCollins Publishers Inc., New York, 1994.

CLAVELL 1983

Clavell James, Editor: *The Art of War;* Sunzi, Bantam Doubleday Dell Publishing Group Inc., New York, 1983.

CLUTTERBUCK/KERNAGHAN 1994

Clutterbuck David, Kernaghan Susan: *Making Customers Count, A Guide to Excellence in Customer Care;* Management Books 2000 Ltd., Oxford, 1994.

COOPER 1995

Cooper Frederic J. et al.: *Implementing Internet Security;* New Riders Publishing, Indianapolis, IN, 1995.

DAVENPORT 1993

Davenport Thomas H.: *Process Innovation, Reengineering Work through Information Technology;* Harvard Business School Press, Boston MA, 1994.

DAVIDOW/MALONE 1992
Davidow William H., Malone Michael S.: *The Virtual Corporation;*
HarperCollins Publishers Inc., New York, 1994.

DAY 1986
Day George S.: *Analysis for Strategic Market Decisions;* West Publishing
Company, St. Paul, MN, 1986.

DUTTON 1995
Dutton William H.: Der Mensch will lesen – Zeitungen, Bücher: *Die
Weltwoche;* No. 29/20, July 1995.

ELLSWORTH/ELLSWORTH 1994
Ellsworth Jill H., Ellsworth Matthew V.: *The Internet Business Book;* John
Wiley & Sons Inc., New York, 1994.

ELLSWORTH/ELLSWORTH 1995
Ellsworth Jill H., Ellsworth Matthew V.: *Marketing on the Internet;* John
Wiley & Sons Inc., New York, 1995.

FOURNIER 1994
Fournier Guy: *Informationstechnologien in Wirtschaft und Gesellschaft,
Sozioökonomische Analyse einer technologischen Herausforderung;* Duncker
& Humblot, Berlin, 1994.

GATES 1995
Gates William H. III: *The Road Ahead;* Viking Penguin, New York, 1995.

GREFF/TÖPFER 1993
Greff Günter, Töpfer Armin, Editors: *Direktmarketing mit neuen Medien;*
Verlag Moderne Industrie, Landsberg/Lech, 3rd edn, 1993.

ITU 1995
ITU, International Telecommunication Union: *World Telecommunication
Development Report, Information Infrastructures, World Telecommunication
Indicators;* ITU, Geneva, 1995.

JANAL 1995
Janal Daniel S.: *The Online Marketing Manual; Integrating Electronic Media
into your Marketing Campaign;* International Thomson Publishing,
New York, 1995.

HAMEL/PRAHALAD 1994
Hamel Gary, Prahalad C.K.: *Competing for the Future;* Harvard Business
School Press, Boston, MA, 1994.

HAMMER/CHAMPY 1993

Hammer Michael, Champy James: *Business Reengineering;* Campus Verlag, Frankfurt and New York, 1993.

HARRIGAN 1989

Harrigan Kathryn Rudie: *Unternehmensstrategien für reife und rückläufige Märkte;* Campus Verlag, Frankfurt/Main, 1989.

HENDERSON 1984

Henderson Bruce D.: *Die Erfahrungskurve in der Unterneehmensstrategie;* Campus Verlag, Frankfurt/Main and New York, 1984.

HODGE 1993

Hodge Senior Cecil C.: *The Electronic Marketing Manual, Integrating Electronic Media into your Marketing Campaign;* McGraw-Hill Inc., New York, 1993.

HUBER-WÄSCHLE/SCHAUER/WIDMAYER 1995

Huber-Wäschle F., Schauer H., Widmayer P., Editors: *GISI 95, Herausforderungen eines globalen Informationsverbundes für die Informatik;* Springer, Informatik Aktuell, Frankfurt, 1995.

KEHOE 1994

Kehoe Brendan P.: *Zen und die Kunst des INTERNET;* Prentice Hall Verlag GmbH, Munich, 1994.

KELLY 1995

Kelly Sean: *Data Warehousing, The Route to Mass Customisation;* John Wiley & Sons, Chichester, 1995.

KOTLER 1984

Kotler Philip: *Marketing Management, Analysis, Planning and Control;* Prentice-Hall Inc., Englewood Cliffs, NJ, 1984.

KOTLER 1995

Kotler Philip: *Marketing nach Mass: Marketing & Kommunikation*, June 6/1995.

KUNESCH 1993

Kunesch Hermann: *Grundlagen des Prozessmanagements;* Wirtschaftsverlag Carl Überreuter, Vienna, 1993.

LARIJANI 1993

Larijani Casey L.: *The Virtual Reality Primer;* McGraw-Hill Inc., New York, 1993.

LEVINE/BAROUDI 1995

Levine Hohn R., Baroudi Carol: *Internet Secrets;* IDG Books Worldwide Inc., Foster City, CA, 1995.

LEVITT 1983

Levitt Theodore: *The Marketing Imagination;* The Free Press, New York, 1983.

MÜLLER VON BLUMENCRON 1994

Mueller von Blumencron Othmar: *Zielgruppenorientierte Massenmedien-konzepte;* Dissertation der Hochschule St. Gallen, No. 1565, DIFO Druck GmbH, Bamberg, 1994.

MUSASHI 1974

Musashi Miyamoto: *A Book of Five Rings, The Classic Samurai Guide to Strategy;* Allison and Busby Ltd., London, 1974.

NIELSON 1995

Nielson Jakob: *Multimedia and Hypertext, The Internet and Beyond;* Academic Press Inc., London, 1995.

NOLDEN 1995

Nolden Mathias: *Der erfolgreiche Einstieg ins Internet;* Ullstein, Franfurt/Main, 1995.

NZZ Nr. 12, 1994

Neue Zürcher Zeitungen: *Dem 'Produktivitätsrätsel' auf der Spur;* No. 12, Commerce page 35. 15th/16th January, 1994.

PEPPERS/ROGERS 1993

Peppers Don, Rogers Martha: *The One to One Future, Building Relationships One Customer at a Time;* Doubleday, New York, 1993.

PITTS/SNOW 1986

Pitts Robert A., Snow Charles C.: *Strategies for Competitive Success;* John Wiley & Sons, New York, 1986.

PORTER 1980

Porter Michael E.: *Competitive Strategy, Techniques for Analyzing Industries and Competitors;* The Free Press, New York, 1980.

PORTER 1985

Porter Michael E.: *Competitive Advantage, Creating and Sustaining Superior Performance;* The Free Press, New York, 1985.

RESNICK/TAYLOR 1994
Resnick Rosalind, Taylor Dave: *The Internet Business Guide;* Sams Publishing, Indianapolis, 1994.

REINHARD 1995
Reinhard Ulrike: *Who is Who in Multimedia, in Germany, Austria and Switzerland;* Springer-Verlag, Berlin, Heidelberg and New York, 1995.

RHEINGOLD 1993
Rheingold Howard: *The Virtual Community, Homesteading on the Electronic Frontier;* Addison-Wesley Publishing Company, Reading, MA, 1993.

RIFKIN 1995
Rifkin Jeremy: *The End of Work, The Decline of the Global Labor Force and the Dawn of the Post-Market Era;* G. P. Putnam's Sons Publ., New York, 1995.

HAUSCHILDT/SCHMIDT-TIEDEMANN 1993
Hauschildt Jürgen, Schmidt-Tiedemann Joachim: *Neue Produkte erfordern neue Strukturen: Harvard Business Manager,* vol. 15, 4th quarter, 1993.

STALK/HOUT 1990
Stalk Georges Jr., Hout Thomas M.: *Competing Against Time, How Time-based Competition is Reshaping Global Markets;* The Free Press, NY, 1990.

STERNE 1995
Sterne Jim: *World Wide Web Marketing, Integrating the Internet into Your Marketing Strategy;* John Wiley & Sons, New York, 1995.

TISCHHAUSER/GERBER 1995
Tischhauser Ulrich, Gerber Heinz: CBT Forum No. 2/95: *Global Teach.*

TURLINGTON 1995
Turlington Shannon R.: *Walking the World Wide Web: Your Personal Guide to the Best of the Web;* Ventana Press, Chapel Hill, NC, 1995.

WALKER/BOYD/LARRECHE 1992
Walker O.C. Jr., Boyd Harper W. Jr., Larréché Jean-Claude: *Marketing Strategy: Planning and Implementation;* Richard D. Irwin Inc, Homewood, IL, 1992.

WÖSSNER 1995
Wössner Mark: Zukunft der neuen interaktiven Informationstechniken: *Bulletin der Schweizerischen Kreditanastalt;* No. 5-6, 1995.

YUDKIN 1995
Yudkin Marcia: *Marketing Online;* Dutton & Plume, New York, 1995.

NOTES

1 Swerdlow, Joel L.; 'Information Revolution'; National Geographic, Vol. 188, No. 4, October 1995, p. 6; This article is a vivid and easily accessible introduction to the achievements and key terms of cyber space.

2 'Artificial Intelligence is here', proclaims Business Week's July 7, 1984, cover story about the industry that develops computers that mimic human reasoning and problem-solving. At that time experts predicted a multibillion dollar industry within the next decade based on expert-systems or knowledge-based systems. Artificial intelligence was not to stay. Today, the activites of emulating decision-making by means of IT use the concepts of neural networks.

3 BLATTBERG/GLAZER/LITTLE 1994: pp. 204–229, Raymond R. Burke presents one of the perspectives on the emerging use of IT-based decision-making: artifical intelligence for designing marketing decision-making tools.

4 The phrase 'information highway' is used in this book to denote any communication options which permit a dialogue between several participants or systems over a distance.

5 ITU 1995: pp. 2–3.

6 ITU 1995: Figure 2.1, the total value of the installed base by 1994 is estimated at 1990 billion US$: telephone lines 48.2%, television sets 29.1% and PCs 22.6%.

7 ITU 1995: Box 3.2.

8 LARIJANI 1993: The connection equipment and different current possibilities of virtual reality (VR) are kept very simple and can serve as a basis to enable anyone really interested to pursue the explosive developments in the VR sector.

9 Mandel, Tom; Confessions of a cyberholic, welcome to cyberspace; Special Issue of TIME, Spring 1995: p. 53.

10 Estimation by the Internet Society at the end of 1995 and publications in January 1997.

11 Meeks, Heidi, Presentation: E-Commerce Anytime, Anywhere with Anyone, Building Information Communities; International Conference Business and Marketing on the Internet, Geneva, September 8, 1995.

12 BARNATT 1995: pp. 74–76.

13 RIFKIN 1995: p. 149.

14 Smolowe, Jill; Intimate strangers, welcome to cyberspace; Special Issue of TIME, Spring 1995: pp. 14–16.

15 TURLINGTON 1995: Walking on the WWW gives a very good taste of the what is on offer in the scientific sector right through to the entertainment and communication scene.

16 RHEINGOLD 1993: pp. 176–196. The membership in a real-time tribe may be temporary or stable.

17 Kirchgeorg, Manfred; Zielgruppenmarketing; THEXIS, St. Gallen, 3. 1995: pp. 20–26.

18 BLATTBERG/GLAZER/LITTLE 1994: p. 10.

19 ITU 1995: p. 1.

20 SCHMID 1995: p. 37.

21 HODGE 1993: pp. 278–283.

22 Cerf, Vinton, Presentation; Internet Strategies on the On-line Services and Internet Service Providers; Internet at Telecom 95; Geneva, October 7 and 8, 1995.

23 Stein, Lee, Presentation; The New Wave of Emerging Internet Application; Internet at Telecom 95; Geneva, October 7 and 8, 1995.

24 YUDKIN 1995: p. 73.

25 Ratan, Suneel; A New Divide Between Haves and Have-Nots; Welcome to cyberspace, Special Issue of TIME, Spring 1995: pp. 17 and 18.

26 PEPPERS/RODGERS 1993: pp. 21–24.

27 BUZZELL/GALE 1987: Share of customers is directly related to high performance in customer-percieved relative quality, which becomes highly important in matured markets with low or no growth.

28 PEPPERS/RODGERS 1993: pp. 106–108.

29 BARNATT 1995: pp. 38–43. The structuring of interface-type into three main areas gives an addi-
    tional insight into the revolution:
        a. Command line – character-based interaction between man and machine.
        b. GUI (graphical user Interface) – friendliness of the interaction by the use of graphic elements.
        c. VR (virtual reality) – man-machine interaction is turning into a man-machine involvement.
30 LARIJANI 1993: pp. 30–35.
31 KELLY 1995: p. 3. The IT-investment trend shifts from automating to informating.
32 Wurman, Richard Saul, Lecture: Information Workers, October 12 1991, St. Paul de Vence. Pre-
    sented the five ring model that encloses information for physical survival to the very abstract form
    of information of cultural heritage, e.g. philosophy.
33 BLATTBERG/GLAZER/ LITTLE 1994: Figure I.1, Information value chain. The validity of the con-
    cept of the value chain in general should be questioned seriously. It is used in this book. The concept
    of the value chain is clearly a paradigm of the industrial age, where value was perceived in those
    processes, that physically shaped a product. In the context of the understanding how marketable
    performance is created, this is not a one way process, but actually a value exchange from both sides.
    This might be illustrated in a business transaction where a product is exchanged for money.
34 US Department of Commerce, Bureau of Economic Analysis, July 1992. *Survey of Current Business.*
35 PEPPERS/RODGERS 1993: p. 52.
36 Direct Marketing Association (DMA), New York 1995. The survey was conducted by Deloitte &
    Touche.
37 KELLY 1995: pp. 131–132.
38 BLATTBERG/GLAZER/LITTLE 1994: pp. 41–54.
39 KELLY 1995: pp. 41–54.
40 Turing, Alan M., On computable numbers, with an application to the problem of decision (1936).
    Reprint in: Martin Davies (Ed.): *The Undecidable: Basic Papers on Undecidable Propositions,
    Unsolvable Problems and Computable Functions;* New York 1965: pp. 116–151.
41 ITU: *World Telecommunication Development Report* 1995: p. 4.
42 HODGE 1993: pp. 119–173.
43 HODGE 1993: pp. 137–153.
44 HODGE 1993: pp. 119–136.
45 HODGE 1993: pp. 175–178.
46 NIELSEN 1995: p. 33.
47 HODGE 1993: pp. 329–344.
48 HODGE 1993: pp. 346–352.
49 HODGE 1993: pp. 364–365.
50 ELLSWORTH/ELLSWORTH 1994: p. 4.
51 TURLINGTON 1995: pp. 5–7.
52 ELLSWORTH/ELLSWORTH 1995: pp. 177–252. This Introduction to the specifics of creating
    web-sites is easy to understand.
53 TURLINGTON 1995: pp. 12–17.
54 Source: Internet-Society October 1995.
55 CANTER/SIEGEL: pp. 98–105.
56 CANTER/SIEGEL 1994: pp. 144–145.
57 ELLSWORTH/ELLSWORTH 1995: pp. 80–82; 123–126.
58 CANTER/SIEGEL 1994: pp. 82–86.
59 JANAL 1995: pp. 75–83.
60 ELLSWORTH/ELLSWORTH 1995: pp. 165–221.
61 JANAL 1995: pp. 60–65.
62 JANAL 1995: pp. 54–59.
63 Jack Davies, President AOL at Telecom 95 in Geneva.
64 GATES 1995: p. 91. The Internet is the most important single development in the world of comput-
    ing since the IBM PC was introduced in 1981.
65 Anthony Bay, General Manager of MSN at Telecom 95 in Geneva.
66 RESNICK/TAYLOR 1994: pp. 321–334.

67 ELLSWORTH/ELLSWORTH 1995: pp. 291–294.
68 O'Connell, Vanessa: US Brokerage Concerns offer On-line Services; *Wall Street Journal Europe,* July 12, 1995.
69 Steinmetz, Greg: Deutsche Telekom to Unveil Upgrade to On-line Service; *Wall Street Journal Europe,* August 22, 1995.
70 CANTER/SIEGEL 1994: pp. 40–45. The survey applies to the USA where it was conducted in July 1994. It shows the massive cost-advantages of the Internet, that are also true for almost any other country in the world.
71 JANAL 1995: pp. 87–105.
72 WALKER/BOYD/LARRECHE 1992: The publication is very useful in formulating marketing programmes in the various states of market life cycle and matching strategies.
73 STALK/HOUT 1990: pp. 214–217.
74 Katzenbach, Jon R., Smith, Douglas K.: *The Wisdom of Teams;* Harper Business, New York 1994, pp. 137–148.
75 Peters Thomas J., Waterman Robert H. Jr: *In Search of Excellence;* Harper & Row Publishers, New York 1982; p. 193.
76 Barabba, Vincent P.: *Meeting of the Minds, Creating the Market-Based Enterprise;* Harvard Business School Press, 1995; pp. 143–149.
77 Davis, Stan, Botkin, Jim: *Harvard Business Review;* The Coming of Knowledge-Based Business; No. 5, September/October 1994.
78 Westwood, John: *The Marketing Plan;* Kogan Page, London 1996, 2nd edn: This book is one other possible blueprint for marketing operations. A standard plan or programme of their own will serve corporations better.
79 WALKER/BOYD/LARRECHE 1992: p. 8.
80 SUNZI 1988.
81 Henderson, Bruce D.: *The Logic of Business Strategy;* Ballinger Publishing Company, Cambridge MA, 1984.
82 PORTER 1980: pp. 34–46.
83 MUSASHI 1974: p. 49.
84 PORTER 1985: pp. 323–336.
85 STALK/HOUT 1990: pp. 131–132.
86 PORTER 1985: pp. 278–297.
87 TIME, July 15, 1996: p. 52.
88 ITU 1995: p. 42 Box Table 3.6 Multi media access.
89 PORTER 1980: pp. 35–40.
90 Kotler, P.: *Marketing Management;* Prentice/Hall, Englewood Cliffs NJ, 1988, 6th edn.
91 RHEINGOLD 1993: pp. 122–131.
92 Belz, Christian, Müller, Roland, Ed.: *Closer to the Client, Outbound Communication;* Verlag Industrielle Organisation, Zürich 1996: pp. 97–105, Kurt Rohner – From the Product of Yesterday to the Serduct of Tomorrow.
93 Quinn, James Brian, Anderson, Philip, Finkelstein, Sydney: *Harvard Business Review:* Managing Professional Intellect: Making the Most of the Best; No. 2 March–April 1996.
94 SCHÜRING 1992: pp. 312–329.
95 Thomas Koch, lecture: at komm '96, Düsseldorf 5th–7th July 1996: Do you know how many PCs there are...?
96 Burke, Raymond R.: *Harvard Business Review:* Virtual Shopping: Breakthrough in Marketing Research; No. 2, March–April 1996.
97 KELLY 1995: pp. 82–89.
98 PEPPER/RODGERS 1993: pp. 91–94.
99 Wiencke, Wolfgang, Koke, Dorothee: *Cards & Clubs – The Customer Club as a Direct Marketing Instrument;* ECON Verlag, Düsseldorf 1995.
100 Rose, Lance: Netlaw: *Your Rights in the Online World;* Osborne/McGraw-Hill, Berkeley CA 1995.
101 Cavazos, Edward A., Gavino, Morin: *Cyberspace and the Law: Your Rights and Duties in the On-Line World;* MIT Press Cambridge MA, 1994.

102 Source: TeleTrust SA, Switzerland.

103 BLATTBERG/GLAZER/LITTLE 1994: pp. 155–166.

104 Gareis, Roland: *Projektmanagement-Forschung im internationalen Vergleich; Projekt Management;* No. 1, 1995, Vol 6: pp. 4–11.

105 BECKER/HABERFELLER/LIEBETRAU 1991: pp. 326–328.

106 Markus, M. Lynne, Keil, Mark: *Sloan Management Review,* If We Build It, They Will Come: Designing Information Systems That People Want to Use. Vol 35, Number 4, Summer 1994; pp. 11–25: Most interesting are the implications for CEOs and CIOs, which the authors pledge for: a. Align the interests of system developers and the managers who must implement information systems. b. Initiate serious reviews of the proposed system design concept and plans for achieving system use and value. c. Put teeth in system investment decisions by measuring and managing system use and value.

107 Frühauf, Karol, Ludewig, Jochen, Sandmayr, Helmut: *Software-Projektmanagement und Qualitätssicherung;* vdf Verlag der Fachvereine, Zürich 1988; pp. 27–30.

108 BOEHM/FUCHS/PACHER 1993: pp. 81–106, The agreement must reflect the chosen procedure which can be designed in a variety of different approaches.

109 Frühauf, Karol, Ludewig, Jochen, Sandmayr, Helmut: *Software-Projektmanagement und Qualitätssicherung;* vdf Verlag der Fachvereine, Zürich 1988; pp. 59–74.

110 SILBERER 1995: p. 230.

111 Esswein, Werner, Körmeier, Klaus: *Projekt Management: Führung und Steuerung von Softwareprojekten im Kapsel-Modell;* 2nd Quarter 1995, Vol. 5,: pp. 26–36.

112 Hesse, Wolfgang, Weltz, Friedrich: *Information Management: Projektmanagement für evolutionäre Software-Entwicklung;* 3/94, Vol. 9: pp. 20–32.

113 Stein, W.: *Objektorientierte Analysemethoden – ein Vergleich; Informatik-Spektrum.* No. 6, 1993, Vol. 16; pp. 317–332.

114 Achatzi, Günter: *Praxis der strukturierten Analyse;* Carl Hanser Verlag, Munich and Vienna 1991: p. 36.

115 Booch, Grady: *Object Oriented Design with Applications;* The Benjamin/Cummings Publishing Company, Inc., Redwood City, CA, 1991; pp. 201–206.

116 Arthur, L.J.: *Measuring Programmer Productivity and Software Quality;* John Wiley & Sons, New York, 1985.

117 BECKER/HABERFELLER/LIEBETRAU 1991: pp. 346–350.

118 Directive of the Federal Office for Organisation: Project Organisation for EDP Projects and mid and long-term EDP planning of 1.9.1973; Swiss Confederation, Bern, Version dated 1.5.1983.

119 HAMEL/PRAHALAD 1994. The authors do stress the first two phases of intellectual leadership and the migration, but not the new market space in the online reality and the vital importance of share of customer.

120 GATES 1995: pp. 243–249.

121 Rohner, Kurt: *Intranet-Management,* Carl Hanser Verlag, Munich 1996.

122 Kotter, John P. : *The General Managers;* The Free Press, New York 1982.

123 Ibid. p. 60ff.

124 Ibid. p. 71ff.

125 Source: ZONA Research.

126 Samuelson, Paul A.: *Economics;* McGraw Hill Book Company, New York 1980, 11th edn.

127 Rayport, Jeffrey J., Sviokla, John J.: *Die virtuelle Wertschöpfungskette – kein fauler Zauber,* Harvard Business Manager, 18th year, 1996, 2nd quarter: pp. 104–113.

128 Rohner, Kurt: Cyber-Marketing, Verlag Orell Füssli, Zürich 1996.

129 Schmid, Beat and associates: *Electronic Mall: Banking und Shopping in globalen Netzen,* B.G. Teubner, Stuttgart 1995: p. 97ff.

130 Tellis, Gerard J., Golder, Peter N.: *Sloan Management Review;* First to Market, First to Fail? Real Causes of Enduring Market Leadership; Volume 37, Number 2, Winter 1996.

131 LEVITT 1983: Most of the things have changed, since this book was written, one fact stands: The mind of the marketeers is the only limit to success — yesterday, now and in the future.

INDEX